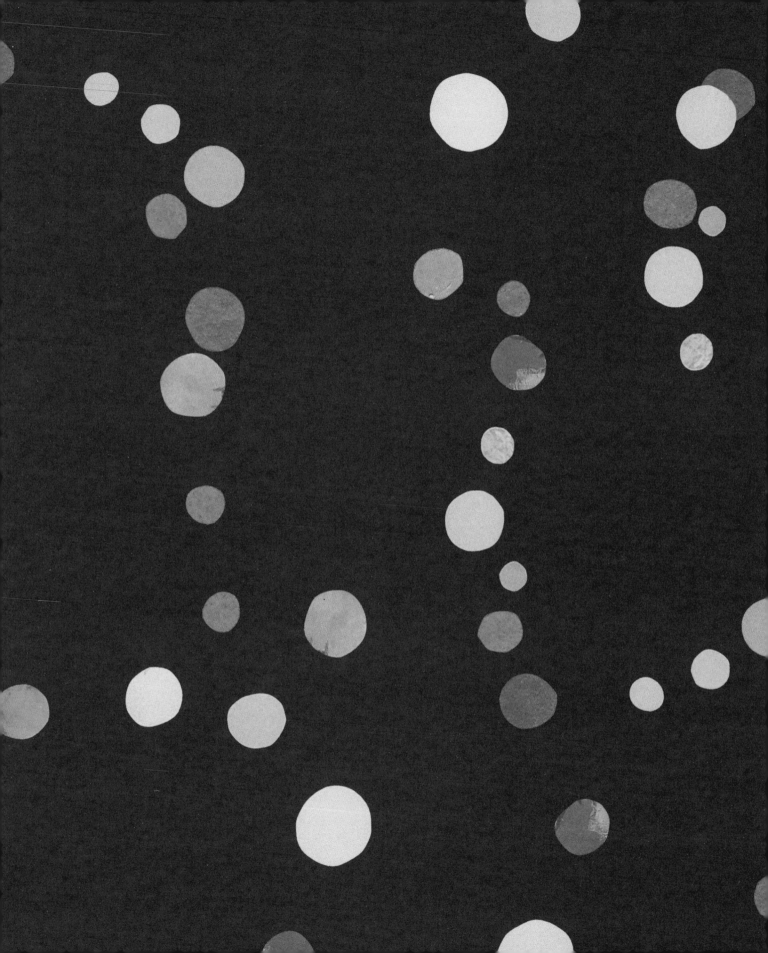

PURPLE RISING

An Imprint of Simon & Schuster, Inc.
1230 Avenue of the Americas
New York, NY 10020

First Atria Books hardcover edition November 2023

ATRIA BOOKS and colophon are trademarks of Simon & Schuster, Inc.

For information about special discounts for bulk purchases,
please contact Simon & Schuster Special Sales at 1-866-506-1949
or business@simonandschuster.com.

The Simon & Schuster Speakers Bureau can bring authors to your live event.
For more information or to book an event, contact the Simon & Schuster Speakers
Bureau at 1-866-248-3049 or visit our website at www.simonspeakers.com.

Manufactured in China

1 3 5 7 9 10 8 6 4 2

Library of Congress Control Number: 2023939146

ISBN 978-1-6680-2321-1
ISBN 978-1-6680-2322-8 (ebook)

PURPLE RISING

CELEBRATING 40 YEARS OF THE MAGIC, POWER, AND ARTISTRY OF
THE COLOR PURPLE

CONCEIVED BY **SCOTT SANDERS**
WRITTEN BY **LISE FUNDERBURG**

ATRIA
BOOKS

MELCHER MEDIA

CONTENTS

BACKSTORIES

I   **TIMELINE** 6

II   **THE 1982 NOVEL** 16
      COVERS ACROSS THE WORLD 28

III   **THE 1985 FILM** 30
      MAKING A FILM IS A TEAM SPORT 36
      GAYLE KING: ALONG FOR THE RIDE 42
      THE MISS MILLIES 58

IV   **THE BROADWAY MUSICAL & REVIVAL** 62
      SHUG ON SHUG 82
      THE BROADWAY SONGS 88

V   **THE 2023 FILM** 94
      CASTING THE LEADS:
      CONTINUING THE LEGACY 112

THEMES

VI   **POWER** 122
      MISTER MEETS MISTER 136
      "HELL NO!" LYRICS 150
      EACH ONE TEACH ONE:
      THE COLOR PURPLE GOES TO SCHOOL 154

VII   **SPIRIT** 160
      THE CURSE 174
      "THE COLOR PURPLE (REPRISE)" LYRICS 180
      A WAY FORWARD 184

VIII   **CONNECTION** 192
      "WHAT ABOUT LOVE" LYRICS 200
      BRINGING *PURPLE* TO BRAZIL 212
      DIRECTING ACROSS THE DIASPORA 218

IX   **JOY** 224
      CELIE'S PANTS 236
      "MISS CELIE'S PANTS" LYRICS 238

NEXT GENERATION

X   **A NEW *PURPLE* RISES** 240
      LOCATIONS 250
      DANIELLE BROOKS:
      ON STAGE VS. SCREEN 260

MEET THE INTERVIEWEES 284

CREDITS AND ACKNOWLEDGMENTS 288

I
TIMELINE

TRACING THE PATH OF
AN AMERICAN MASTERPIECE

"Keep in mind always the present you are constructing. It should be the future you want."

—Alice Walker,
The Temple of My Familiar

1944

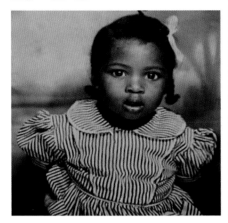

Alice Malsenior Walker is born in Wards Chapel, Georgia, a rural community on the outskirts of Eatonton, on February 9. Alice is the youngest of eight children born to Willie Lee and Minnie Tallulah Grant Walker, who work as sharecroppers on a 600-acre cotton farm. Alice's older brother Bill recognizes Alice's fearlessness and independence early on, when she's "just an itty-bitty little girl."[1]

1952

While playing a game of Cowboys and Indians with her brothers, eight-year-old Alice Walker is shot in her right eye with a BB gun. The scarred, blinded eye that results turns the formerly outgoing child inward. She finds refuge in books and begins writing poetry. Six years later, Alice's older brother Bill, who lives with his wife and baby in Boston, invites Alice to spend the summer with his family. Unbeknownst to her, he and his wife, Gaynell, have arranged eye surgery for her. Though Alice's sight cannot be restored, the surgeon removes her unsightly cataract, liberating Alice from an acute self-consciousness. According to Bill, the first thing Alice does after surgery is to attend a Johnny Mathis concert. Alice later writes that the surgery restored her confidence, allowing her to "raise her head"[2] once again.

1961

Alice enrolls in Atlanta's famed all-women HBCU, Spelman College, having been awarded a scholarship for the "handi-capped,"[3] which was linked to her injured eye. Alice is sent off by her mother with three essential tools: a suitcase, a sewing machine, and a typewriter. At Spelman, she finds two mentors in social action, professors Howard Zinn (above, in 1991) and Staughton Lynd. When Zinn dies half a century later, she writes this tribute: "I was Howard's student for only a semester, but in fact, I have learned from him all my life. His way with resistance: steady, persistent, impersonal, often with humor, is a teaching I cherish. Whenever I've been arrested, I've thought of him. I see policemen as victims of the very system they're hired to defend, as I know he did. I see soldiers in the same way."[4]

1963

Alice transfers to Sarah Lawrence College, in Bronxville, New York, where she will complete her undergraduate education. She arrives "in the middle of winter, without a warm coat or shoes."[5] A professor, the writer Muriel Rukeyser, shows Alice's poems to her own literary agent.

1966

Alice begins to weave a life of social activism and writing. She heads to Jackson, Mississippi, where she meets law school student Melvyn Leventhal. Both work for the NAACP, taking depositions from disenfranchised Black citizens.

1967

Alice marries Melvyn, now a civil rights attorney, despite the disapproval of family members (his object to Alice being Black, hers object to Mel being white and Jewish). "I loved Mel because he was passionate about justice and he was genuinely passionate about me,"[6] Alice said.

1967

Langston Hughes presents Alice's first published short story, "To Hell with Dying," in his collection *The Best Short Stories by Negro Writers: An Anthology from 1899 to the Present*. In his introduction, Hughes writes, "Neither you nor I have ever read a story like [it] before."

1968

Alice's first book, a collection of poetry titled *Once*, is published.

1969

Alice and Melvyn have a daughter, Rebecca Leventhal Walker, on November 17. Rebecca grows up to become a novelist, editor, artist, and activist.

1970s

Alice co-founds a New York–based group of Black women writers who call themselves The Sisterhood. They periodically gather, as seen here in June Jordan's Brooklyn apartment in February 1977, where, literary scholar Courtney Thorsson notes, they would share work, discuss politics, and eat gumbo. Members included Nana Maynard, Ntozake Shange, Louise Meriwether, Margo Jefferson, Vertamae Smart-Grosvenor, Audrey Edwards, and Toni Morrison, among others.

1973

Alice locates the unmarked grave of writer Zora Neale Hurston in Fort Pierce, Florida, and places a marker there. "Her work had a sense of Black people as complete, complex, undiminished human beings, and that was crucial to me as a writer. I wanted people to pay attention. I realized that unless I came out with everything I had supporting her, there was every chance she would slip back into obscurity."[7] The headstone reads:

ZORA NEALE HURSTON
"A Genius of the South"
1901–1960
Novelist, Folklorist
Anthropologist

1974

Alice signs on as a contributing editor to *Ms.* magazine, cementing what will become a lifelong friendship with its founder, Gloria Steinem. Forty years later, Steinem would say of Alice, "Her writing is activism, and her activism is writing. Of anybody I've ever known or could possibly imagine, she's the most true."[8]

1982

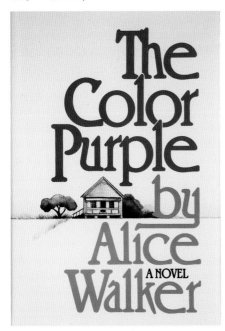

Alice's third novel, *The Color Purple*, is published, having been preceded by *The Third Life of Grange Copeland* (1970) and *Meridian* (1976). *Purple*'s story, which chronicles the life of a Black woman in the American South between 1909 and 1949 and which draws inspiration from Alice's own family history, wins the Pulitzer Prize, making Alice the first African American woman to win the prize for fiction (Gwendolyn Brooks won for poetry in 1950). *The Color Purple* also wins the National Book Award.

1983

Hollywood producer Peter Guber (above, left, with former business partner Jon Peters) secures film rights to *The Color Purple*. Guber promises Alice he'll hire "the *best* people in all categories."[9]

1983

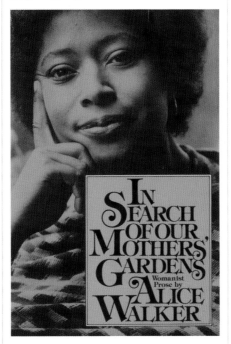

Alice coins the term *womanist* to mean "a Black feminist or feminist of color."

1983

Actor and standup comedian Whoopi Goldberg is driving through Berkeley, California, with her daughter when they hear Alice reading from *The Color Purple* on the radio. "We pulled the car over to listen because it was so extraordinary," Goldberg recalled. On hearing that it's to be made into a film, she writes Alice a letter, professing her desire to be involved. Goldberg goes to New York, where she performs *The Spook Show*, her one-woman multi-character play. Director Mike Nichols sees the show and convinces Goldberg to let him produce it on Broadway, where it has a successful run. "A letter from Alice is waiting for me in New York," Goldberg recalls, "saying, 'Dear Whoopi, I already know about you. I live in San Francisco. I've been to all your shows. I know what you do. I already sent your stuff.' She said, 'When they know what they're doing, someone will reach out so you can audition.' Because I had said to her, 'I'll play the dirt on the floor.'"[10]

1984

In February, director Steven Spielberg and producer Quincy Jones fly from Los Angeles to San Francisco to meet with Alice, in what Spielberg later calls his "audition." Alice is apprehensive at first, as she notes in her journal: "Quincy had talked so positively about [Steven] I was almost dreading his appearance—but then, after a moment of near I don't know what, uneasiness, he came in & sat down & started right in showing how closely he has read the book. And making really intelligent comments. Amazing. And Quincy beamed."[11]

In March, Quincy Jones flies Alice to Los Angeles to see Whoopi Goldberg audition for Celie at Spielberg's studio. Goldberg enlists some of the characters she developed for *The Spook Show*. Years later, Spielberg tells Goldberg that her performance instantly convinced him. "I knew you were Celie probably before you took your fifteenth breath,"[12] he says in 2016.

1984

Copy of Alice Walker's comments (undated) on Oakland School Board action in banning THE COLOR PURPLE.

(School Board later rescinded the ban, after hearing from a panel of experts on literature. Early 1985).

I feel certain that the Oakland Board of Education felt they were doing right when they banned my book, The Color Purple, for ~~Oakland~~ high school students. Of course I do not agree ~~with~~ with them. Some of my most intelligent readers are high school students, many from Oakland, from whom I receive dozens of letters each month. I would ask my young readers, who are not only intelligent readers but understanding and loving ones to try not to feel insulted and patronized by the board's decision. But to remember that if The Color Purple can be banned today, the Color Blue may be outlawed tomorrow.

Groups around the U.S., mostly parent-led, propose banning the novel from school libraries and reading lists. They charge that the book contains "troubling ideas about race relations, man's relationship to God, African history, and human sexuality."[13] For decades to come, *The Color Purple* will make the American Library Association's top 100 list of banned and challenged books.

Alice launches Wild Trees Press. Ex-partner Robert Allen (above) and friend Belvie Rooks join her, and they publish six books over the next four years, including Black writer and playwright J. California Cooper's story collection *A Piece of Mine*.

1985

Spielberg's film is released to both acclaim and protest. As film historian Donald Bogle noted in 1986: "For Black viewers there is a schizophrenic reaction. You're torn in two. On the one hand you see the character of Mister and you're disturbed by the stereotype. Yet, on the other hand, and this is the basis of the appeal of that film for so many people, is that the women you see in the movie, you have never seen Black women like this put on the screen before. I'm not talking about what happens to them in the film, I'm talking about the visual statement itself. When you see Whoopi Goldberg in close-up, a loving close-up, you look at this woman, you know that in American films in the past, in the 1930s, 1940s, she would have played a maid. She would have been a comic maid. Suddenly, the camera is focusing on her, and we say 'I've seen this woman some place, I know her.'"[14]

1986

Whoopi Goldberg wins a Golden Globe award for Best Actress in a Film Drama for her portrayal of Celie in *The Color Purple*.

1986

Critic Gene Siskel tells Oprah Winfrey, who plays Sofia in the film, she should bronze the roll from the Oscar nominee luncheon, since there's no way she'll win against fellow nominee Anjelica Huston (*Prizzi's Honor*). Oprah bronzes the roll.

1986

Whoopi Goldberg brings actor Michael J. Fox as her plus-one to the Oscar awards ceremony. The film wins no awards. *Out of Africa*, which Alice condemns as reactionary and racist, wins seven. "It patronizes Black people shockingly, and its sly gratuitous denigration of the Black woman is insufferable," she later writes. "But it is a worldview the Academy understood and upheld."[15]

The Color Purple receives eleven Academy Award nominations. Notably, Best Director is not among them. Critic Roger Ebert credits Whoopi Goldberg wtih giving one of the most amazing debut performances in movie history and predicts, "Here is this year's winner of the Academy Award for best actress."

The Director's Guild of America names Steven Spielberg the year's best director for *The Color Purple*, the first (but not last) time he will win this award.

1994

Alice changes her middle name from Malsenior to Tallulah-Kate, honoring her mother (pictured above with Alice's father) and paternal grandmother.

1996

Alice publishes *The Same River Twice: Honoring the Difficult: A Meditation on Life, Spirit, Art, and the Making of the Film* The Color Purple *Ten Years Later*. She includes the screenplay treatment she wrote for the 1985 film, which was not used, as well as reflections on the mixed experience of having her novel adapted for the screen.

1997

American singer Erykah Badu releases her album *Baduizm*. In the music video for its Grammy Award–winning hit single, "On and On," Badu portrays a character that borrows heavily from both Celie and Shug as they were portrayed in the 1985 film.

1997

Producer Scott Sanders approaches Alice with the concept of a Broadway adaptation. He makes his pitch, to which she responds, "Well, you seem like a very nice young man, but no."[16] Months later, he flies her to New York to see Broadway shows and speak further about adapting the novel to a musical for the stage. Reassured and encouraged, Alice gives him the go-ahead.

1998

Alice visits *Sesame Street* and helps The Count count raindrops.

2002

Alice is inducted into the Georgia Writers Hall of Fame.

2004

Alice Walker: A Life is published. Written by journalist Evelyn C. White (above), with the cooperation of Alice and over the course of ten years, the biography is hailed by the *New York Times Book Review* as "never less than fascinating."

In September, Sanders and his fellow producers preview *The Color Purple* musical outside of New York, at the Alliance Theatre in Atlanta, a mere 80 miles from Alice's hometown of Eatonton. The month-long preview draws sold-out audiences and breaks the Alliance's box-office record.

2005

Sanders's creative team includes song-writers Allee Willis, Brenda Russell, and Stephen Bray (above), as well as director Gary Griffin and playwright Marsha Norman. Roy Furman and Quincy Jones sign on as producers. In July, they produce a pre-Broadway workshop of the musical's book, choreography, and score, which is staged in New York. *O Magazine* Editor-at-Large Gayle King attends.

In September, Sanders's cell phone rings. It's Oprah Winfrey. "How can I help?"[17] she asks, and they agree that she'll sign on as a producer. "It's been a secret dream of mine to be part of Broadway," she will later tell *The New York Times*. "I hope to be able to do for this production some of what I've been able to do for books—that is, to open the door to the possibilities for a world of people who have never been or even thought of going to a Broadway show."

2005

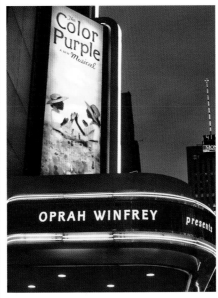

In addition to making a financial investment, Winfrey lends her name to the marquee above the show's title. That November, she features *The Color Purple* cast on her television show. Ticket sales skyrocket.

The show premieres December 1st at the Broadway Theater, featuring LaChanze (Celie), Felicia P. Fields (Sofia), Kingsley Leggs (Mister), Elisabeth Withers (Shug), Brandon Victor Dixon (Harpo), and Renée Elise Goldsberry (Nettie). Stars and celebrities flood the red carpet, from Sidney Poitier to Cicely Tyson, Angela Bassett, and David Bowie.

2006

In June, the show garners eleven Tony nominations (a number eerily reminiscent of the film's 1986 Oscar nominations). The Leading Actress in a Musical award goes to LaChanze, who begins her acceptance speech by acknowledging Alice. "Thank you for allowing these characters to come through you and grace us all with this human, powerful story, that I get to experience every single night."[18]

2012

Northwest School of the Arts in Charlotte, North Carolina, is one of the first high schools in the country to mount a production of *The Color Purple*. Under the tutelage of drama teacher Corey Mitchell, the show wins a spot at Nebraska's International Thespian Festival in 2013.

2013

British director John Doyle refashions the stage show into a shorter, sparer production. The revival features Cynthia Erivo as Celie and debuts at the Menier Chocolate Factory in London in July.

Beauty in Truth, a documentary about Alice and directed by Pratibha Parmar, is released. Filmmaker Ava DuVernay describes the film as "an intimate, exquisitely rendered portrait."[19]

2015

Northwest School of the Arts drama teacher Corey Mitchell is awarded the inaugural Excellence in Theatre Education Award by Carnegie Mellon University and the Tony Awards.

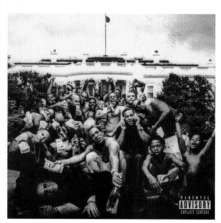

American rapper Kendrick Lamar opens his song "Alright" with a line from Sofia's character: "Alls my life I had to fight." In response, Alice says, "I think he's understanding that this is the truth of it. Especially for poor people and people of color in this country. We've had to fight all of our lives. And it's a good thing that we can talk to each other across generations."[20]

2015

The revival, still under John Doyle's direction, opens on Broadway in December and features Cynthia Erivo (Celie), Danielle Brooks (Sofia), Jennifer Hudson (Shug), Isaiah Johnson (Mister), Joaquina Kalukango (Nettie), and Kyle Scatliffe (Harpo).

2016

The revival wins two Tony Awards: Leading Actress in a Musical (Cynthia Erivo) and Best Revival of a Musical.

2018

In January, *The Color Purple* musical opens in Johannesburg, South Africa, with an all-South African cast.

Scott Sanders meets with Warner Bros.' Niija Kuykendall, executive vice president of film production, to pitch the idea of adapting the musical into a feature film. "I'd never met Scott before," Kuykendall says, "and I immediately loved the notion, because doing the musical for screen felt like new news."

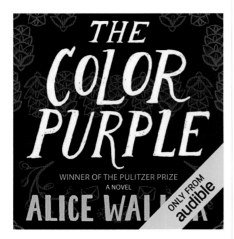

Alice records an audiobook version of the novel.

2020

Actor Samira Wiley (*Orange Is the New Black*, *The Handmaid's Tale*) records an audiobook version of the novel. "I honestly feel like, sometimes, that Miss Alice Walker was writing just for me," Wiley says of the book.[21]

2021

Scholar, cultural critic, and activist Salamishah Tillet's book *In Search of The Color Purple: The Story of an American Masterpiece*, is published. *Elle* magazine calls it "a love letter to *The Color Purple* and the Black women who came before us."

2022

The musical film begins its shoot on location throughout Georgia.

2022

Gathering Blossoms Under Fire: The Journals of Alice Walker, 1965–2000, edited by Valerie Boyd, is released. "I want the journals to be used so that people can see this working through of disappointment, anger, sorrow, regret," Alice says. "So in that sense, it's a medicine book."

2023

In December, the musical film is released.

II

THE 1982 NOVEL

TAKING IT TO THE PAGE

*If it is true that it is what we run from
that chases us, then* The Color Purple *(this color
that is always a surprise but is everywhere
in nature) is the book that ran me down while
I sat with my back to it in a field.*

—Alice Walker,
preface to the 1992 edition of
The Color Purple

Dear God, ~~I Trist See with ret~~

Shug Avery is coming to town! She coming with her orkestra. She ~~a big time singer.~~ She going to sing in the Lucky Star out on Coalfield road. Mr. ~~———~~ going to hear her. He dress all up in front of the glass, look at himself, then undress and dress all over again. He slick back his hair with pomade, then wash it out again. He been spitting on his shoes & hitting it with a quick rag.

He tell me, Wash this. Iron that. Look for this. Look for that. Find this. Find that. He growl over holes in his sock. ~~I'm not spose to know what~~ Going on.

I move round ~~from~~ doing this, ironing, finding handkerchifs ~~another.~~ Anything happening? I ast.

Whatumean? he say, like he mad. Just trying to git some of the hick farmer off myself for a change. Any other woman be glad.

I'm *is* glad, I say.

Whatumean? he ast.

You looks nice, I say. ~~Handsome.~~ Any woman be proud.

LISTENING TO THE ANCESTORS

ALICE WALKER (author of *The Color Purple,* **1982):** I completely changed my life to find a place where this story could be born. That meant leaving a marriage, New York City, my job as an editor at *Ms.* magazine, as well as a lovely home I had created in the Park Slope section of Brooklyn and that I had assumed I could coax my characters to visit me in. No luck. My characters basically wanted to live somewhere like the Georgia they were born in, but one where a Black creative person could relax. So I moved a few hours north of San Francisco, to a valley flanked by modest mountains, close to a river and redwoods. Twenty minutes from the coast.

EVELYN C. WHITE (journalist and author of *Alice Walker: A Life***):** In 1982, I was living in Seattle and working as an advocate for battered women with the city attorney's office. I was among a staff of four or five women who would accompany women to court who had filed charges against their abusers. I read *The Color Purple* because everybody was talking about it. I read it almost in one sitting. I just went right through it. I knew immediately that it was historic because it was written in the epistolary style, the letter form, and because it

dealt with a Black girl from the South [Celie] who had been sexually abused. It was written in Black dialect, or what people back then might have called Ebonics. It was so vivid, so heartfelt, so personal. And at the same time, very, very large.

There was beginning to be more public talk about childhood sexual abuse. That topic was beginning to come out of the closet. I had read Alice's novel *The Third Life of Grange Copeland* as part of the research I was doing for a book on battered Black women. So this whole notion of the abuse that Black women and girls were suffering at the hands of their mirror reflection was coming to the fore.

When this novel appeared, it captured the attention of all good people who were reading literature. It was artistic, it was political, it was breaking a silence. The craft of it was magnificent. It was groundbreaking on every level. I had no trouble entering the language, the—as Alice would call it—Black folk language. I understood every word of it. Coming from the spiritual slice of Black life, this girl writing to God, I got it. And I was so grateful to be on planet Earth at the same time as when this novel was published.

SALAMISHAH TILLET (scholar, critic, and author of *In Search of the Color Purple: The Story of an American Masterpiece***):** I first read the book when I was fifteen

Alice Walker as a young girl, 1950

Alice Walker (center) and her parents,
Minnie Tallulah Grant and Willie Lee Walker, 1963

years old, in the summer of 1991. As a lover of literature, it gave me access to a world that was foreign to me because it was so long ago. At the same time, the novel creates a Black world on so many different levels. Alice creates it on the level of structure, with Celie writing to God, or Nettie [Celie's sister] and Celie writing to each other. And then the use of Celie's voice and African American Southern vernacular as the primary language in which we understand this story. And then also, while white characters are present—and in a disturbing way—the majority of characters in this book are Black. I grew up in Boston and then Trinidad and Tobago, but I grew up in predominantly Black communities. This idea of being enveloped in this Black world was familiar to me.

Shug Avery is based on. Shug Perry was the woman that Alice's grandfather, Henry Clay Walker, really wanted to marry, but his father, Albert Walker, who would become Old Mister, thought that Shug Perry was a loose woman.

According to Ruth, Albert Walker, who was fairly wealthy and owned land, basically forbade his son to marry Shug Perry, real name Estella Perry, because she was lowlife. Albert insisted that Henry marry a woman named Kate, who was from an upstanding family. Henry did, but he never loved her. He always maintained a relationship with Shug Perry, who had moved to Cleveland but would come back and visit. And apparently, whenever she came back to town, Henry would begin his relationship with her.

"I was dealing with some skeletons in the closet in the family, wanting to bring light to very murky corners."
—Alice Walker

Then there are parts of it that really woke me up and helped develop my Black feminist consciousness. Because there had been domestic violence with my mother and my stepfather, this idea that Black women and girls could be vulnerable was familiar to me. My mother was also a sexual assault survivor. Alice Walker's clear-eyed depiction of violence against Black women, and the vulnerability of Black women and girls, articulated that and also provided an alternative at the same time.

EVELYN C. WHITE: When I started work on the biography, Alice did not suggest to me that I go to Hollywood and talk to Steven Spielberg or that I go to Chicago and interview Oprah Winfrey. She sent me immediately to interview her brother Bill, who had been instrumental in having the scar tissue removed from her eye [following a childhood accident], and her sister Ruth. I stayed with Ruth for maybe ten days. She was an incredible storyteller, and I think she appreciated having the opportunity to tell me about Alice's step-grandmother, Rachel, who was basically Celie, and Shug Perry, who was the woman

As Ruth told me the story, Kate decided that two could play at this game, so she had an affair of her own with a man in the town. This upstanding, Sunday school-teaching woman apparently began to feel guilty about it, so she wanted to end it. One day, sometime in the 1920s, she and her son Willie Lee Walker, Alice's father, were heading home from a Fourth of July gathering. This man Kate was having an affair with came out of the bushes, and she told him, "I don't want to do this anymore." Apparently, he didn't want her to quit him. He put a pistol in her chest, it went off, and she was shot. Alice's father witnessed that, unloosing her corset as he sat with his dying mother. Ruth told me he was traumatized by it forever.

As a result, Henry, who was basically Mister, was left with five kids, so he was not so much looking for a wife as he was looking for someone to take care of the children. Henry went to a neighbor wanting to hire his daughter, Rachel Little, a young Black girl about Willie Lee Walker's age. This man said, "You can't have her as a nanny or a housekeeper, but I'll let you marry her."

Apparently, he was concerned about the propriety of his daughter going to the household of a known womanizer. So that's why Henry married Rachel, who was Alice's step-grandmother and who became the model for Celie in *The Color Purple*.

And so Old Mister is Albert Walker. Mister is Henry Clay Walker. Willie Lee Walker is Alice's father and is more or less depicted in the character Harpo. Sofia is based on Alice's mother, Minnie Lou Walker. And Nettie takes the name of Alice's maternal grandmother. Minnie Lou Walker's mother was named Nettie and apparently took some abuse from her husband.

ALICE WALKER: In writing *The Color Purple*, I was dealing with some skeletons in the closet in the family, wanting to bring light to very murky corners, wanting to have my grandmother back who had been murdered, and wanting to understand what had happened to my father, who was required to basically try to raise some wild sisters as a boy because his mother had been murdered in the road. Also, the grandfather that I adored was a horrible person when he was younger because he was a drunkard, a wife-batterer, a philanderer, you name it. He was also someone suffering very much from the botched job of Reconstruction. That was a piece that it took me even more years to struggle with, because of course, nobody was going to tell us why we were sharecropping the same land in which we'd been enslaved.

Unlike my older siblings, I knew our grandfather when he was old and had quit drinking, or, as he used to say, drinking quit him. He had a sense of humor. Without being an alcoholic and the damage that wrought to his body, his spirit, his psyche, he was a sweet old man, and he really loved me. He wasn't abusive; you just felt that solid presence of someone old, who deeply cared, and who was just going to be there for you. I sense that we were very similar in our love of quiet nature.

I was actually in Greece when he died. I had gotten a divorce that almost killed me, and I just took off and left the country, so I wasn't there at the funeral. I knew I should have been. In a way, out of that realization that I had missed saying goodbye to this person in person, was part of why I wanted to write about his transformation. I really suffered from not being there. I don't go to funerals much now because I went to so many as a child. I mean, just funeral after funeral. I should have been there.

EVELYN C. WHITE: Ruth told Alice the story about one time when Shug Perry returned to Eatonton [Georgia]. Whenever she would come, she would hang out with Henry Clay, her lover, and Rachel accepted it because, as Ruth said, he was nicer when Shug was around. The conversations were better. They had better food. He was totally in love with her. And so Rachel accepted it.

Shug Perry had come there one summer, and they all had come from church. Ruth was five years old, and they were cutting across the field to go to the outhouse. Ruth witnessed Shug Perry sitting in the outhouse toilet with her panties dropped and Rachel saying to her, "Oh, give me those pretty pink panties." Shug Perry kicked the panties off and handed them to Rachel, who was basically her lover's wife. And Ruth told me that she shared this story with Alice, and Alice later said she'd kept that in mind, that her family history had one Black woman giving another Black woman her underwear. That became the nugget of the relationship between Shug and Celie.

Members of Alice's family, including her step-grandmother, Rachel (second from right), who inspired the character of Celie

ALICE WALKER: Well, imagine that your husband has a lover he's just crazy about, and there you are, this homely—well, to quote them, "homely" mainly because she was thin—drudge. The woman he adores wears panties like these. Now, there you are in bloomers. I don't know a whole lot about bloomers, but some of the old people still referred to panties as bloomers. There you are in your homemade bloomers that sag down the side and to the knee almost, and his lover is wearing these frilly, satin, probably hot pink, scandalous panties that obviously were driving him crazy. And then Shug gives her a pair. She says, "Here." There's so much wonderful solidarity in the way they both approached their common fate as women. One was adored, but not really supported—children gone to the wherever—and the other a drudge with no agency whatsoever.

A DIFFERENT ENDING

EVELYN C. WHITE: Alice's work in *The Color Purple*, as well as in *Meridian* and *The Third Life of Grange Copeland*, is about Blacks in relation to each other. Of course, there's always the backdrop of white oppression, but Alice is saying, "Let's look at how we deal with each other. Just because the white man is dogging us doesn't mean that we go and disrespect and disparage each other." And people were not ready to hear that message.

> ## "When the book came out, there was already this robust literary movement happening within Black feminist thought."
> —*Aisha Harris*

AISHA HARRIS (co-host/reporter, National Public Radio's "Pop Culture Happy Hour"): In 1982, when the book came out, there was already this robust literary movement happening within Black feminist thought. All these Black female artists were reckoning with their position in society and how that position both aligned with and diverged from the Black men in their lives. Michele Wallace really homed in on that with her book *Black Macho and the Myth of the Superwoman*. She laid out how the idea had been festering since slavery that patriarchy in many ways rules over everything, even racism. And this was how we saw Black men adopting this idea of Black liberation that often excluded Black women or put them to the side.

SALAMISHAH TILLET: Walker was exploring and exposing these issues of gender-based violence in the '80s. These were taboo topics, and she paid a cost for exposing what she understood to be the fragile condition of Black women's lives. Something I learned only from the process of writing my book was that these weren't just characters in *The Color Purple*, these are actually her family members. And so when Walker encounters attacks in the media and in the Black community from people who claim that she is reproducing stereotypes of Black men, she's like, "But this is real life. These are the lived conditions of the women I know." In a sense, it's not a fantasy that she was creating; she was actually trying to give her grandmother a different ending.

Learning about Rachel Little humanized Celie in a way that I didn't know was possible. If you're thinking of these people simply as characters, that's one thing. But if you think of them as a wish fulfillment for a Black woman growing up in the South in the early to mid-twentieth century whose life is filled with drudgery, it's different. Then you really are cheering Celie on. She's speaking for all Black women, and that's why it resonates with people, because you don't have to know about Rachel Little to appreciate Celie's revelatory song at the end of the musical. But knowing it gave me a deeper appreciation for what was at stake in Celie's arc.

NIIJA KUYKENDALL (former production executive, Warner Bros.): I'm in the movie business, and I love it. I feel very blessed. But my road to being in the movies really started with being a bookworm from third grade on. And so my first experience with *Color Purple* was the book when I was probably eleven, twelve. All throughout

Alice Walker with the quilt she worked on while writing *The Color Purple*, 1980s

"*The Color Purple* was what church should have been, what honest familial reckoning could have been, and it is still the only art object in the world by which all three generations of Black artists in my family judge American art."

—KIESE LAYMON
Award-winning author

From his foreword to the 40th anniversary edition of *The Color Purple*, 2022

Left to right: Alice Walker, Barbara Christian, Mary Helen Washington, and Paule Marshall, members of the Black female writers' group the Sisterhood, 1984

[my] preteens and then into college, I was leaning into Alice Walker and Ntozake Shange. I was in this space of becoming a woman and gravitating toward Black female authors. I remember being struck by it, being like, "OK, this is one that I need to keep and that I'm going to revisit." There were a few like that. There was this. There was *Sassafrass, Cypress & Indigo* from Ntozake Shange. There was the autobiography of Assata Shakur. I was in this phase of consuming and reading these books that opened my eyes to both empowerment and to the challenges and the history of being a Black woman in this world. And then also, of course, the relatability of certain awakenings with these women. I remember reading it for the first time and thinking, "I've got to reread this. I don't know if I understood everything, but going forward, this is one that's going to go with me."

EVELYN C. WHITE: The editor on *The Color Purple* was a man named John Ferrone, who basically told me that Alice had submitted a manuscript no one believed was going anywhere. He told me they were astounded by it: Black English, epistolary, about a Black girl who'd been sexually abused in the South. He said they couldn't wait for the novel to vanish so Alice could go into the next thing. He had no faith, no belief in it whatsoever. They wanted it to drop and to vanish. They saw potential in Alice, but this *Color Purple* thing, they were not feeling it at all.

There was this surge of Black woman writers they wanted to be in on because they perceived it as being commercially profitable. At the time *The Color Purple* emerged, Toni Morrison had done *Song of Solomon*. Toni had been on the cover of *Newsweek*. Ntozake had done *For Colored Girls Who Have Considered Suicide/When the Rainbow Is Enuf*, which had been a huge success. There was this atmosphere of wanting to get in on the Black women writers thing.

I think everybody was completely blindsided by the Pulitzer Prize. We might not have the Alice Walker we have today if *The Color Purple* had not won the Pulitzer, had not been made into a film. I believe, as Alice believes and Ruth and others believe, that it was this divine story that Alice was determined to write, no matter what the publishing world said, and she did. She was dead set on telling the story and organized her life so that she could listen to Shug and Celie and Mister and Nettie. She moved purposely out of New York City to the countryside of California to write that novel. She gave herself five years to do it, and she did it in a year, and she wept when it was over.

ALICE WALKER: When I finished writing the book, I was in tears, but they were tears of just such deliverance, because I felt I had really sussed this out, the whole rigamarole of the lives of these people that

I loved, and that I mostly made up, really, based on something that was fragmentary, to say the least. So, I was free.

QUINCY JONES (executive producer and composer, 1985 film; producer, 2005 Broadway musical, 2015 Broadway revival, 2023 film): I first became aware of Alice Walker and the novel when the book was published in 1982. The book was a sensation and deservedly catapulted Alice into that rarefied air of being one of the country's most important literary voices.

I've stayed connected to it over all these years because, simply put, Alice penned a brilliant and "real" novel. She carefully painted the lives of the characters in

very short. Very short. I tried to insist that they keep the title of the book, that it should be the Romanized words for "color purple" in Japanese. That original title is so striking and should not be changed. But the publishing company said no. They chose *Tremblance of Purple*. I didn't like that, the sense of shivering when it should be more direct. But I was too weak against the giant publishing company. So I lost. I was so unhappy and disappointed. And then Steven Spielberg made the film, and the publisher at last understood. In less than six months, which is highly unusual, they came out with the pocket edition and changed the title to *The Color Purple*. So I am pleased. And it's now in its forty-first printing.

"When I read those first lines, 'Dear God, I am fourteen years old,' I thought, 'How does Alice Walker know about my life?'"
—Oprah Winfrey

such a beautiful way that it was something I couldn't turn away from. It's heavy, but it matters, because it forces you to face it head-on. It is our truth. And that truth needs to be passed down.

YUMIKO YANAGISAWA (Japanese literary translator, 1982 novel): The book came out in 1982, and in 1983 I traveled to the United States for the first time. I went to meet with people I knew in the women's movement. I traveled from San Francisco to New York, and almost everybody I met was talking about *The Color Purple*. I bought the book, and on my flight home to Tokyo, I read it. I was so impressed, and I was moved, and I thought, "I have to translate this." I had been translating books from Swedish into Japanese since 1979, but I had never translated English.

I had a connection with Shueisha, a big publishing company. I went to them and said, "I would like to translate this." They said they had the translation rights and I think they had somebody in mind, but I came there with such eagerness that they gave me the chance. I translated in one stretch, in four months, which is

STEPHEN BRAY (music and lyrics, 2005 Broadway musical, 2015 Broadway revival, 2023 film): I love words, and I love the written word. I love anybody who has that facility with creating characters and telling a really, really, powerfully disturbing story in some regards and then still somehow managing to make the whole thing end up being uplifting and life-affirming and love-affirming and forgiveness-affirming. I can't think of another book that does that. I would like to think it helped cement my belief in those things.

OPRAH WINFREY (Sofia, 1985 film; producer, 2005 Broadway musical, 2015 Broadway revival, 2023 film): I was obsessed from the moment in 1982 when I read the *New York Times* review of the novel. I got out of bed, went to get the book at the bookstore around the corner from me, came home, and read it straight through. When I read those first lines, "Dear God, I am fourteen years old," I thought, "How does Alice Walker know about my life?" Obviously, I was moved by the story because at fourteen years old, I became pregnant and had to hide it and the baby died. But I also knew that if I had been so

Author Alice Walker wins a Pulitzer Prize

From Press Dispatches

NEW YORK — Georgia native Alice Walker won a 1983 Pulitzer Prize Monday for her novel "The Color Purple," making her the first black woman to win the award for fiction.

■ *Alice Walker didn't know there was a Pulitzer Prize for fiction. Page 1-B.*

■ *Complete list of Pulitzer winners. Page 5-B.*

Another Georgian, Claude Sitton, editor of The News and Observer in Raleigh, N.C., since 1968, won a Pulitzer for commentary. Sitton, a native Atlantan who graduated from Emory University, now is editor of the Raleigh, N.C., News and Observer and writes a weekly column on national and international issues as well as regional politics.

The 67th annual Pulitzer prizes in journalism and the arts, most of which carry a $1,000 award, were announced by Michael I. Sovern, president of Columbia University, which administers the prizes.

Ms. Walker's novel, published in 1982, is the story of Celie, a teenage bride with a family in the rural American South, and Nettie, her sister, a missionary in Africa.

Ms. Walker, a native of Eatonton whose mother still lives in the middle Georgia town, now lives in San Francisco.

Sitton, 57, received the award for his 1982 Sunday columns, including commentary on civil rights, the Environmental Protection Agency, public education and Sen. Jesse Helms (R-N.C.), the prize board said. He served as the New York Times' Atlanta-based southern correspondent from 1958 to 1964 and was the newspaper's national news editor from 1964 to 1968.

Georgian Alice Walker

Syndicated columnist Russell Baker of The New York Times was awarded the Pulitzer for his autobiography, "Growing Up." The prize for distinguished play went to "'Night, Mother," by Marsha Norman, the story of a woman who decides to commit suicide.

Atlanta Daily World announces Alice Walker's Pulitzer Prize for Fiction, 1983

---

moved by the story, at least a million other people would also have this feeling.

I was still in Baltimore then, doing a talk show. We probably tried to have her on, but Alice Walker wasn't coming to Baltimore for a local talk show. There was no way of having that conversation. Instead, I was trying to force the conversation with other people one-on-one, literally one-on-one: "You need to read this." If I could have put on a sandwich board and gone out into the street, I would've.

I used to carry a backpack to and from work, just to give out the book. I would empty out the bookstore every week, buying all their stock. I would walk down the street with at least ten or twelve books, until I'd lightened my load, and then I'd go back and buy more.

I'd open a conversation with, "How are you today? Have you read *The Color Purple*?" and give the person a book. They'd be like, "Huh? What is this?"

I have never done that with anything before or since. I was buying books and handing them out on the street. I was telling people I worked with, "If you don't read it, then you can't be my friend." I was going to beauty salons I didn't know on Saturdays and handing out the books. I'd be looking at people under the dryers and thinking, "I wonder, does she read? Even if she doesn't, she can give it to somebody else." At the time, I didn't have any kind of platform or way of having that conversation about what Celie was saying. I didn't have a way of having the conversation about Black women's empowerment in a way that I felt comfortable.

COVERS ACROSS THE WORLD

Book jacket designs for Alice Walker's novel, which has been translated into more than two dozen languages, speak not only to design trends but also to how each culture aims to capture the book's core message.

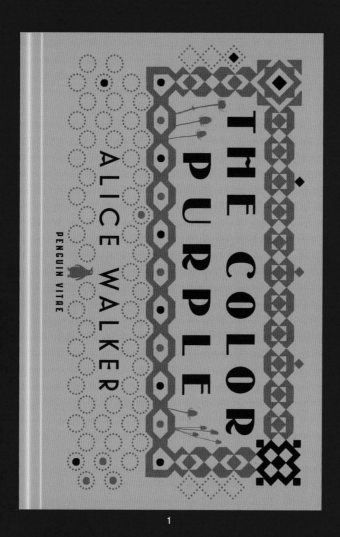

1

1. Penguin Random House, 40th anniversary edition, 2022
2. دار المدى , Arabic transaltion, 2018
3. বাতিঘর, Bengali translation, 2023
4. Samlerens Bogklub, Danish translation, 1985
5. Maartin Muntinga, Dutch translation, 1987

6. Ecco Verlag, German translation, 2021
7. Robert Laffont, French translation, 2022
8. Frassinelli, Italian translation, 1984
9. Shueisha, Japanese translation, 1986
10. Suma de Letras, Portuguese translation, 2018

2

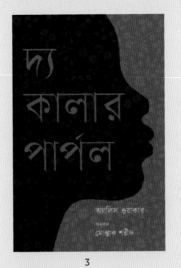

3

4

5

6

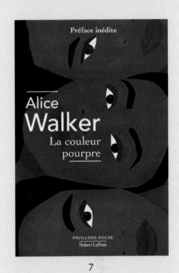

7

8

9

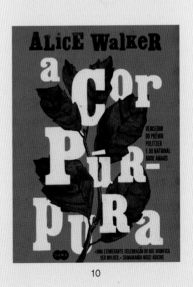

10

III

THE 1985 FILM

TAKING IT TO THE SCREEN

*For me the filming of my book was a
journey to the imagined and vastly re-arranged lives of
my mother and father and grandparents before I was born
(among other things); it was a re-created world I
hoped desperately my mother would live long enough to
enter again through film. I used to amuse myself, on
the set, watching Steven work, and thinking of the gift
he was preparing for a woman he had never seen.*

—Alice Walker,
The Same River Twice

Swain (Laurence Fishburne, left) and Harpo (Willard E. Pugh, right) take Shug (Margaret Avery, center) to see the juke joint, 1985 film

PUTTING TOGETHER
THE PEOPLE AND THE PIECES

SALAMISHAH TILLET (scholar, critic, and author of *In Search of the Color Purple: The Story of an American Masterpiece*): This story has such a weird lineage. The number of people who have become obsessed with *The Color Purple* and who want to do something with it and who have the power to do something with it is interesting, starting with Peter Guber, the Hollywood producer. He's a key person because he's the one who first optioned the film rights. Then he found Quincy Jones. Jones then brought on Steven Spielberg.

Years later, Scott Sanders worked for Peter Guber doing TV. After a time, Scott went off on his own, and he came up with the idea of the musical. He went back to Guber to ask for the rights; Guber no longer owned them, but he introduced Scott to the people who did.

ALICE WALKER (author of *The Color Purple*, 1982): I was very taken by Quincy and Steven when they came to meet me at my house, and if I had not been, the answer would've been no. But I really liked them. In fact, I loved them. If I don't feel it, I just will never miss you. "It's nice seeing you, and no, and goodbye." But they were so down-to-earth and warm and fun, and even more than that, they had read the book.

My characters knew nothing of Hollywood, nor did I. I don't think of either Steven or Quincy as being especially Hollywood, and that's probably because I am still innocent in a way about that world. They just seemed really alive and creatively thoughtful about producing a movie we might all enjoy. Our evening together plotting what *Purple* might become made us, all three, bubbly with joy. It was quite a miracle, really, that these two men whom I'd never met and barely heard of—I'd never heard even of Steven; [my daughter] Rebecca took me to see *ET*, which I adored—just completely met my own enthusiasm about the loveliness of Shug and Celie and Sofia and other characters. What were the odds? But since this is the way I live—from wonder to wonder—it seemed perfectly right. I was very happy.

QUINCY JONES (executive producer and composer, 1985 film; producer, 2005 Broadway musical, 2015 Broadway revival, 2023 film): My production deal at the time was at Time-Warner, and Steve Ross—one of

Quincy Jones and Alice Walker
on the set of the 1985 film

my business mentors and the chairman of the company—loved the idea of *The Color Purple* and that Steven Spielberg and I would be teaming up together on it. So he was kind of our guardian angel throughout the entire filmmaking process, from production all the way through to the release of the film.

REUBEN CANNON (casting director, 1985 film): When I first read *The Color Purple*, I thought, "What an amazing piece of work." At the time, Reuben Cannon & Associates was the largest and most successful casting office in Hollywood, and it wasn't just with Black projects. Because of the success of my company, I never had to pick up a phone and ask for a job. My attitude was that if you want to buy a Rolls-Royce or a diamond, you know where to go. Quality sells itself.

I heard that Quincy Jones was producing *Color Purple*, and I thought, "Well, they'll call me." But the phone didn't ring. I loved the book, and I believed wholeheartedly that no one in Hollywood could do a better job than me. No other casting director had my experience and reputation as well as my cultural connection to the novel. But mostly it was my passion for the material. I knew I would be really pissed off if I went to see this movie and saw another name under "casting by." So I wrote a letter to Quincy saying, "I know

Moon Song, the code name
for the original film's screenplay

"Everyone—
famous, well-known
actors as well as
talented unknowns
—was crazed and
obsessed, wanting to
play a role."
—*Reuben Cannon*

you're one of the executive producers of *Color Purple* and I'd love to be considered." Right before I mailed it, the phone rang. It was Quincy, and he said, "You need to meet with Steven Spielberg regarding casting *The Color Purple."*

Once it was known—even under the pseudonym of *Moon Song*—that Reuben Cannon was casting *Color Purple*, my office was inundated. I was inundated. Every Black actor in the country wanted to be cast—or at least given the chance to audition. Everyone—famous, well-known actors as well as talented unknowns—was crazed and obsessed, wanting to play a role. At that time, there were so few Black projects being produced that *The Color Purple* became a focal point of increased anxiety and desperation among Black actors.

When Steven and I first talked about the casting concepts, we agreed this film would be better served with a cast of unknown actors. Steven wanted to work with Danny [Glover], who had been in *Witness* and *Places in the Heart*, but he was maybe the only actor in the cast that you could say was known. The story was the star.

Sofia and Shug were the hardest roles to fill. Obviously major names came up, like Phyllis Hyman and Patti LaBelle. Tina Turner came in and met with Steven. I was there for that meeting. It was a hot summer day, and she was wearing a summer dress, and she just had a spellbinding aura about her. I remember sitting next to her,

and she was sweating. Someone handed her a tissue and she wiped underneath her arms and was wondering what to do with it. Without even thinking, I extended my hand and collected it. I must have been having an internal conversation: "I am so in awe of you, Miss Turner, I'll take the sweat from your armpits." I should have kept it! I really should have.

Quincy knew Tina and was pushing for her to play Shug. But she said, "Look, I went through this with Ike. I'm not going to go through it again. Anna Mae Bullock experienced that. Tina Turner does not want to."

So we continued the process of casting. Actors would read for me. If I found someone really exceptional, I would videotape them and share the tape with Steven, and he'd select the ones to come in for a callback. I was seeing people; I was making trips; I had other casting directors around the country also videotaping actors. Because who knows? There might've been someone in Minnesota or somewhere that I wasn't aware of. No one had jumped out at me, and then Margaret Avery sent me a letter.

MARGARET AVERY (Shug, 1985 film): I had just come back from Jakarta, where I was singing, and I had all kinds of messages on my answering service from other actors, saying, "Margaret, have you heard about *The Color Purple*?" I called my agent, and they said, "We've been trying to push you, but they don't want to see you. Reuben says that you're just not the right type."

I knew Reuben Cannon. I'd been doing television for twenty years, and Reuben had cast me for several roles. So I wrote him a note and I said, "Reuben, I know where you live, and if you don't see me for this role I'm going to sit at your doorstep until you see me."

A couple of days later I heard from him: "OK, Margaret, come on in."

I went out and bought the book. I thought everyone had me right for Celie, but when I read the book, I gravitated to Shug. I could really relate to her. Because Q [Quincy Jones] was a producer and a music person, he was looking at the big star singers at that time. So when I went in and actually read, Reuben was blown away. He said, and these are his very words, "Margaret, I know you're not right for the role." And he said that because

he knew what they were looking for. "But your read is so worthy, I want you to tape, and I'm going to show it to Steven."

REUBEN CANNON: So Margaret came in. I knew she was a skilled actress, but I didn't know anything about her musical talents and how she could flow. So she was part of that final callback for Steven [Spielberg]. All the actors came in on point that day. They were so ready. During this final screen test, the chemistry between the actors was evident. For instance, Harpo, played by Willard Pugh, and Sofia, played by Oprah, were magical, like nitro and glycerin together. An all-star roster would've been a distraction. Part of the novelty and the freshness is that you're telling a story that hasn't been told before. You don't want to be preoccupied with who's who.

Shug (Margaret Avery) at Harpo's Juke Joint, 1985 film

MAKING A FILM IS A TEAM SPORT

An interview with Peter Guber, the Hollywood producer who stumbled upon the novel, recognized its filmic potential, and struck the deal that led to the iconic 1985 film.

Peter Guber and the cast and crew of the 1985 film
celebrate their eleven Academy Award nominations, 1986

Before there was Steven Spielberg or Quincy Jones, there was you. You approached Alice Walker to buy the film rights to her novel in the first place. Why?

PETER GUBER: I was at the beach with friends, and a couple of the women were reading the book. It wasn't a big bestseller yet; it had just been published in hardcover. I was intrigued by what interested them: the journey of Celie and the aspirational desires she had against all odds, at a time where women were not equal in the world, and Blacks were not equal in the world, and Black women were not equal in the world.

In the movie business then, there were not a lot of women's stories, and certainly not Black women's stories, but I was curious about why these two white women I was with were so motivated by it. Because I was in the movie business and had run Columbia Pictures, I always was listening to the audience. That's the way I got my clues: You don't have to invent anything to be really good.

So I read the book. It was very esoteric, even in the way it was written. It was not traditional. And I decided to acquire the book. I was a formidable player in the entertainment business then. I'd made a lot of movies, run big studios, run big music companies. At the time, I had a relationship with the head of the studio at Warner Bros., Terry Semel. My production company [Guber-Peters Entertainment Company] had a deal there. I went to see Terry about it, and he said, "Sure, we'll read it." They came back and said, "It's not a movie. It's prose. The antagonist is interesting, but maybe that woman who's the protagonist isn't the key to the picture." I said, "No, no, the woman's the key to the picture." They ultimately said, "We're not interested."

That it would get passed on was to be expected. It wasn't a studio picture for that time: an African American woman lead, a period picture, not an escape film, no physicality. It just wasn't in the zeitgeist then.

I decided to buy the rights myself. I didn't know if I could pull all the pieces together, but I wanted to give it a try. So I put up my own money. When I made the offer, Alice Walker's agent said, "Do you have a studio?" I said, "No, the studio passed on it." Her agent said, "I don't think she wants to sell it to you." I didn't know what "to you" meant, but I took it to mean "to anybody."

I thought, "I'm going to go and see her," which was also unusual for me, because I was a major producer and my credentials were strong. I called Alice Walker on the phone and introduced myself. I said, "Could I at least come and talk to you about it?" She was reluctant, but she said OK.

I flew up to San Francisco, knocked on her door, and said, "I'm Peter." She looked at me like, "Oh!" I think she expected maybe an African American guy. She was very polite, but she was not exactly like, "Come on in!"

We talked for about twenty minutes and had a nice conversation. She said, "I've had a couple of calls, but I'm not super-interested in the movie thing." Then we talked more. She said, "You want some tea?" We sat and had tea for another half-hour talking about what movies I made. I told her about *Missing*, which was a very difficult movie to make. Very, very difficult: Jack Lemmon, Sissy Spacek, set in Latin America. And of course it won the grand prize at Cannes and was an Academy Award–nominated best picture. So I had the credentials of taking a challenging picture about a complex subject and making it work.

She said, "This is a difficult picture in America today." I said, "It doesn't bother me that it's difficult." We talked more. She was welcoming as a human being, but she wasn't encouraging as the author of the book. And what happened next was either I saw a picture in her house or she asked me about my background, but somehow it came up that I went to law school. She said, "My husband went to law school. Where did you go?" I said, "I went to NYU." She said, "He went to NYU," and then mentioned his name. I said, "Ah, he's my friend! He sat right next to me!"

She wasn't married to him anymore, but that changed the whole conversation. We talked about that for at least another hour, just about what a terrible job law school is. She didn't disparage her ex-husband, but it was just such an odd coincidence that both of us were struck by. Really? I mean, *really*?

Both of our moods changed. I became more interested as she told me about the story and how it was formed. She said, "OK, let me think about it." It was better than a no. She said she enjoyed meeting me. I had no desperation, I had enthusiasm for the idea, and I think she was impressed that I didn't have all the answers for it right away.

Shortly afterward, I said to myself, "You know something? I'm not an African American. I need to have a partner who understands the culture, the personality, the considerations better than I." So I went to Quincy Jones, who was a friend of mine. He'd composed a lot of music for the movies, and I was also in the music business. I said, "Why don't you produce with me?" He knew the book and said, "OK, I'll do it."

Why do you think Alice Walker eventually decided to sell you the film rights?

You try to convince somebody of your earnestness, your enthusiasm, your attention to detail, your track record—and then you cross your fingers and hope they get it. I think it was because I had done pictures that were really hard to get made, and I made them well. Plus, Quincy was a formidable guy, and he was supportive of it, of us, and she believed in Quincy. That was probably the reason why.

He says, "Well, we would be interested in it."
"Wait a minute, you passed on the project."
"Ah, not really."
"Well, yes, you did."
We went through that argument for a couple of days, and I could tell he was very, very, very anxious. Terry knew I had a deal with Warner Bros., but because they had passed, I could go anywhere I wanted. And Terry had a boss he had to answer to, Steve Ross.

I let him stew in his own juices for a few days. And then I said, "OK, if Steven [Spielberg] wants to make the picture, he can be the boss and we'll be the executive producing company." It was best for the picture. So Steven took over.

Here's another element that might be of interest, but again, I'm saying this is to the best of my recollection.

> ## "You try to convince somebody of your earnestness, your enthusiasm, your attention to detail, your track record—and then you cross your fingers and hope they get it."
> ### —Peter Guber

I'm doing my best to remember forty years ago. Four weeks ago is a challenge for me. Forty years ago, Holy Christ. The deal got put together. Menno [Meyjes] was writing the screenplay. Then Quincy told me he had mentioned it to Steven Spielberg. He said, "I think Steven really wants to do this." Steven was as hot as could be. He was the *plat du jour* at that time. But even so, he wasn't African American, he wasn't a woman, and he hadn't done pictures like that.

Life is about serendipity. So now, the book was going up on bestseller lists, I have a screenplay, and I've got Quincy Jones and Steven Spielberg. And Terry Semel calls me and says, "Hey, listen, remember that project you mentioned to me?"

I might have been born at night, but not last night. So I played along: "I don't remember any project. What project could that be? I don't know what it is."

Could I be off 10 percent? Yeah. Could I be off 20 percent? Maybe. I'm not off 50 percent and definitely not off 100 percent. So Steven had made the movie. A few days before the Academy Awards, I got wind that Steven may want to make a sequel of this movie, but he wanted to produce it himself.

I got a call from Terry Semel. He's talking about this and that, he's talking about tennis. And I'm thinking, "He didn't call me in to talk about tennis."

Terry said to me, "Spielberg may want to make a sequel of this thing, but he wants to do it himself. So we'd like to buy out your rights."

OK, I'm listening. I'm not in show *show*, I'm in show *business*. And I said, "You'll have to deal with Alice." He said, "Yeah, we know that." This was two days before the Academy Awards, and the picture had eleven nominations, including best picture.

What is Terry thinking? He's thinking we're going to win best picture and seven Academy Awards, and we're going to make the sequel and own all the rights. I sat there and thought to myself, "He's a smart guy, but I am too, and I know life is round. There are no guarantees on anything." So I said to him, "OK, you want to make that deal? Here's the deal: We close it by tomorrow, five o'clock, completely documented. No 'Maybe, we'll get to it, we'll work it out.' Completely signed and executed deal."

They would control the remake rights and would pay us for this movie and our other rights. It was an extraordinarily formidable thing; we argued about that for two hours. I said, "We can argue till tomorrow, but at six o'clock, when the Academy Awards start, there's no deal. We don't need the money. This is the deal." I knew he needed the deal because Steven wanted to do the picture. So we made the deal, went to the Academy Awards, and *Color Purple* got no awards. Today, they would've won all eleven awards. But it was a different world.

Peter Guber and Whoopi Goldberg, 1980s

You went into the film knowing it would be a challenge. How did it turn out?

I thought Steven did an unbelievable job as a white male filmmaker in capturing the quintessence of that story. I thought he did a brilliant job. All the actors were fantastic. I was lucky to be associated with it, but luck comes to those who are trained and experienced. You have to have a certain kind of position in the business and a certain kind of awareness to be able to even get into the equation. But I'm proud of the film. I'm proud of my friends Quincy and Steven. If you let go of your ego, you can get a lot of things done. You have to know how to fit, where to fit, when to pass, when to punt.

And you have to know when you don't know something, which is what you were saying about bringing in Quincy.

I looked in the mirror and said, "This film is about an African American period experience. I'm neither of the period nor African American." I felt I could be a piece in the supporting cast of the film and be content with it. I didn't have to be holding the trophy up. I just thought, "Wouldn't that be neat if we could get this movie made? I'll bet you it will be successful."

Making a film is a team sport. There's a real quarterback like Spielberg. There's a real owner like Alice. There's a real playmaker like Quincy. And if you're part of the team, whatever contribution you make, you feel good about it.

What kept you connected to this story, even though there were so many ways in which it wasn't your own?

There were two things that I felt were important to the film. The moment that Celie says, "*No más.*" I liked that. "*No más*: I'm going to be active in my own rescue. *No más*: Not one more inch." That, to me, is a character who stands on the firing line and wins. But I also liked Celie's redemption. That's what made it so powerful to me. When Danny Glover walks past Celie and Nettie at the end, there was no vindictiveness or meanness in Celie. She had won, but his demise wasn't her victory. Her victory was solely her victory. And his recognition that she won and that he had wronged her was also important. And the fact that there was some contrition on his part. Each character had an evolution. I looked up at the film, and I said, "It really worked."

MARGARET AVERY: I think the process of developing Shug is my proudest moment from that film. I had thirty days to prepare, so I went to a coach. He said, "Whatever you do every day, do it as Shug. If you're holding a cup or the way you walk." And that's why that "You sho is ugly" line was very personal to me, because I worked so hard on that laugh.

OPRAH WINFREY (Sofia, 1985 film; producer, 2005 Broadway musical, 2015 Broadway revival, 2023 film): It all started when I read the book, which changed my life. And then I found out they were turning that book into a movie. And I knew I had to be a part of it. So I really literally prayed to God every night so that I could be a part of *The Color Purple*. I thought I would just carry water for whoever was in it. You know when you go to movies, at the end of the movie it has "best boy"? I thought, "I'll be the first 'best girl.'" It didn't even occur to me that I could actually play a role in it until one day when Quincy Jones was in Chicago. He had just flown in on a red-eye and was in his hotel room. At the time, I had just started on television there. I was doing a show called *AM Chicago*. And he saw me—he came out of the shower, the TV was on, he saw me.

QUINCY JONES: I've always been blessed with a knack for just seeing "it" in someone, whether it was Lesley Gore, Will Smith, Tevin Campbell, or taking Michael

Jackson solo. I can't explain it, but I've always been able to recognize that special thing in someone.

So when I was in Chicago to testify in a plagiarism case over the recording of "The Girl Is Mine," and I turned on the television and saw Oprah on *AM Chicago*, she just jumped out at me. I remember thinking, "If she can act, that is Sofia." I could just feel it in my soul. I told Steven about her and we brought her out to read, and she just killed it. That strength and independence that are at the core of the Sofia character, that is Oprah. And man, were we right on the money.

REUBEN CANNON: The principal roles all had unique challenges, especially the roles of Sofia and Shug Avery. The actress who would play Sofia needed to have not only strong acting skills, but she also had to have a physical power to be believable in a scene where she knocks a man out with one punch.

Often during the casting process, serendipity and happenstance will come into play. This was true when I received a call from Quincy, who happened to be in Chicago. He called me from his hotel room and said, "I'm watching TV, and I'm looking at the woman who could play Sofia." I said, "Well, I'll be coming to Chicago in three days when I finish casting in New York. I'll meet with her." Quincy said, "Her name is Oprah Winfrey."

I called Debbie Di Maio, who was Oprah's show producer, and told her I was coming to Chicago and that I'd like to meet with Oprah. I asked whether she could send me any materials prior to the meeting. And what she sent me was not from Oprah's local television show. She sent me Oprah's VHS. That tells you the time period—it was a tape of Oprah going around on weekends and doing one-woman shows.

OPRAH WINFREY: I had started doing those shows in Baltimore in 1977, on stage at the Morgan State University theater. I was very church centered at the time, and I put together that first show to raise money for my church. I called it "To Make a Poet Black and Bid Her Sing," which was a nod to the Countee Cullen poem "Yet Do I Marvel."

I started with pieces from Sojourner Truth's *Ain't I a Woman*, Fannie Lou Hamer's speeches, a piece from Margaret Walker's *Jubilee*, just picking African American women from history and doing poetic essays put to music by Bernice Reagon and her group, Sweet Honey in the Rock.

Harpo (Willard E. Pugh) and Sofia (Oprah Winfrey) at their wedding, 1985 film

REUBEN CANNON: Even though the video was crude, pretty low in terms of production values, I was impressed with her acting. I told Debbie, "I'll be in Chicago to audition actors for another film, and I've reserved time to meet with her." And she said, "What's it about?"

I said, "It's just a meeting." She said, "Is this for *Color Purple*?" I said, "It's a meeting." Debbie said, "Oprah will be there."

I arrived in Chicago on one of the coldest days of the year. Although I'm from there, it was so cold even my own family wouldn't come down to the hotel to visit me. My mother said, "It's too cold. We'll see you next time." I was using a local casting office and had from 12 to 3 blocked out for Oprah's appointment.

Oprah came to the door and said, "I'm here to meet Reuben Cannon." I said, "I'm Reuben Cannon." And she said, "Look, mister. I have a temperature of 102 degrees. I don't have time to play games. I'm here to meet Reuben Cannon."

It never occurred to her that Reuben Cannon could be Black. We went through that awkward moment and then had a laugh about it. I said, "I saw your one-woman show. It's impressive." And she said, "Let me tell you. I know this is for *Color Purple*, and I'm destined to play Sofia." I said, "Really? Why is that?" She said, "Because Harpo spelled backwards is Oprah." I said, "Well, that's interesting. I'll be sure to tell Alfre Woodard that. I'm sure she may have a similar reason why she thinks she's destined to play the role as well."

I decided to just fess up to her that it was actually for *The Color Purple*. Based on her video tape and our meeting, I had a feeling she should definitely be a candidate for Sofia. I gave her the audition scenes and suggested she work with a local acting coach to prepare for her screen test with Steven.

I sent her the material. Oprah was over the moon with excitement and calling every day, checking in on the status of the role. And apparently, according to Oprah, on one of the phone calls I said, "Why are you calling me? You don't call me, I call you."

OPRAH WINFREY: Reuben denies that he said that, but you never forget it. I actually wrote it in my journal, and you never forget when somebody says that to you. I got off the phone and cried.

It didn't make any sense to me. Why had I gotten the call if they didn't want to consider me? Nobody's

ever called me ever, nor since, to ask, "Would you be interested in being in a movie?" Why would that all happen? God, why did that all happen?

At first I was so excited, and then so disappointed and confused that I had come as far as I'd come. I had to surrender, and the process of doing that was life-changing. It altered the course of my actions in life, that act of surrendering in that moment and saying, "All right, Alfre Woodard's going to get the part. I'm not going to get the part."

I blessed Alfre Woodard. I blessed her because as I was praying and crying, I would be like, "OK, I can let it go, but when the movie comes out, I won't be able to see the movie. OK, God, help me be able to get to the place where I can see the movie. Now, help me get to the place where I can see the movie and not feel like, 'Oh, I should have had that part.' Now help me get to the point where I can not only say that and feel that, but say, 'I bless you that you have this part, that it was supposed to be for you.'" And right then, I got the call.

I never wanted anything more than to be a part of *The Color Purple*. That prayer has been fully answered. It's been answered for forty years straight. God has answered and answered and answered and answered again.

"When I turned on the television and saw Oprah on *AM Chicago*, she just jumped out at me. I remember thinking, 'If she can act, that is Sofia.' I could just feel it in my soul."

—*Quincy Jones*

GAYLE KING:
ALONG FOR THE RIDE

Emmy-winning broadcast journalist and editor Gayle King has been friends with Oprah Winfrey since 1976, when they worked together at a Baltimore television station. Along the way, King has encountered *The Color Purple* in all manner of unexpected ways and in unexpected roles.

Oprah Winfrey and Gayle King on the set of the 1985 film

"*The Color Purple* has been with me from the very beginning. I read the book because Oprah had strongly recommended it. I can't say it's something I would've picked up, but she was just raving about it. And of course it delivered.

"The first time I got to go on a set was when they were shooting the movie. It was Oprah's first movie, so I was just going as a looky-loo just to see what she was doing because I was so psyched that she had gotten a part. Not only a part, but a bona fide part. I was her friend and was just going to cheer her on. I was like, 'Can I come?' We'd already been friends for at least ten years, and we were clearly best friends, so that didn't seem like an inappropriate ask. I was a news anchor in Hartford, Connecticut, at the time, and I took vacation days to go. I'd never been on a movie set before, so I thought everything was cool: I was not one of those people who said, 'Let me stand in the back row.'

"Twenty years later, when I was editor at large for Oprah's magazine, I ended up at a table reading of the Broadway show. No props, no costumes. I was just going to make a pop-through to be polite because Scott [Sanders] had asked me, and I was going to leave halfway through. I didn't know what we were going to see. I couldn't even understand how that movie could translate on a stage. Almost from the moment they began, though, I was so blown away. It was the power of the words and their voices. I said, 'Oh, I need to see how this ends.' I called my office and said, 'Call my lunch plans and say something has come up.'

"What brought me to tears was the voices and the words to the songs. 'Dear God – Shug,' 'I'm Here,' 'The

"I still am trying to figure out how I ended up in a costume in the wedding scene, because I certainly didn't ask to do that."

—Gayle King

the craft table, lights, camera, action, all the costumes. And then to see her in her first acting job—that added to it.

"I still am trying to figure out how I ended up in a costume in the wedding scene, because I certainly didn't ask to do that. I would've never dreamed of asking. Either Oprah said something or a producer said, 'Would your friend like to be in the movie?'

"'Doing what?'

"'All she has to do is just stand there.' I didn't even know what I was agreeing to.

"Look, if you blink, you will miss me. You actually have to go frame by frame to catch me. Put it in slow motion. But that was OK. I was excited to get a wardrobe and be told where to stand. And I realized that moviemaking is a very long, tedious process, because you do take after take after take after take. To say that I am in the movie is being generous. I'm just standing there. I did try to stand next to Oprah, so at least I wouldn't get totally cut out.

Color Purple,' 'Too Beautiful for Words.' I mean, I was mesmerized. And I called Oprah and said, 'You should really pay attention to this. This is something very special.' I said to her, 'I can't even describe to you what I just saw and heard. But it literally made the hair stand up on the back of my neck.' She said, 'I'll come and see it.' And she felt what I felt. And the rest, as they say, is history.

"I saw the Broadway play seventeen times. Anytime somebody would come into town, I would say, 'You've got to go see this.' LaChanze from the very beginning to Cynthia Erivo and all of the permutations in between, I saw.

"And now, with Blitz Bazawule's film, you have the third interpretation. It's interesting that this one piece of work can have all these adaptations and forms, and all of them are still brilliant and still beautiful.

"Am I in the new movie? No. Uh-huh. No one asked me to do anything, including Oprah. No one said, 'Hey, would you like to be in it?' All they said when I visited the set was, 'Hey, Gayle.'"

Quincy Jones and Menno Meyjes
on the set of the 1985 film

MARSHA NORMAN (playwright, 2005 Broadway musical): Alice and I won our Pulitzers on the same day in 1983. The story on Page 1 of the *The New York Times* read, "Prizes were awarded yesterday to *'Night, Mother*, a play by Marsha Norman, and to *The Color Purple*, a novel by Alice Walker." You can imagine how that felt! I knew Alice's book and loved it, as did the world, so my agent and I began our search for the person making the movie. Spielberg flew me out to L.A. to talk to him about writing the screenplay. Unfortunately, we disagreed on some things and I didn't get the job, but Quincy Jones, who was in the meeting representing Alice, took me to lunch. We had a great time talking about Petula Clark and Michael Jackson. With Quincy, I felt like I belonged to the great throng of Alice Walker's admirers.

QUINCY JONES: Steven had *Hook*, *Schindler's List*, *Always*, all these pictures. He said, "The first one that gets the best script is the one I'm going to do."

REUBEN CANNON: I remember the excitement when Menno Meyjes' draft came in. He had found a way to stitch it together, to create a compelling screenplay that captured the essence of the novel.

BRENDA RUSSELL (music and lyrics, 2005 Broadway musical, 2015 Broadway revival, 2023 film): This is funny. My first encounter with *Color Purple* was through my friend Kathleen Wakefield, who worked at Warner Bros. This is about 1982. She said, "We're doing this movie called *The Color Purple* and do you want to audition?" I said, "Sure." I'm not even an actress. I don't know why I said sure. But I did. I went and auditioned for Shug. I bought the book first and read the book. Then I auditioned. I didn't get the part, but the same guy [Reuben Cannon] who held my audition, years later, was sitting next to me as we were watching the stage production.

GETTING THE SCRIPT RIGHT

REUBEN CANNON: My question was, "How do you adapt this book?" It was so original in its form, it almost defied adaptation to the screen. Multiple writers, novelists, playwrights, and screenwriters, including Athol Fugard and even Alice Walker, had tried their hand at it. In fact, Steven didn't commit to directing until there was a script that lived up to the quality of the book.

MAKING THE MOVIE

STEVEN SPIELBERG (director, 1985 film; producer, 2023 film): So many of the cast had never acted before in a film, and I felt rehearsals would rob them of the magic, terror, and spontaneity of saying the lines for the first time while the cameras rolled.

The brutal separation of sisters was hard felt by audiences because Desreta [Jackson] as Young Celie and Akosua [Busia] as Nettie was unrehearsed and their relationship with each other was so strong behind the scenes. I filmed it in real time with several cameras over the course of a day, which meant the actors had to relive their being torn apart again and again from the different camera angles. We were all sick to our stomachs that day, and even in my editing room it was difficult to watch.

The summer of 1985 in North Carolina was like a summer camp, and everyone in the company bonded and forged long-enduring relationships that made the film even more authentic and emotional.

Mister (Danny Glover), 1985 film

Celie (Whoopi Goldberg) listens to Shug sing at Harpo's Juke Joint, 1985 film

DANNY GLOVER: Some of the magic is what happens from the words on the page and some of it is what happens among the people there. And because of their presence with each other, and their presence on a daily basis, and the brilliance of Steven Spielberg to put it together, we're still talking about *The Color Purple*. We're still talking. Generations who weren't even born at that time are talking about *The Color Purple*.

BLITZ BAZAWULE (director, 2023 film): Whoopi. Whoopi. I'd never quite seen a character who, due to the mechanics of the character, lacked propulsion. And one thing they tell you about good characters: They make change. They're changemakers. That's why the audience is rooting for them. But when you have a character who is on the docile side, that's a hard character to play because other people are the propulsion for this person. For a very long time in the film—until Celie stands up for herself—other people lead. And I have to say, it's so masterfully directed, the Spielberg version. And the acting, particularly from Whoopi. Her ability to play in its subtleties, and how she was able to maintain that empathy throughout—but not the kind that you go, "Well, this character's not doing anything, so I'm checking out." It is a magical thing that both Steven and Whoopi were able to achieve cinematically and through acting.

STEVEN SPIELBERG: My favorite scene both in the script and in the finished film was Celie and Nettie's reunion after so many harrowing and fallow years. I didn't have a lot I could say to the actors. I saved the last scene for the end of the schedule, and the the actors all knew who they were by then, so their reactions were genuine and deep and unprompted. We were all crying behind the camera. I'd say "action" and then "cut," and then I'd change the setup with hardly another word spoken. It was unforgettable. It was so joyful in its justice.

FRANCINE JAMISON-TANCHUCK (costume supervisor, 1985 film; costume designer, 2023 film): I had not read the book yet when [head costume designer] Aggie Rodgers asked me to work with her on the [1985] movie. Once I knew that I was going to be part of it, I decided to buy the book, and I tell you, I was in tears. I literally was in tears, and I thought, "I am so honored to be a part of this project." I think everyone felt that as well, especially in the costume department. The

Celie (Whoopi Goldberg), 1985 film

work was very difficult because we spanned between five and six different periods. We would fit 1940 in the morning and then 1909 in the afternoon. Then, just before we're all calling it a day, after we had probably put in a good fourteen or fifteen hours, we're fitting 1920s or 1930s. It is incredible the work that we did, but we all felt so honored and connected in order to bring this movie to the screen. It was hard, but it was really fulfilling.

FANTASIA BARRINO (Celie, 2005 Broadway musical, 2023 film): I know I was very young when I first saw the movie, and I think Celie's life resonated with me. Her skin tone, little things that I would deal with in school. It was also the music in the movie, like Shug singing "Maybe God Is Tryin' to Tell You Somethin'." So around the age of five, six, it was just my go-to, which for some people is like, "Really?" Some people say, "I couldn't watch it. It was this, it was that." But funny now that I'm sitting here talking about it, it was just something about Celie, something about the music, that drew me into it. I watched it over and over.

Madame Walker's
Speech Clinic
and
Tarot Readings

OPPOSITE PAGE, CLOCKWISE FROM TOP LEFT:
Alice Walker and Whoopi Goldberg; Steven Spielberg,
Oprah Winfrey, Akosua Busia, and Alice Walker; Alice
Walker; Whoopi Goldberg, Alice Walker, and Danny
Glover; Steven Spielberg, Whoopi Goldberg, and
Menno Meyjes; Alice Walker's chair

THIS PAGE: Actor Bennet Guillory (top left) and Alice
Walker (in car) with crew members; Alice Walker
entertaining young cast members

QUINCY JONES: It is impossible to tell the story of the African American experience without the music. Our story in this country from our arrival is told through our music. *The Color Purple*, Celie's story, is the blues. The physical and emotional pain, the self-loathing and, ultimately, the desire to love and be loved. The sense of self-preservation and the determination to be free to live despite the circumstances, the music—our music—embodies all of that. The music is the "emotion lotion" of the film, as Steven and I called it.

OPRAH WINFREY: When the filming was over and they were making the movie poster, I had not started my talk show yet, so my name didn't make the cut. When I saw the design, I went to Steven and said, "Look, I think I'm

going to be famous because I just signed this deal for a show. He said, "What kind of show?" And I said, "It's a talk show." And he said, "On radio or what? What is it?" I said, "No, it's on TV. It's kind of like Phil Donahue, only it's me." And he says, "No, we can't put your name on the poster."

I got $35,000 for doing *The Color Purple*—the most money I could have imagined for it, and my agent at the time was asking for more. I said, "Please, don't ask for any more. Please, please, please. I'd do it for free."

REACTION SHOTS

EVELYN C. WHITE (journalist and author of *Alice Walker: A Life*): The film really touched people's hearts. I saw it in December 1985, right when it came out. I was in Phoenix, and the audience was almost 100 percent Hispanic people. They totally got it. They were cheering, they were crying. When Celie spits into Old Mister's glass, people were yelling, *Beberlo, beberlo!*" meaning, "Drink it! Drink it!" When he finally did, everyone started laughing. I later saw it with my housemates in Oakland, a married couple. The man was from an affluent WASP family of longstanding San Francisco lineage, and all of a sudden, I heard what sounded like crying. The husband was weeping. I later found out that his parents had divorced when he was young, and he basically never got over this disruption in his family. The scene where everybody comes back together and Mister's on the horse watching the reunion had touched him profoundly. So, it was deeply moving on many, many levels. And at the same time, I would cross paths with people, primarily Black American males, who said, "Alice is destroying Black culture. This is all made up. She's just making Black men look bad"—that whole controversy.

E. R. SHIPP (journalist and academic): I went back and reread the *New York Times* article I wrote ["Blacks in Heated Debate Over 'The Color Purple,'" January 27, 1986], and as I reread the complaints, mostly from men, it occurred to me that this was a #MeToo moment without us having come to that realization. It was some years ahead of the actual #MeToo movement. Finally, someone is validating what we have experienced. I had a quote from Danny Glover in the piece where he says, "Lots of

The promotional poster for the 1985 film

Alice Walker and then-partner Robert Allen at a screening of the
1985 film held in her hometown of Eatonton, Georgia, 1986

times we sweep our own problems under the rug under the justification of upholding Black history and the Black man." More women were saying that than men, but I think they were recognizing that while this was not the intent of the film, necessarily, to be an opportunity for reckoning, there was truth in the story.

At the same time, politicians were using terms like "poverty pimps" and "welfare queens." Within that atmosphere, those who were most critical of the film saw it being used as further evidence for political policies that the Reagan administration and others already had in mind. Also in that mix was an enduring battle between Black men and Black women: Over the years, you'd hear that Black women have it easier than Black men, that Black men have always been targeted. All of these things had absolutely nothing to do with the film itself or the book itself. The film just became this rallying point for these other issues.

If that same movie, by Spielberg as opposed to someone else, had been done now, it might land differently. People would think, "It's just a movie." In 1985, we didn't have as many choices. We didn't have as many Black people or Black women greenlighting projects,

directing projects, producing projects. So any movie would be subjected to extra scrutiny, because the idea was that if this was the only way other people get to see Black people, what message were they going to come away with?

Many males who were critical were saying, "This is going to make white people think we're just beasts." And some women were saying, "They're going to think less of Black women for allowing ourselves to be victimized, for being involved in these relationships in the first place." Everybody was thinking of how white people would see Black people, and if this is the only way they'll see us, what does that mean?

When I was a child in Conyers, Georgia, not everybody had a television. Those people who had televisions would open their houses so we could all come and watch, maybe somebody on *The Ed Sullivan Show* or a repeat of *Imitation of Life*. We would all gather for those rare moments of seeing Black people on television. And that later became an obligation to watch any show that had Black people in it, even if it was a genre you didn't care about. You felt, "Well, it's Black people. I've got to support it."

"You could have made this movie with an all-Asian cast; you could have made this movie with an all-Puerto Rican cast; you could have made this movie with an all-French cast and the story would be the same because this is a universal story. And that, I think, is what keeps it going. It's what people feel when they see it for the ninety-ninth time and still weep uncontrollably. It is one of the best movies ever made because it's about us. Humans."

—WHOOPI GOLDBERG
Actress, comedian, and television personality
who played Celie in the 1985 film

From "The Making of *The Color Purple*," Warner Bros., 2003

Steven Spielberg on the set of the
1985 film

I think we've gotten beyond some of that. Today we see more diverse depictions of Black life, from tragic to joyous. We've seen depictions of homosexuality normalized in Black culture, in film, and on stage. We've seen a greater appreciation of our connection to Africa than might have been understood then. We have a better understanding of feminist traditions that hark back to our Africanness. So I think we as an audience probably have a deeper appreciation of some of the subtleties in the message that Alice Walker was trying to convey.

SALAMISHAH TILLET: Alice Walker said she was so taken aback because she was basing these characters after people in her family, but also her love of Black men. She was really surprised that this was going to be the

DANNY GLOVER: I was doing an Athol Fugard play at Steppenwolf Theater in Chicago when the movie came out. There was a National Council of Negro Women conference there at the time, and I was invited to speak. I remember the woman who introduced me said, "I see this young man is a good young man, but first I'm gonna go out to my car, get my skillet out of the back, and hit him on the side of the head."

Sometimes we want more out of cultural productions than just to be entertained. And that's what *The Color Purple* was. We want more out of culture because we want to see ourselves and understand through that. That's what a cultural product is. Historically, that's what it's always been about. And particularly for the African Americans using film as a platform to understand, not

"Many people who spoke about the book and trashed the book and all of that, they hadn't read it at all. I really feel so sad for us that that was true."

—Alice Walker

nature of the attack. And as a civil rights activist, and how much she'd fought for Black freedom, she was now being attacked for selling out Black people. She was a SNCC [Student Nonviolent Coordinating Committee] activist who then was seen as a sellout. So that's a quick trajectory.

REUBEN CANNON: Look at how few studio-produced films, films of importance, were made for Black audiences in the mid-1980s. The scarcity of Black films meant those that were made had to satisfy the entire culture as well as prove that such projects were bankable. That was the weight placed on *Color Purple*, that this is hopefully going to be the movie that will give us some credibility—"us" being Black folks in Hollywood. The burden on a project like this was that it had to satisfy the entire culture. It's impossible for one movie to carry that burden. You can't be all things to all people.

only to say, "This is who I am," but understand who I am at the same time. And that's what I felt about *The Color Purple.*

On the other hand, you only grow and learn to love through debate and through the kind of discourse that's difficult for this country to have.

ALICE WALKER: Many people who spoke about the book and trashed the book and all of that, they hadn't read it at all. I really feel so sad for us that that was true. It was a real missed opportunity for us as a culture.

AISHA HARRIS (co-host/reporter, National Public Radio's "Pop Culture Happy Hour"): On the pop culture front, in the '80s there were barely any Black-cast dramas being made. You had outliers here and there: Richard Pryor, Eddie Murphy. But the rest of their casts were white. They were the one person of color in that realm. All these potent and touchy issues are percolating within Black culture, and this is all happening as *The Color Purple* is being made.

Look at the reactions. The NAACP protested the film, and then when it didn't get any Oscars, they were upset. But this goes back as far as *Gone with the Wind*, when the NAACP was upset with that film, but they were also happy to celebrate the fact that Hattie McDaniel won the Oscar [for Best Supporting Actress]. You'll see that often. Anytime these movies would come up, someone from the NAACP or another activist or even James Baldwin would say, "This movie is embarrassing. It's terrible, it's bad for our race, but yet this performance still rises above the text." That absolutely played out in the same way with *The Color Purple* reactions: "We're happy to see all these Black people getting work, and we're happy to see them giving these amazing performances, but why did it have to be this film?"

Left to right: Akosua Busia, photographer Gordon Parks, Oprah Winfrey, Alice Walker, Quincy Jones, and Robert Allen on the set of the 1985 film

LONG LEGS

DEON COLE (Alfonso, 2023 film): My first introduction was the movie itself. I remember seeing the trailer, and I remember seeing these two little girls skipping through these weeds and that the movie was made by Steven Spielberg. That's all that really took for me. I was like, "Wow. I want to see this."

JON BATISTE (Grady, 2023 film): The film came out the year before I was born. Quincy Jones did the score for it and was a producer, and the cast featured all of these incredible figures that, when I was growing up in the '90s and early 2000s, were household names. In particular, being from a musical city like New Orleans, and an entertainment family, and a Black American family, you could imagine how that film was such a monumental part of the canon. And then realizing, after watching the film a few dozen times, that there's this incredible book by Alice Walker.

There were probably three to five films that were so entrenched in the canon that you could almost recite the words as the film was playing. You watch it every Thanksgiving and on television every summer. You identify with the characters. It's an African American story, but that's not what you're thinking about. You're not looking

at it and thinking about, "Oh, this is a Black-forward narrative, and that's why I like it." The story is great. The quality is of a level to where it becomes canon. Like *Forrest Gump*, another film that I can remember that had that same sort of impact in our household. You had *Coming to America*. There's only a few, and I think it definitely played a role that there weren't as many of those types of narratives in films in that era.

NIIJA KUYKENDALL (former production executive, Warner Bros.): I saw the movie fairly early, but I don't know exactly when. I didn't see it in theaters, but I recall in high school, my friends and I would always quote the movie and reference the movie. It was a big part of our culture in the Black female community.

LAWRENCE DAVIS (hair department head, 2023 film): I watched it for the first time as a kid, but I think I've watched it maybe thirty-five times since then. It's this comfortable place for me, knowing the dialogue and knowing the storyline. But there's always something different that I see every time. Knowing the story, I know that in the end, she did win. She got what she desired. It's become this thing in the Black community, for those who are fans of it: We know the lines and finish their sentences because we've watched the characters over and over.

COLMAN DOMINGO (Mister, 2023 film): My first time was in a movie theater back in 1985, when it first came out. It was one of those huge events, not only because Alice Walker's incredible book was being adapted but also because of all the people who were involved. I've always been a history buff and trying to investigate more of our history, and I think this film did that in many ways. I know that there was some controversy around the film as well, but I loved it. I've always been a Spielberg fan. I think he's a master storyteller, and I was interested in seeing how he guided this story, how he poured his heart into it.

COREY HAWKINS (Harpo, 2023 film): I grew up in my household with the sayings "You told Harpo to beat me" and "You and me must never part." It was this lore, especially growing up in a Black household in D.C., which is kind of the South. We all knew *The Color Purple*, but I don't think I had actually seen *The Color Purple*. So it's weird in that there were all these things about the film that I've known but didn't put together until I actually watched the movie. And that was some years later, maybe high school. That's when I first encountered these brilliant, wonderful, raw, human, funny, visceral characters who I identified with in many ways. And then also other ways I was like, "Wow, that is so completely not what I thought." "You told Harpo to beat me" was a funny line that I'd hear friends say. But the reality of it for these women, how they lived, of these men, how they lived—that was something that didn't hit me until much later.

A short-lived Christmas visit from Sofia (Oprah Winfrey, center), 1985 film

"The 1985 movie was ahead of its time in that it showcased multiple Black women and their concerns."
—Aisha Harris

For me it was something my family had grown up on, because it was really my grandmother and my mother's generation that knew that film. It wasn't really my generation, given that I was born three years after the film came out. Even the song: "Sister, you've been on my mind." My grandmother would be ironing or whatever and just humming it. So it was crazy how I knew it on a cellular level, but didn't know it until I saw and read it.

AISHA HARRIS: The 1985 movie was ahead of its time in that it showcased multiple Black women and their concerns. When you think about this cast of mostly unknowns being introduced to the general public, that was something that didn't really happen. And for it to be such a big commercial success and Academy success—even if it didn't win, it still got nominated for eleven Oscars. Most movies still don't get nominated for eleven Oscars. So it was ahead of its time in how it centered Black women's perspectives and foreshadowed TV series like *The Women of Brewster Place*. And then *Waiting to Exhale* and other films showed Black women were audiences and wanted to see these things. Even though it didn't necessarily translate immediately into getting more of those movies made, it did help lay the groundwork that others were able to build off.

REUBEN CANNON: When you talk about longevity, the term in the industry is about a project having legs. Very few people can tell you who won the Oscar for best picture in 1985, but *Color Purple* lives on. It lives on and lives on. The race doesn't always go to the swift. Slow burns are sometimes better.

THE
MISS MILLIES

An interview with the two actresses who play Miss Millie, a character Alice Walker offered up to show how even the slightest encounters could have enormous consequences when racism and associated power dynamics were at play.

Miss Millie (Elizabeth Marvel), 2023 film

Miss Millie (Dana Ivey), 1985 film

What makes it possible for you to play an unsympathetic character?

ELIZABETH MARVEL: I feel like we are all big houses with many rooms, and some of those rooms we choose not to open the doors to. In this story, there's a respect for our nation's history that we need to honor and show. And if I can be a useful conduit to the truth of what's happened in our country, what continues to happen in our country, then I'm grateful to be able to use my toolset to do that. This was such a loving and generous set to be on, and Danielle Brooks, who I was working with most of the time, and I know each other, and I know she

women like that through my grandmother—women who are innocent and not very well educated. They actually would help anybody do anything, but they had the instilled fears of the time in them, and I don't fault them for that. I didn't find any difficulty playing it and I don't think of her as a bad character. She's a character in a story, and she's a foolish woman, but we are all foolish sometimes.

ELIZABETH: That's fascinating, because for the story we were telling with my Miss Millie, I definitely worked with a power dynamic and a need to control another person—a need to have a person at my command, my whim.

> # "There was no concern at that time about anything other than just telling the story in the book, a story that was written by somebody who wrote well and wrote good characters."
> ## —Dana Ivey

felt safe with me. I felt safe with her. We were very clear on the task at hand and the work we were doing, so I felt honored to participate. I also never shy away from the ugly, the difficult. That's part of my job. But I'm curious to hear what Dana has to say because I'm curious to hear what that set was like. What was your experience?

DANA IVEY: I had a wonderful time. We shot in North Carolina. I only worked for a couple of days, and everybody was very nice. There was no concern at that time about anything other than just telling the story in the book, a story that was written by somebody who wrote well and wrote good characters, and we just embodied the characters. Most of the people I've played over my life have been considered hard-nosed or difficult. I didn't think of Miss Millie that way at all. I thought of her as not malicious, but like a childish character. Having had the benefit of growing up in the South, I felt like I knew

Miss Millie was so limited as to what she could control that she was driven to manipulate another person.

Dana, your Miss Millie beautifully conveys her foolishness, especially in the car scene when you don't trust anyone but Sofia to drive. Your helplessness is so powerful. And at the same time, you're wielding power that upends her life.

DANA: Yes, but it's unconscious power. She does not do it deliberately. It's nothing that's done to make herself feel better. It's nothing that we would psychoanalyze today in terms of some kind of conscious manipulation at all. In the Old South, their feelings of superiority didn't need to be reinforced by them. It just *was*, so that's just something that you live with. That's a given and doesn't need any effort on her part. That's just my feeling about it from the experiences I had. I mean, my grandfather was a very bigoted man, but kind. Just because you're bigoted doesn't mean that you're mean or ugly to people or anything. It's a mindset, but it doesn't necessarily act out in malicious ways.

ELIZABETH: Interesting. I'm curious about the set, too, because I was so excited to be on this set with Blitz, who was our director, who is an unbelievable, amazing, beautiful visual artist, too. But ours is a musical. I had never been involved in a musical, which was thrilling, and it was the first time I'd been on a dominantly African American set driven by African American artists. I was usually the only Caucasian on the set. It was such a new experience in so many ways, and I loved it. I loved being in this crazy musical world, which was all new to me, and standing by artists like Danielle and Fantasia when they sing. It's bananas. It's just rapture. I'm curious what your set was like.

DANA: Well, we weren't musical, of course, so we were just telling the story. I've been in several musicals, on Broadway and off, and musicals have their own way of telling stories, which are not necessarily the way you tell a straightforward logistical play. I wouldn't know how to do it in a musical movie, but I've done a lot of musicals on stage, and I recognize what their particular constraints are. I'm sure that this *Color Purple* takes the

Miss Millie (Dana Ivey) asks Sofia (Oprah Winfrey)
to work for her, 1985 film

"It helped that this was a musical, not just a new film."
—Elizabeth Marvel

stage musical and opens it up, but it's very different than telling a story with people only talking to each other, not conveyed through music or song at all. Those are different energies.

Dana, what's it like to have participated in such an iconic film?

DANA: Isn't that funny? I didn't know it would become iconic. I'm very grateful. I get letters or fan mail, and a lot of that comes from other movies I've done, but some of it's about *The Color Purple*. I met Alice Walker; I got her to sign my copy of the book. That was special. It was before Oprah was Oprah, so that was a different time completely, and it just seemed like a quiet little thing to do.

Elizabeth, did you have a sense that you were going into a role with a giant legacy?

ELIZABETH: Oh, yes, absolutely. I've always been a fan of Dana and have seen her on stage and on screen for a very long time, so I was well aware of that. And of course, the conversation on set between actors referenced that film, and we talked about it a lot, so it lived in our consciousness. It helped that this was a musical, not just a new film version. It was a very different beast, so we weren't worried about comparisons. It runs parallel to the movie instead of trying to intersect it. It's another way to engage with it instead of trying to remake it. That would have been ridiculous.

DANA: And also, the original film is an iteration of its original material as a book. Everything you do is going to be different and build on or take from whatever's gone before, but be itself.

Sofia (Danielle Brooks), Buster (Stephen Hill), and Celie (Fantasia Barrino) drive into town prior to the confrontation with Miss Millie, 2023 film

ELIZABETH: That's right. The magical realism in this new film, for example, is so magnificent. Blitz is such a gorgeous artist and human being. I'm very excited for his vision to come out to the world because I think his talent as a filmmaker is something else.

Do either of you have favorite aspects from your *Color Purple* experiences?

ELIZABETH: I saw the original film before I read the book. I was a pretty young person, a teenager. Maybe this is a weird thing to take away from it, or maybe it's an obvious thing to others, but I remember that the celebration and the treatment of bisexuality was profound and moving and radical.

DANA: That's true. It was approached with a lot of love and understanding, which was very interesting at the time.

ELIZABETH: Yeah. And race and gender. It's just such a generous and loving film in so many ways for such brutal territory. That hit me very intensely as a young person and has stayed with me.

DANA: I remember that it was such a surprise and an honor to be able to get the part. I had just two or three days in North Carolina, and it kind of went like a blip. The experience I had was wonderful. The iconicness that has developed with the film that I was honored to be in speaks to the fact that we can talk about Black people and white people, but it's just a human story that's really well told. And over time, that's the thing that keeps sticking in my head: It doesn't matter what color people are, it's about people finding ways to survive, persevere, continue, and love under all kinds of life circumstances. That's why it's so inspirational. These human beings in really difficult circumstances find a way to be kind and loving and persevere and have good lives. That's inspirational to all of us, and I think that's what makes it such a great story.

IV

THE BROADWAY MUSICAL & REVIVAL

TAKING IT TO THE STAGE

*I have fallen in love with the imagination.
And if you fall in love with the imagination, you
understand that it is a free spirit. It will go anywhere,
do anything. So your job is to find trustworthy
companions and cocreators. That's really it.*

—Alice Walker,
The World Has Changed

Church ladies (Left to right, Maia Nkenge Wilson, Virginia Ann Woodruff, and Kimberley Ann Harris), The Broadway Theatre, New York, 2005

TAKING IT TO THE STAGE: THE 2005 MUSICAL

SCOTT SANDERS (producer, 2005 Broadway musical, 2015 Broadway revival, 2023 film): I always thought *The Color Purple* had music in its soul and was a universal story that had to be told again. I told Peter Guber, who was my boss at the time, that I'd like to turn *The Color Purple* into a musical for Broadway. He suggested I speak to Alice and was willing to give me an introduction. He called Alice, Alice agreed to meet with us, and Peter was kind enough to fly up to Berkeley with me in the summer of 1997 to meet at her house. After a half-hour, she said, "You seem like a very nice and smart guy, but no." I asked her why, and she said, "It was adapted for Steven's film, and I've moved on. I'm writing other books."

I went back to New York somewhat discouraged, but I stayed in touch with her and said, "Hey, I have ideas about how the musical would differ from the film, particularly in the relationship between Celie and Shug, as well as the portrayal of the men in the story. Would you be willing to let me fly you to New York and go see some shows together and continue to talk about this vision for how it might work?"

She said yes, which surprised me. I brought her to New York; we went to see several shows. One was *Bring in 'da Noise, Bring in 'da Funk*. Another was *The Fantasticks*. One night she surprised me and brought Gloria Steinem with her, which made it hard to watch the show, because I kept thinking, "I can't believe I'm sitting in the theater with Alice Walker and Gloria Steinem."

At the end of that week, I chartered a cruise around Manhattan. I invited people I had worked with over the years. I told Alice to talk to anyone on the boat and ask for a reference, whether or not I was worthy of her trust. It was [theater owner] Jimmy Nederlander, Diana Ross and two of her daughters, and a bunch of other people.

The next day we had dinner, and I was holding my breath, wondering what she was going to say. She said, "I've decided to let you do this. I trust you to do this."

GARY GRIFFIN (director, 2005 Broadway musical): I thought it was a good idea to make a musical of *The Color Purple* partly because the characters used music to survive—in the church, in the juke joint, in their solitude. It's part of their faith. So that made it a no-brainer for me.

The show I thought about, although it ended up being nothing like that, was *Fiddler on the Roof*, which was also telling a story about a change in a way of life. As our way of life changes, musicals can often capture that well. *West Side Story* is about the change of a way of life. In *The Color Purple*, it was the idea of "What do we do now?" post-slavery.

From the very first time Scott said to me, "I want to make the musical of *The Color Purple*," I thought, "What a good idea." Rarely does that happen. You normally have to go home, read it, spend time with it to think if it's a good idea. But I had an immediate, visceral instinct that it was a good idea. So there was that. Then, how? How do you make it a musical?

You could make an eight-hour version of *The Color Purple*. The material is dense and vast enough. So it became this act of sculpture: Take away everything that isn't a Broadway musical. Find the characters that most vibrantly speak on a musical stage. Find the moments in the story best served by a musical. Whenever someone says, "You can musicalize anything. I could take a book off your shelf and we could make it sing," that doesn't mean it's a musical.

There were lots of skeptics, as you can imagine, because the movie starts very dark. I'd argue that many dark things happen in *West Side Story*, *Fiddler*, and *Sweeney Todd*, and they're awfully great musicals. Music is the way we transcend the darkness into the humanity.

You look at what you can do that nobody else can do. Movies can have these delicate, small gestures. Lovely moments in a film, but what do I do for the poor person sitting eight hundred feet away? A lot of times how we handled that was to bring Celie downstage so she could be close to us. You exploit all the things you can do that

> ## "Music is the way we transcend the darkness into the humanity."
> ## —*Gary Griffin*

Lef to right: Alice Walker, Scott Sanders, and Oprah Winfrey at the opening night curtain call for *The Color Purple*, The Broadway Theatre, 2005

Left to right: Stephen Bray, Marsha Norman, Brenda Russell, Fantasia Barrino, Allee Willis, and Gary Griffin, 2007

nobody else can do. That larger vocabulary you have when you are creating a musical: We can do that through dance, we can do that through song, we can do that through ballet. Those are wonderful opportunities to say things that in other mediums aren't as successful.

SCOTT SANDERS: I was clear that I wanted to hire artists of color and women to author this show. Most musicals, including Black musicals like *Dreamgirls* and *Porgy and Bess*, were written by white men. It was challenging to figure out who was right for this project. I engaged Brenda Russell, Allee Willis, and Stephen Bray to write the music and lyrics. When it came to the book [for the musical], knowing that they had not worked in the theater before, I knew that I had to have not only a great book writer, but also, in some regards, a leader and mentor. The first writer we hired wasn't working at the same pace as the songwriters, so we knew we had to change horses.

By the time we met with Marsha [Norman], we had several songs but no book. Marsha came in and started to weave the book together into a structure. In the author collaboration, Marsha really was the team leader in the storytelling. I'm sure the songwriters could tell you firsthand how valuable that collaboration was, and how she was able to streamline this forty-year story into a two-act musical and bring authenticity to it. Obviously,

she's not Black, but I think her background of being from the South was very, very helpful. It ended up being a really wonderful, successful team.

MARSHA NORMAN (playwright, 2005 Broadway musical): When the project of the musical appeared, I begged to talk to the producers, but as I wasn't a Black woman, they said no. Then one day, as I was about to leave for Paris, my agent got the call: Could I be in rehearsal on Monday? They had a full cast for a workshop reading, but no book.

Naturally, I canceled my flight and showed up that Monday to see LaChanze, Felicia Fields, Brandon Victor Dixon, and the whole glorious cast of what would become the stage musical. For two weeks, they spent mornings learning the songs and dances, and I sat in the room with them writing the book and talking with the composers, whom I loved on first meeting. It was both exhilarating and really hard. Initially, some of the cast seemed suspicious of me and didn't know how devoted I was to the book and Alice. Then on one break, they all left the room, and I went over to sit with Felicia Fields [who played Sofia], just to chat. We talked about, of all things, bad men we had known. When the cast came back, she gave them a look that must have said, "She's OK. She's with us." And from that moment on, I was one of the gang, for which I am still eternally grateful.

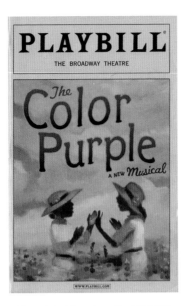

The original Broadway Playbill, 2005

Left to right: Krisha Marcano, Renée Elise Goldsberry, Gary Griffin, Elisabeth Withers, and LaChanze, Broadway opening night, 2005

I didn't watch the [1985] movie again while I was writing. I knew I had to make some different choices, because the theater is such an entirely different medium, so I watched a group of "person up against it" musicals, primarily looking for how a main character gains the trust of the audience, not just their pity.

QUINCY JONES (executive producer and composer, 1985 film; producer, 2005 Broadway musical, 2015 Broadway revival, 2023 film): When [producer] Roy Furman approached me to join as a producer, my only concern was how it would be presented on the stage, how the story would be maintained in an honest and emotional way that would be faithful to the essence of the novel and the [1985] movie. Once that concern was addressed, no one had to convince me to get involved, because it was a project that branched off from the film.

SCOTT SANDERS: Our first New York venue turned out to be unavailable, and by the time we secured a second, the Broadway Theatre, we had only four or five months to create interest in the production before it went into November previews. I said to our publicist, "I know this is atypical, but I feel like we need to bring long-lead publications in to look at the workshop reading we're going to do in early July." Magazines often work months in advance, so if I wanted to get any press whatsoever in

November, this was the only time that I had anything to show and tell.

My publicist and I both asked the question, "What about *O* magazine?" None of us knew Oprah. None of us knew Gayle. I called Quincy, who put me in touch with Gayle. We talked for about twenty minutes, and Gayle said, "I don't know about musicals, but I sure am interested in why a white guy wants to do this." I said, "Well, that's not the story. I really want you to come see the show." She said, "All right, but I have a lunch, so I'll only be able to stay for the first part."

Not only did she stay till the end, but before she left, she said, "I just emailed Oprah and told her you're doing her proud." I thought, "She has Oprah Winfrey's email address?" My colleague Carol Fineman was the one who had to tell me, "You do know she's Oprah's best friend, don't you?" I said, "No, I didn't know that." Carol said, "How do you not know that? Everybody knows that."

Gayle called me the next day and said, "Hey, listen, I have a friend who might want to invest in the show." I said, "We've pretty much raised all the money, but if it's somebody who's a really close friend of yours and it's a small amount, I might be able to move some things around and do it."

She said, "Scott, it's Oprah," and I almost dropped the phone. I said, "Oprah wants to invest in the show?" She said, "Yeah, she's going to call you."

"Being a part of this production is a huge deal as well as a huge opportunity and responsibility. It's like God has placed a gift in my lap and it's going to help other people. There are so many hurting people in the world. There are so many people that have experienced all the things that Celie went through. A lot of people think, 'Oh, I wish I was Shug, because she just loves love.' It's a big responsibility when you're telling a story every night. You have to move yourself out of the way and be submissive to the story you're telling."

—ELISABETH WITHERS

Actress and singer who played Shug in the 2005 Broadway musical

From "Berklee Today" by Rob Hochschild, Berklee College of Music, 2006

Celie (LaChanze), The Broadway Theatre, New York, 2005

TODD JOHNSON (producer, 2005 Broadway musical): Scott and I were walking down the street in SoHo when Oprah called and said, "Maybe we can meet." I remember when the phone call came in. It was her, and Scott did his Scott thing of, "Well, I've got to do such and such on such and such a day," and I just punched him in the side as hard as I could and was like, "Whenever she says! If it's ten minutes from now, we're going."

OPRAH WINFREY (Sofia, 1985 film; producer, 2005 Broadway musical, 2015 Broadway revival, 2023 film): I decide what I'm going to invest in or support, first and foremost, by what speaks to me. I have known since my early days of performing in front of audiences as a young girl, my early days working as a television reporter and paying attention to what people respond to, that if I feel this thing, somebody else is feeling it too.

I am drawn to what makes me feel: what makes me feel that the work is meaningful, what makes me have an "aha" moment, meaning my heart has opened to the point where I see myself differently, or see other people differently. Anytime I was ever doing a show and got goosebumps or teared up, I'd always pause within myself because I knew, "Oh, if I'm connecting, then other people are also connecting." So I make these choices purely on instinct, purely on what I feel.

When Gayle called me and said, "Oh, you have to hear this," and then she said, "Oh, you have to come," I flew to New York to watch a rehearsal and made the call instantly. I wanted to be involved with it because of how it made me feel. I am stirred. I am opened. I feel more alive. I feel more connected. I feel a sense of vibrancy.

If I have to go away and think about it, usually I don't choose it. It's just instant. I feel like, "Wow, this is big." Same thing with choosing books for book clubs. I remember seeing the rehearsal and feeling it then. That's when I committed.

TODD JOHNSON: I had worked with Scott as a consultant on other projects, and when this one came along, it was a no-brainer. The novel had been transformative for me: Growing up in the South, I had heard that language all my life, but I had never seen it represented in literature. It changed the way I thought about reading. It changed the way I thought about writing. It changed the way I thought about books because Alice had given real voices to these voices that I had only heard but never seen before. It was groundbreaking.

Primarily my role, while Scott was doing everything else, was to stand alongside the creative team and shepherd that process, which at times was challenging because we had to make some changes in that creative team along the way. And because there were a number of producers, I was tasked with being the voice of all those producorial notes going to the creative team, which is a delicate matter when a project is at a very initial stage. So I'm not sure I was very popular. But what they don't know is that I only gave about 20 percent of the notes that I was given, and the rest went into the trash. And those are for me to know, and no one to find out. I spent over four years with it, getting it to Broadway, but it was invigorating because I got to watch the project evolve from nothing into something.

SCOTT SANDERS: Oprah said, "How can I help?" It was like walking down the beach and finding a bottle, pulling out the cork, and a genie says, "What wishes can I grant you?" She said she wanted to invest, and when I told her I didn't need money at that point, she said, "Well, you're the first person who's ever said to me, 'I don't need your money.'"

I said, "Broadway's market research indicates that this past season, of all shows combined, the African American attendance was 3.8 percent. If we don't deliver a meaningful African American audience to the theater to see *The Color Purple*, then I will not have done my job. You can help me with that."

She agreed to let me put "Oprah Winfrey Presents" on the theater marquee, and in November she had the cast on her TV show to sing a bunch of songs. While her show was live on the air, on the East Coast at 4 p.m., I got a call from the Shuberts, who own Telecharge, the ticket-selling mechanism for all the Shubert theaters. They said, "We sold $3 million worth of tickets in the last ten minutes. We have to add more bandwidth to Telecharge in order to handle all the orders."

I admire the way she expresses herself as a woman. I admire the way she expresses herself as a writer. And to have this exceptional novel that she's written be turned into a musical where I am portraying her main character? That could be stressful, but all I kept thinking was that if Alice Walker is happy with my work on this, then I don't care what anyone else thinks. At the end of our reading, she got up, walked across to the table to where I was sitting, took a ring off of her finger—it was a purple amethyst—and put it on mine. And didn't say one word. That's when I knew. I said, "OK, I did it. I did my job."

ALICE WALKER (author of *The Color Purple*, 1982): I did that because LaChanze was carrying her responsibility to be this character in the best way. I was

"The pressure I felt to get it right didn't come because of the history or the celebrity around the story. The pressure I felt was Alice Walker."
—LaChanze

LACHANZE (Celie, 2005 Broadway musical): It was 2003 when I auditioned for it, and I was like, "*Color Purple* the musical? What's that going to be like? It sounds oxymoronic." But then I heard the music. At the time, "Dear God – Shug" was the *Color Purple* song. That was the only song I had to learn. I immediately connected with it and felt like it was my anthem, my own LaChanze anthem. It spoke so beautifully to me, and I really understood Celie's struggle. It's sad, but it's a common real-life experience of dark-skinned Black girls in the South. And being a dark-skinned Black girl from the South, I could identify with Celie's isolation, with discrimination against her because of her dark skin. All of that I could easily tap into, so when I auditioned for it, I knew who the character was.

The pressure I felt to get it right didn't come because of the history or the celebrity around the story. The pressure I felt was Alice Walker. The first reading that we did for her, I was extremely nervous because I value her writing, her words, her presence, her energy. Everything that she has brought to light in her time on this earth I admire.

commending her. I'm not much of a talker. It didn't feel right to go over and try to converse after she had just performed something so beautifully. I knew she would get that I was approving by doing this, just giving her whatever the ring was. I guess I haven't missed it, but I'm sure it was beautiful.

BRANDON VICTOR DIXON (Harpo, 2005 Broadway musical): Creating Harpo for the stage was fairly practical, and it contained only a percentage of the consciousness with which I approach things now, because I was only twenty-three, twenty-four years old at the time. I had only one professional production prior to that, and this is the first original show I was a part of. We first did a reading in New York and then went to Atlanta to develop it out of town.

I think the nature of Harpo, the nature of all the characters in this inception, came as a result of the connective work we did as an ensemble. It's one of the first shows I did where our interaction as actors and creative team members really helped make the story rise in this

> ## "The nature of all the characters in this inception came as a result of the connective work we did as an ensemble."
> —*Brandon Victor Dixon*

medium. Because you can't take the exact components of a thing and translate them to a new medium and have them have the same effect. So how do we balance them in this space? For me, it was the ensemble work that helped direct me to the character of Harpo: how he should be portrayed, how he operated in this world, and how he could be most effective in the overall propagation of the story and the message of Alice Walker's work.

TODD JOHNSON: Scott and I stood in the back of the Alliance Theater in Atlanta, and when the production opened there regionally, it opened with a funeral of Celie's mother. We looked at each other and we said, "We can't do it." There's so much difficult material in this story anyway, that we realized that the expectation of a musical theatergoer is perhaps in some ways different from someone who's opening a novel, and that they have to be coaxed into the story a little more gently than a scene in which we learn that Celie's mother has died, and that Pa [Alfonso] has raped her and given her two children. We went out of that production and reinvented the whole opening of the show. I say we, meaning the creative team, obviously.

What's so great about the theater is that it happens in real time with bodies in the room. And so it was a feeling in Atlanta; it wasn't anything that we saw or heard that was different. It was the feeling of being in that room with hundreds of people and then knowing in your gut that it couldn't be that way. I don't mean to be vague about it, but that's exactly what differentiates the theater from any other medium, is that it happens in flesh and blood.

GARY GRIFFIN: What distinguishes our version from all the others is that we committed to it being a Broadway musical. The movie is the movie, and it's a very good movie. The novel is genius. The revival was very different, and I respect it very much. I've done that kind of revival myself with other shows. But our charge was to make sure this felt like a Broadway show. That we used, intentionally, the values and the tenets of a Broadway musical: storytelling through dance; cast size; more of a poetic approach; not trying to be literal. Color: The whole show's about, "Don't walk down the path and not notice the color." So the color choices weren't drab and natural. They reflected a higher hue of tone. I was very clear in those choices. They heightened the energy of the show.

MARSHA NORMAN: I relate to Celie. I have always said my personal writing theme was "trapped girl." My plays are all about this subject because of my own recovery from a violent childhood. There was a great aunt who saved me over and over again, teachers who stepped in to help me—probably why I teach so much today—and ultimately my college education, whose genius was in making my scholarship work be accompanying the dance group rehearsals. The first day, as I started tinkling some Chopin for them, the teacher came over and said, pointing to a book on the piano, "The girls like to do their pliés to 'Edelweiss.'" And thus, over three years, three days a week, I learned the entire Broadway songbook.

The primary delight of writing the book for *The Color Purple* was listening to the music all day. Brenda Russell, Stephen Bray, and Allee Willis are geniuses. You can't sit in your seat without moving to the music they made. I watched them write a song one day, and it started with Stephen beating on the radiator. Then Brenda began to hum, then Allee started smacking the table and saying, "Yeah, yeah, *yeah!*" until a rhythm evolved. Brenda then began making a musical line with her stunning voice, and Allee chimed in with words, until finally, she was singing the song they just wrote. It was a miracle. They'd never worked on a musical before, and yet they produced one of the most glorious scores in the whole history of musical theater. In the biz, we say that a show has legs if it runs. But this show has a whole damn body to communicate with, which it does with all its huge heart.

Harpo (Brandon Victor Dixon) and
Sofia (Felicia P. Fields), The Broadway
Theatre, New York, 2005

Shug (Elisabeth Withers), Celie (Fantasia Barrino), and other cast members, The Broadway Theatre, New York, 2007

ALL THE WORLD'S A STAGE

STEVE SPIEGEL (CEO, Theatrical Rights Worldwide): It's the most important musical I represent. I have quite a collection of Broadway properties in my catalog, but *The Color Purple* is the centerpiece, the one I'm the proudest of.

My career has been in the licensing of musicals, and now also plays, to theater companies of all levels. Schools, community groups, professional groups, tour companies, summer camps, park and recreation departments—not only here in the United States but around the world. We deal with 150,000 groups in sixty-eight different countries.

For something as well-written as *The Color Purple* to be adopted by producers and actors around the world is very meaningful to me. I always say, "If all the world's a stage and music is the universal language, then musical theater bridges everything—the entire world and all languages."

Color Purple is something I'm so proud of because, first of all, Marsha Norman's writing is at such a high level. Most of the time in musicals we want to have a quality book, but we want to get to the songs. In *The Color Purple*, the book has so many nuances, and it's so important and complete. There's truly a beginning, middle, and end. There's Celie's growth as an individual,

as a person, from her younger years to her adult years. All of the characters are richly developed and have so much to say and reveal about their lives.

MARSHA NORMAN: I wanted to write the book for the musical because I knew the technical problems the book had to solve. First of all, the novel is written in letters. Second, Celie, though she is the center of the story, is not the most charismatic or dramatic character on the stage. Neither is Nettie. They become those heroic main characters because they overcome such incredible obstacles. So I made the unwritten but often spoken rule that Celie is always present. If you as another character come on stage, it's because you want something from Celie. Yes, you can have a sexy song between Harpo and Sofia late in the show, but that's just a release from the tension around them. Otherwise, Celie is the center. That keeps her from having her show stolen by the much louder, sassier, and funnier characters like the Church Ladies, who will try to steal every scene they're in, or Shug or Sofia or Squeak. You cannot ever forget Celie because she's always there.

STEVE SPIEGEL: I was already a huge fan of Marsha Norman's. I was a huge fan of Allee Willis's. Obviously, I loved the movie. But when I was sitting in the audience in 2006, I was moved by not only what I experienced on the stage, but also off the stage. A lot of people look at

Audience members await a matinee showing of
The Color Purple at The Broadway Theatre, New York, 2006

Chaz Lamar Shepherd (Harpo, left) and fans outside
The Broadway Theatre, New York, 2007

Purple Rising

The Color Purple and think, "This is such an upsetting story." And it is a serious story, but there's comedy in this script. There are moments to breathe and moments to even laugh. But what I really experienced was an audience that usually doesn't go to the theater. People of color, specifically. They might go to their church performances, their church choirs, but the show opened up a new audience, which is so important to me, because I'm a salesman.

The first time I saw it, I remember thinking, "This is the highest quality of musical theater. Great songs, great characters, great story." The audience, as I looked around, were talking to the stage and commenting on

DANIELLE BROOKS (Sofia, 2015 Broadway revival, 2023 film): My first encounter with The Color Purple was in 2005. I had won this competition back in South Carolina, where I grew up. It was this diversity competition where they were allowing fifteen or twenty students to go for free to New York with a parent. We would service their diversity initiatives while getting to explore New York.

One of the days we had there, my dad took me to see The Color Purple because at the time the only Black shows that were on Broadway were The Color Purple and The Lion King. Other people think Lion King is an animal show, but that's a story for another day.

> # "In the biz, we say that a show has legs if it runs. But this show has a whole damn body to communicate with, which it does with all its huge heart."
>
> ## —Marsha Norman

the action, and I could see that reacting to what was happening on the stage was empowering. I thought, "I need to represent this show because this is a show that has a meaning."

COREY HAWKINS (Harpo, 2023 film): You watch this story and you can feel it has a tight hold on the world. It's the lean-in factor. If it gets you to lean in and feel like you are not just witnessing it but feeling it in your bones—that's what I feel every time I think of The Color Purple. That's what I felt when I was a student at Juilliard and first heard LaChanze sing the music. I remember thinking, "This story is ours, but it's also for everyone." Spielberg did a fantastic job when he directed it. But also that was a sort of microcosm of where we were then, and it reflects who was deemed able to tell this story onscreen. But it doesn't take away from the art, because the source material stands the test of time. It's just so strong.

I was fifteen years old, and we sat in the mezzanine. I remember the first scene, seeing Renée Goldsberry and LaChanze sitting in a tree and singing, "Hey, sister, whatcha gonna do?" My jaw dropped. I was like, "This is what theater is? OMG!" I was already doing theater back in South Carolina, but of course it was nowhere close to this scale. The story took me on such a journey. I was so impressed with the music, the acting, the set design, the lighting, everything. Blew my mind.

I sat there bawling my eyes out. While my dad sat in discomfort from the tiny theater seats, I sat in awe. Jaw on the floor with a stream of tears running down my face, I was mesmerized by the performance.

I knew the story from the movie. As a fifteen-year-old intern at my church summer camp, we would watch the film after the younger kids left for the day. But in my head, my first encounter has always been the Broadway show. That was the moment for me. It changed my life. It truly changed my life. I remember just saying, "This is

Nettie (Renée Elise Goldsberry, left) and Celie (LaChanze), The Broadway Theatre, New York, 2005

what I want to do for a living. I don't know how I'm going to get to that, how I can manifest this goal, but this is what I want to do." For me to then step into the play ten years later was a full-circle moment. I couldn't have written it any better than God had orchestrated it.

OPRAH WINFREY: When Gayle said they were making a musical of *The Color Purple*, my first thought had been, "How are you going to do that? How are you going to take that story and make some singing and dancing around Celie and her troubles?"

What was so poignant for me was that Scott [Sanders] had the vision to see what it could become, and then to surround himself with a cast and crew of such talented people who could bring that vision into fruition. I give him all the props for that. In our first conversations, it was clear to me that he understood what *The Color Purple* was. It was also clear that he wasn't in any way fearful of or anxious about being in this space and around Black people. He was comfortable enough with himself and comfortable with the idea. From the moment I saw the rehearsal, I could see that this wasn't just talk.

I understood from my conversations with him that he understood the spirit of it and knew how to bring that together, whether it was hiring the musicians, the writers, the technicians, and all the other people who were required to make it work. No better way to express it for me than I got that he got it, that he really got it. It wasn't just one of those peripheral conversations that people have that goes around the center of things, where you come away and you go, "I don't even know what that was."

He has been an ally. He has been a devotee. He has been an uplifter. He has been a champion for this in a way that no one else has—other than Quincy Jones, who's been there since the start.

QUINCY JONES: I was blown away by the performances of the Broadway show and the staging of it. One of the things that made the original *Color Purple* movie so successful, I believe, was the emotional power and pull of the film. With the Broadway presentation, you feel that power and pull in an even more visceral way. That is what a live performance can do. It was not a reinvention or a new interpretation of Alice's novel, but what I would call a rebirth of it. It was beautiful to see audiences experience and embrace it all over again.

> "I remember seeing Reneé Goldsberry and LaChanze singing, 'Hey, sister, whatcha gonna do?' My jaw dropped. I was like, 'This is what theater is?'"
> —Danielle Brooks

GARY GRIFFIN: What stays with me all these years later is the incredible honor it was to get to do it. That is a big one. I mean, I've never gotten over that I got to do *The Color Purple*, and I never will. And working with the cast. I had an amazing company of artists—there was great trust and debate and love. I could sense there was pride from the beginning of getting to do it.

We knew there would be revivals. But we were the first. I take that away, nightly. We're rounding twenty years. That's hard for me to believe. But I'm proud of the show. I'm very proud that it's having this new life as a film with Fantasia. I hope it means more people will hear the story and hear the story through the material we created. That means a lot to me.

PHYLICIA PEARL MPASI (Young Celie, 2023 film): The first time I ever heard of this musical, I was on my way to school, and on the radio they were talking about Fantasia about to make her Broadway debut. I remember listening to it on a Black radio station at home in Silver Spring, Maryland, and everyone was saying, "We're so proud of our girl Tasia. We're so excited for her. Can't wait to see her." That's the first time I'd ever heard of *The Color Purple*. I was like, "What is that?"

TAKING IT TO THE STAGE, AGAIN: THE 2015 BROADWAY REVIVAL

SCOTT SANDERS: The first version played in New York and toured for five or six years. I thought that would be the end of my experience with *The Color Purple*, because normally you don't revive a show for at least a decade. But when I went to Africa with Oprah when she opened her girls' academy, I had a burning desire to bring *The Color Purple* to Africa. Tom Schumacher, who ran Disney Theatricals, introduced me to local presenters in Johannesburg and Cape Town, and both said, "We'd love to bring it here, but your show's too big and too expensive."

I start thinking, "What's the scaled-down version of the show?" I thought of the Menier Chocolate Factory, a

Academy Award winner Jennifer Hudson, and when she said yes, I put the money together and announced *The Color Purple*'s first Broadway revival. That production went on to win the Tony and a Grammy.

CYNTHIA ERIVO (Celie, 2015 Broadway revival): This was not only my Broadway debut, it was my first experience performing in the U.S. I don't know that it even had been a fantasy, because I'm not sure I thought Broadway was in my future. It wasn't something that was talked about in the U.K., and certainly not at drama school. So it wasn't something that I thought was a path for me. When it was mentioned, I actually, genuinely thought they were joking. I'd done this performance at the Chocolate Factory, and when someone said, "Oh, we might go to Broadway. Would you go with?" I was like, "Sure, if you'll have me." That was legitimately my answer: "Sure, if you'll have me."

> ## "This one woman got up on her feet and just pointed at me. And then people started stamping their feet on the ground."
> ### —Cynthia Erivo

theater in London that has only three hundred seats, and they creatively reimagine musicals for their space. Their artistic director, David Babani, loved the idea of doing a production there, and we both agreed to go after John Doyle to direct it. He's done smaller versions of *Sweeney Todd*, *Company*, and others.

I called eight of my co-producers from the original Broadway production and said, "We can make this work. I'll be the first to invest. If nothing comes of it, we're going to all lose our money. But if we can get a functional, powerful, small version of this musical, we can take this to other parts of the world, starting with Africa."

In doing that Chocolate Factory production, we discovered Cynthia Erivo. Opening night in London, I looked her in the eyes and said, "I have to bring you to New York." All my partners said, "You're out of your mind. The show just closed five years ago." I said, "If I can pair Cynthia with a star to play Shug, I will do it." I went after

And then when it happened, my mind was a little bit blown, to be honest. Broadway is a world of its own. There's this familial energy that Broadway has, so that you are not there in your own show—you are there with your show and everyone else's show. I made lifelong friends doing that show, and a lot of them weren't necessarily from my show. So I've got friends who I love and care about from the show I was in, and then from next door's show, and from the show that was two streets over. It was wonderful.

STEPHEN BRAY (music and lyrics, 2005 Broadway musical, 2015 Broadway revival, 2023 film): Over the years, if I had nothing to do, I would fly to weird places and see the show—somewhere outside of Pittsburgh or some regional place where they had no idea that the authors were sitting in the audience. I just wanted to see, not to catch them doing anything.

Celie (Cynthia Erivo) and cast members, Bernard B. Jacobs Theatre, New York, 2015

The Color Purple brought a lot of new people to the theater. I'm so proud to see that it plays in different regions and different cultures. My wife and I went to see it in London where we were told that how the audience was reacting was not at all common for them. The artistic director and the general manager told us that their audiences never made the noises that they made. At the end of the show, when they would applaud, they would start stomping their feet. Cynthia Erivo earned every second of it, I'm sure. I mean, it's Cynthia Erivo. But yeah, we were told that it was a cultural shift for them to respond the way they did.

CYNTHIA ERIVO: I'd never seen anything like it. I remember one performance, we had finished the show and we were singing the final "Color Purple," and people started clapping. And then this one woman got up on her feet and just pointed at me. And then people started stamping their feet on the ground. This is in London. That's not a usual thing. It doesn't happen—ever. And that is what was happening over and over. People stamping on the ground, ovations. But that particular night, I've never experienced anything like it. It was so wild because she just locked in with me.

SHUG ON SHUG

To many, Shug Avery is either a symbol of liberation or a wounded bird who hides behind bright plumage. Alice Walker saw her as both, but also as the bringer of a new gospel. Margaret Avery and Jennifer Hudson speak to each other about embodying this complex character.

Shug (Margaret Avery), 1985 film

Shug (Jennifer Hudson), 2015 Broadway revival

MARGARET AVERY: Jennifer, when I auditioned for the role of Shug, I had done TV but never been in a film, so I had to fight to be seen. You were already known as a wonderful singer from *Dreamgirls* and other realms. What was your experience like in taking on the role?

JENNIFER HUDSON: I actually received a call from Oprah saying, "Jennifer, would you be interested in playing Shug Avery in the revival?" I hopped at the chance because, first of all, I'd always wanted to do a Broadway show. And I was so inspired, obviously, by the original film and your portrayal of Shug Avery.

Shug was one of my favorite characters, although at first I saw myself more in line with the character of Celie. Once I said yes, I tapped into my inner Shug. For me, her personality was a combination of Tina Turner, Rue McClanahan's Blanche [from *The Golden Girls*] and

that stage. I was so happy to see that. I loved everything about your version.

Now, I think I had an advantage in that I had never seen the character before. What I felt about Shug was that she was a woman looking for love. So often in real life, if you're a woman who didn't have a connection with your dad, you get into relationships that you probably wouldn't have if you weren't looking for love. In the film, you see that so clearly when the father is driving by and Shug is saying, "Hey, I's married now," trying to get his love, his attention.

I felt that Shug was looking for love, but at the same time, she was promiscuous and loved sex. At that time in history, women weren't free with their bodies like that, but she did want Celie to know how sex feels when you are loved. You saw much more of that relationship in your version.

"Shug helped all of them find their strength and see what women can be."
—Jennifer Hudson

Jackée Harry's Sandra [from *227*]. In all the stage versions I'd seen, everyone who portrayed Shug had their own interpretation to a certain extent, but the original premise and fabric of the character—where she was built from—was what came from you and the novel. I had my own journey with it. I wish, though, I wish I got to sing songs from your film.

MARGARET: Oh, really?

JENNIFER: Oh my God, yes. I loved "Sister," and then what was that song when you go back to the church?

MARGARET: "Maybe God's Tryin' to Tell You Somethin'."

JENNIFER: Oh my God.

MARGARET: The music was totally different for the stage version; it came from a new set of songwriters and not Q [Quincy Jones]. And when you came, you just lit up

JENNIFER: My Shug is a bridge for Celie, and a lot of that comes across through song. You had "Push Da Button," which worked as the introduction of Shug. Then you had "Too Beautiful for Words," which was my favorite. It's such a beautiful duet, and it sums up the love story that is Celie and Shug's relationship. In the musical, the music is the journey. It's the narrative. It pushes the story along. My job as a character was to connect everyone together. Shug helped all of them find their strength and see what women can be.

I wonder for you, Ms. Avery, what did you pull from to create this womanly figure who did not exist during that time? Look at Celie; she didn't even have a voice. Sofia was strong but still in the mode of the times to a certain extent. But Shug was the representation of the future of what we could be. I had you as a reference, but I wonder what reference you had to develop such a Shug Avery who could show the other ladies, "This is who you can be. This is what it is, and I'm OK being that way."

MARGARET: From working on the stage, I've learned to write out a backstory for my characters. All the secrets that no one knows about, all the things that would hurt them to reveal. With film, a lot is about the eyes and what you're thinking under the lines or when you are saying nothing, which is something you don't get the benefit of on stage. In film, having a backstory reveals itself when you're talking or having no lines at all.

I remember that Steven [Spielberg] let us see dailies, and the first thing I saw was the juke joint scene. I had gained almost thirty pounds for the role, and when I saw my face and my movements and all, I thought, "Damn, I worked so hard on that character...and I look like my mom."

Then, for myself, no matter what role I'm playing, I like to add whatever is within me. Some characters can be so different from you that you're like, "Oh my God. I have nothing here to connect myself to this character." So at some point you have to pull, at least in my process, a piece of yourself and put it into the character. With Shug, I could relate in songs, or in knowing what it's like to be a child of God, and growing up in the church and those restrictions or beliefs. To understand Shug that way, to understand what her battle was with her father, her relationship with men. So I feel like my biggest connection with my Shug is in song, in music.

The Color Purple is such a classic, and seeing Shug in that first film was the vision of beauty. I will say, I think

"For me, when you're building a character, especially in period pieces, you have to ask yourself, 'What does she pull from?'"

—Jennifer Hudson

I said, "I'll be damned. I thought I was doing this on my own." But in my subconscious, I guess I re-created my mother. I think there's something Freudian about that. I don't know. Then I thought, "How would I compare my mother to Shug?" There was a lot of parallelism, because my mother was an alcoholic, and I think it was all her pain that she tried to suppress. Maybe this looseness that Shug had was looking for love and suppressing the pain that she had not being close to her father.

JENNIFER: For me, when you're building a character, especially in period pieces, you have to ask yourself, "What does she pull from?" You've got to consider the time she's in and how women existed then: the circumstances, the environment. I approached it no differently than I did when I later played Ms. [Aretha] Franklin or even Effie [from *Dreamgirls*], which all overlapped some of the same time periods.

she is the sexiest character I have ever played. To step in that space was very different and new for me, and even then I was like, "Me as Shug? Oh, wow."

MARGARET: I was mesmerized when you were on that stage with all that height and that beauty and that costume. Oh, God, you were wonderful. Really wonderful.

For me, I knew going in that it was going to be a very important film because this was the first Black film since *Sounder*, which had come out in '72. It was my first film ever, and I felt a lot of pressure, but I did my personal best. When I saw the film for the first time, I said, "Oh, God, thank you." I was in tears saying, "Oh my God. I think I really did do a good job after all."

JENNIFER: I'm honored to even be in the same interview space as you, Ms. Avery. I'm thankful to speak with you, and I'm thankful for my Shug Avery, your Shug Avery, and *The Color Purple*, which is so special and dear to us all.

Shug (Jennifer Hudson), Bernard
B. Jacobs Theatre, New York, 2015

Mister (Gavin Gregory) and Harpo (J. Daughtry), Bernard B. Jacobs Theatre, New York, 2015

We didn't think it would happen again, but when we went to Broadway, in the first preview, people stood up in the middle of the show after "I'm Here." I was blown away. The first time it happened, I thought it was a fluke. So I plowed on. Then it happened again, and I was just like, "OK, I have to skirt the line between giving respect to the audience so they feel what they feel but make sure that they know we have a story to continue."

But I just was breathing with everyone because the way this show was done meant that we really had to listen to everything around us. You could hear a pin drop sometimes. And if someone's phone went off, you could hear it and you could hear the audience gasp. And so you have to think, "It's OK. We know the phone's ringing. We're just going to wait, and then we'll go on." So we're playing this wonderful tennis match back and forth between us. I could hear people crying. I could hear people audibly willing Celie to go on. I could hear frustration in people's voices. It was wonderful. It was crazy.

Purple Rising

STEPHEN BRAY: The abstract language of music doesn't need a translator. Even though you're from the middle of the country, or the East Coast where everything's super-cool, or the West Coast where everybody's super-jaded, it still manages to work on people. But that's a testament to Alice, too. The true believers really, really respond to it.

CYNTHIA ERIVO: This was a long run, and I loved doing this show. The show changed my life. But during my very last performance, I could barely get through "I'm Here." I could hear my cast members on either side of the stage yelling to keep going. They were watching this final part of the song—they were watching. I can't tell you how held I felt at that moment. It was one of the most...how do I even describe it? I don't know why, but the word *ascent* comes to my mind. It felt like I was being lifted into it.

It was my thirtieth birthday also. So all of the things had come around. It was the beginning and the ending of something. And my cast is there and they're holding me. They were yelling. They didn't care. They were like, "Sing!" It was amazing. It felt like I was in a ring of energy because the audience was up on its feet. Then my cast members were side stage. I was totally surrounded. And it was wonderful.

FANTASIA BARRINO (Celie, 2005 Broadway musical, 2023 film): To be honest—and I'm the one who's always going to be very, very honest—I didn't want to play the role again for the new film. Scott [Sanders] called me and had a long conversation with me. The role for me when I played it on Broadway was very tough. When I stepped into Celie's shoes, I stepped into her life. I woke up Celie, I went to bed Celie, all day long I was Celie. I had Celie's problems and I had Fantasia's problems and they were similar. And they were dark. And it was hard. Times have changed, but it was hard for me being a young mother, having dropped out of school in the ninth grade, having been molested—I've been through a lot of things. I was piling her stuff on top of my stuff.

TODD JOHNSON: Fantasia was not a trained actor. And so the first time I heard her read—because of course I had heard her sing—it was almost as though I couldn't breathe because it was so raw. So something

"Playing Celie is not a walk in the park. It's hard."
—Cynthia Erivo

in Celie resonated with her so deeply that it was almost as if she didn't have to act. She just had to let it out. It could only have been exhausting for her because I believe she was 100 percent there every single time on an emotional level that was more intimate and personal than we can know.

CYNTHIA ERIVO: Playing Celie is not a walk in the park. It's hard. For the first couple of weeks, you can differentiate what's you and what's her. And then your body doesn't really know what's real and what's not; it just knows you're going through something. So for two-odd hours every night you are getting abused and called names and called ugly. All of those things you are hearing, they're still in your ears. It's your brain, it's your mind. So the whole thing is connected. And after a while, it does get hard to separate the two. Because quite frankly, it's easier to get into if it's not separated at all. And so the job actually is to know what to do when everything comes to an end and how to let that go. That's actually the difficult part, because for all intents and purposes I don't have to work so hard to get into Celie for performance three hundred and something.

But at the end of performance four hundred and something, when it's the end of the thing, what I have to do to get out of a character and let her go will not take me a day. It'll take me a week, two weeks, a month, maybe. There are habits that never leave. I'm never going to forget Celie. I'm probably never going to forget how she moves, because it was part of me. That's the thing I battle with. I tend to battle with it with a lot of characters I play. If you're in them for long enough, they stick with you, and you have to know when to really let them go and say, "Thank you for your service. I'll never forget you. You have to go."

THE BROADWAY SONGS

Stephen Bray, Brenda Russell, and Allee Willis teamed up in 2000 to write the book for the original Broadway musical. All were established, successful songwriters in the pop and R&B worlds, but none had ever written for the stage before taking on this project.

Left to right: Stephen Bray, Brenda Russell, and Allee Willis

STEPHEN BRAY: Back in 1986, Allee [who passed away in 2019] was the visual consultant on a music video for my band, the Breakfast Club, and our song "Right on Track." The director said it was going to be as if the band rehearsed at Pee-wee's Playhouse, and Allee was going to bring all the visuals together. It was amazing. I mean, literally the drum set I was playing was made out of hubcaps and tires. I thought, "This is a very creative person." Years later, she called me, and by then I'd found out that she was the great Allee Willis, the songwriter behind "September" and "Boogie Wonderland" for Earth, Wind & Fire, and the Pointer Sisters' "Neutron Dance." Allee called and said, "Can you come help me with some scores?" which I hadn't done a lot of, but it was Allee, so it was going to be fun. At one point she said, "Do you know Brenda Russell?" I said, "I used to play her records all day long. I'd love to meet her." Allee's reasoning was that we'd go faster if there were three of us.

BRENDA: As we were sitting together, working at Allee's, I looked up and said, "We need something bigger." Because I could feel something was happening in that room with the three of us. I just looked up at the universe and said, "We need something bigger." And sure enough, something bigger came.

STEPHEN: Scott Sanders had been developing *The Color Purple* for years already at this point. He came to Allee and said, "I'm moving on from my last writing team, and I'm hoping you can help me identify some fresh blood. I don't want predictable, expected Broadway music."

BRENDA: Scott told Allee that he was holding auditions, and did she know Brenda Russell? He was looking for me to write the music. She said, "Yeah, she's on her way over to write with me and Stephen right now, and you should let us audition." And Scott said, "OK, but no special favors."

> ## "I looked up at the universe and said, 'We need something bigger.'"
> ### —Brenda Russell

BRENDA RUSSELL: I was very good friends with Allee. We were an unusual combination because we were so different. But we somehow connected. I didn't really know Stephen until I went to Allee's, and then I just fell in love with him because he's an amazing human being.

STEPHEN: We managed to have a lot of fun working on those scores, as well as a never-heard theme song for Liza Minnelli's reality show. Mood-wise and temperature-wise and character-wise, Brenda and I were probably in a similar place in terms of personalities. But when it came to the emotional relationship with the work, Allee and I were more aligned. If you said to us, "That's terrible, write a different one," Allee and I were like, "OK, let's do it." Whereas it would take Brenda a while. Brenda would say, "What do you mean you don't like it? It's beautiful. It's so beautiful."

STEPHEN: We didn't know anything about musical theater other than what we had gleaned from experiencing it from time to time. But obviously the mountains and the valleys are where the music comes from in a musical story. So we tackled what we thought was one of the bigger scenes, which was Shug Avery's arrival in town. We likened it to the Wells Fargo wagon in *The Music Man*. Allee, true to form, was like, "Let's make this sound really different." So we went to her kitchen and we got egg beaters and we got cheese graters and we got any kind of metallic thing that would make rhythms. We designed the whole scene. We had the horse hooves. Then we did a song called "She Be Mine" about Celie seeing her baby in the store.

BRENDA: We wrote two fantastic tunes. We arranged them. Most Broadway demos are just piano and vocal, but we put in the strings and the horns, and then we sent it to Scott by FedEx.

STEPHEN: We sent it off, and then you just kind of sit there going, "OK, are they going to hate it? Do they love it? Is it as good as I hope it is? Is it terrible?"

BRENDA: We knew when he was going to get it. And we're waiting. And we're waiting. And he doesn't call.

STEPHEN: The weekend went by and we hadn't heard anything. We finally called, and Scott said, "Oh, yeah, I forgot to tell you. I played it for Alice. Alice drove around with it, listening to it in her car. She consulted her circle, and everybody signed off on it. Everybody loved it. So yeah, you guys are in."

BRENDA: He said, "I would never hire people on just this, but I feel like this is it."

Nobody said that to us when we started, and we had to learn it the hard, slow way.

BRENDA: When we first got the job, we saw every show we could see. And Allee hated musicals. But we would read to each other from Alice's book. Alice was our guiding light because that woman is like a goddess. She is so full of light, and she would bow to us when she would leave the room. She's amazing. At our first meeting with Alice, she didn't know what to expect. She looks at us and says, "Well, you look beautiful." And Allee says, "Yes, well, we're doing an all-white version." And Stephen said, "And we're doing it in Swedish," or something crazy like that. But then we all laughed. I almost fell under the table.

"We wrote a version of 'What About Love?' that was very poetic, with lines like, 'Cold as the edge of a knife.' And when we played it for Gary and the others, they were like, 'I don't know what that means.'"

—Stephen Bray

STEPHEN: It was a very, very high moment for us. I think we immediately went to the bookstore and got *How to Write a Musical*. Pop songs are all about hooks and catchiness and singability—nothing to do with moving a story from here to here. Nobody said that to us, so we wrote a few songs that were probably quite listenable, but they did not do the job. [Director] Gary Griffin, God bless him, and [book writer] Marsha Norman were incredibly respectful of our naivete and ignorance about the storytelling part of it. If you ask me now, I'd say, "Well, in a musical the song is a scene. It's got to have a beginning, a middle, and an end. You want your character to be somewhere different emotionally or story-wise than when you started or you probably don't need that song."

STEPHEN: We watched everything we could find. This is before streaming and on demand. There's a concert version of *Sunday in the Park with George* we watched a million times. [Stephen] Sondheim's work to me is just the pinnacle of intelligent musical theater writing because it's funny, it's musical, it's musically complex. He tells the story with songs in a modern, contemporary way. And then *Pippin* and *Godspell* appealed especially to Allee because she was a sucker for rock musicals.

BRENDA: We got along really well, considering. But it was a lot of pressure. When I first started writing, all I could think about was the millions of dollars that were resting on my shoulders. But then I had to release

Left to right: Allee Willis, Alice Walker, Brenda Russell, and Stephen Bray, 2005

everything and let it go, just let it flow through me and not think about that.

STEPHEN: Brenda's superpower is that she goes into her mode where clearly she is channeling. She has some angelic sources that feed her gorgeous music and gorgeous chord progressions.

BRENDA: We all did everything, but some were stronger at some things than others. Stephen is a drummer, first of all, and the only one of us who could actually read music. Structurally, lyrically, melodically, everything. He was really good. Allee was extremely good with lyrics and melodies. She would hear a melody—it was fabulous. I would be at the piano, fumbling, because I'm a writer who plays piano. I'd play three notes and she'd say, "That's it!" She had an instinct that was fantastic. Stephen's greatest line to me was, "There's only one of us in the room—one spirit. It's all one." And I was like, "Oh, I love that. OK. I'm in."

STEPHEN: We wrote a version of "What About Love?" that was very poetic, with lines like, "Cold as the edge of a knife." And when we played it for Gary and the others, they were like, "I don't know what that means." It was hard for Brenda to hear that. I definitely held her hand

while she cried. Because we'd never been in a situation like that. I like polishing things until you rip it from my grasp, so I was fine. Allee had the uncanny duality of loving every idea she had but being willing to let go of it just as quickly as it came on. Between the three of us, "we lived through it."

BRENDA: The most important thing I learned about writing for Broadway is rewriting, because we came from pop songs. In pop, you write a song, give it to someone, and they say, "I like this song, I'm going to record it." They don't say, "Can you rewrite the chorus for us? Or can you take away one verse?" On Broadway, that's all they do. I felt like they had one of those sickle things, just cutting those songs, slashing. I was so stressed out. Scott would run after me saying, "It's OK, Brenda, we're not going to ruin your music." I had to separate my heart from the project a lot. But you get attached, and you're not used to people saying no when you have written a very good song.

Mister's song ["Celie's Curse"] was like writing with a team, a bigger team than the three of us. We had the director, the choreographer, the costume person. Everybody had something to say. So it made it a bit harder to figure out what you want the song to be. We wrote Mister's song about four or five times. The singers

Shug (Taraji P. Henson) and
Celie (Fantasia Barrino), 2023 film

were amazing, though, because they would learn something overnight and come back and sing it. We were like, "How are they doing that?" The talent was astronomical.

One of the most fun songs we wrote was "The Color Purple," because you could feel the energy in the room when we found the hook. Allee would say, "Take a Valium, now," and then she would read a line and we'd go, "Oh, that's perfect." When I found those chords, and she had the lines, and Stephen was directing, suddenly it was magic when we started singing it.

STEPHEN: I can't say that I have a favorite song. I am extremely proud of "What About Love?" because it's a historical lesbian love song that I don't think had happened before we put it on stage. And seeing the audience react to it, 2004 to 2022, being part of that vanguard in terms of same-sex relationships on stage, I feel really proud of that song. And obviously "I'm Here." Nailed it.

BRENDA: "I'm Here" was hard to write, because we couldn't get total agreement from that huge team. When we finally landed on it, it was a beautiful thing because it was a struggle to get there.

STEPHEN: We had iteration after iteration of that song, and when we'd turn in a version they'd say, "OK, but what has Celie learned?" At one point, Brenda asked LaChanze, "Well, what do you want to do when you come into all your fullness? What do you want to become? What will your behavior be?" And LaChanze's answer was where those lines came from about putting your shoulders back and flirting with somebody.

BRENDA: "Hell No" is the song where Sofia decides that she is not going to let Harpo beat her ass. It was always an anthem to us, an anthem for women not to accept brutality from men. The audience reaction was always fantastic because women like to stand up against brutality, and they really love it when someone else says it too. It makes them feel stronger. They would scream. They loved it.

STEPHEN: "Push Da Button" and "Any Little Thing" are tied for the most fun songs. Also "Miss Celie's Pants," when Celie gets to finally say, "Look who's wearing the pants now." They wanted to kill that song because it was going to be expensive to stage and they weren't sure the story needed it. We had to fight for that. I remember saying, "Listen, we've written a moment for all six of the principal women to come to the front of the stage and revel in each other's beauty." That makes me super proud.

BRENDA: When we got "The Color Purple" right, we were very, very happy. We knew. You can tell by the feeling of it more than anything else. Something happens. I don't know how to express that, except that it's a feeling of energy in the room when something starts ringing in harmony.

And once the show was live, we loved to sit in the audience and watch the people respond to it. Because I'm telling you, people don't yell on Broadway normally, but in *Color Purple*, people were loud. "Go ahead, girl! Sing the song!" We heard before we opened *Purple* that Black people don't come to the theater. We were like, "Well, yeah, they're not coming to see *Oklahoma!*, but they might come to see our show." And they did. Buses. I'm talking buses from across the country. People are flying in. Mothers, sisters. It was a totally mixed audience, but a lot of Black ladies with church hats. We loved watching guys trying to pretend like they weren't crying. People would talk to the stage, because my Black people are very expressive and interactive, right? At one point, Sofia's walking across the stage after coming out of jail, all messed up. And the woman in the front said, "It's gonna be all right, Sofia. It's gonna be all right."

Handwritten notes on the
"What About Love?" sheet music

V

THE 2023 FILM

TAKING IT TO A NEW GENERATION

I believe movies are the most powerful medium for change on earth.

—Alice Walker,
The Same River Twice

GOING FOR A GREENLIGHT

SCOTT SANDERS (producer, 2005 Broadway musical, 2015 Broadway revival, 2023 film): This is a timeless story. There are new generations of women and men and people of all ages and colors who need to see this, and I realized that to make someone go to a destination and pay $100 or $150 for a [Broadway] ticket makes it limiting. I thought, "I'd love to do it as a movie."

Back in 2016, I had thought about airing it live on NBC from the theater with Cynthia Erivo on the last night of that production, but that didn't happen. Then it sort of went away for a bit. Then the Black Lives Matter movement came into full force, and I called Oprah and I said, "We have to make this as a movie. We just have to," and she called Steven [Spielberg]. I said, "Let's all do it together," and here we are.

NIIJA KUYKENDALL (former production executive, Warner Bros.): I was at Warner Bros. for thirteen and a half years, ultimately as an executive vice president of production, and over the years, various people had brought up the notion of doing something with *The Color Purple*. Warner Bros. owned part of the rights, but the rights were tricky. And also, how would you do that? It's such an iconic piece of culture. Not just iconic entertainment, but actually iconic—it emotionally means something to the world and to a community. It always felt like one of those things that you don't touch.

My colleague Kevin McCormick came to me one day and said, "I want to introduce you to a dear friend of mine, Scott Sanders, and he may want to talk about *The Color Purple*." I'd never met Scott before. As soon as he started talking, I could see that he clearly had a path. He had a relationship with Alice. He had a relationship with Oprah. His notion of doing the musical for screen felt like a way for new generations to access the material. That's what got me excited: the idea of doing something that could be wildly different from Steven's very revered version of it.

Also, Scott and I immediately fell in love with each other and felt like this could be a great partnership. It felt like we could really tackle this together. He's definitely aware when there is a challenge or when something is tricky, but he's willing to roll up his sleeves and figure it out. Which is generally my attitude. So I love that about him.

SCOTT SANDERS: Studios rarely tell you "in the room," as they say, that they're interested in moving forward on a pitch. Normally, the executives have to caucus with their bosses, caucus with their colleagues, and then come back to you several weeks later. Niija was crystal clear before we paid the check at breakfast that she wanted to do this.

SHEILA WALCOTT (senior vice president of creative development, Warner Bros.): At Warner Bros., when I was still a junior executive, Niija Kuykendall pitched that we should remake *The Color Purple*. And I thought, "Ooh, I don't know if we want to mess that one up. I don't know, girl. I don't know." Because Niija's such a formidable force, of course she was able to push it through all the hoops that it needed to go through.

I was the only African American junior executive at the time, and once I saw they were going to make this movie, I said, "I have to be junior on this movie. Nobody else can touch this movie because this is ours. This is a Black woman's movie. We have to get this right, and I have to be at the table to make sure we get this right." I kept lobbying and lobbying, and then Niija put me on it, and we had our first meeting with Oprah. We went to her office in Hollywood. Again, similar to *The Color Purple*, Oprah is Black royalty. So we were both walking in like, "Oh my God, I can't believe this!" Niija is very stoic and put together, so for her to be that excited was a big thing.

I remember at the top of the meeting, I was just waiting for Oprah to levitate. I was thinking, "She's not going to show us her superpowers, but maybe she'll accidentally levitate. Let's see if she's going to float."

We talked about finding a writer. We had these lists we were going through, and she knew people on the list. I thought, "How on earth does she have time to know who these people are?" I assumed she was just in the meeting to get updated. But she was like, "Oh, no, I don't like that person's sample."

I was thinking, "What? She reads stuff, too? Surely she's going to levitate, I just know it." I remember we left that meeting and Niija and I were like, "That was nuts."

TURNING THE DREAM INTO A SCRIPT

MARCUS GARDLEY (screenwriter, 2023 film): When I heard that Warner Bros. and the producers were looking for a screenwriter for the adaptation, it became my mission to get the job.

SCOTT SANDERS: There were a lot of questions, creative and otherwise, that needed to be answered as we began to embark on the film. Is it a straight adaptation of the Broadway show? Do all the songs from the musical remain in the movie? If not, which ones don't? Are there new songs we want to add? If so, what are they? Who's going to write them? That's really how it started.

musical, it needs to be grounded in something powerful. So what is it like to get into Celie's imagination?

One thing I struggled with in conceptualizing this screenplay was that we have a central protagonist who's not using language as often as other characters. Then her journey is one in which she's not necessarily active. The sister is active. There's this great moment where Nettie says, "I want to be a doctor" and "I want to see the world." And Celie says, "I want to make you a dress." For a 2023 audience, that's not going to cut the mustard, even though the book is very much about that. But how do we go deeper with this character and give a new experience to audiences who love the book, who love the musical, who love the movie? How do we go deeper with Celie's character but also obey the tenets of the book? I

> ## "I wanted to introduce magical realism to this world, to bring some levity to the more somber, tragic moments in the story. Even though it's a musical, it needs to be grounded in something powerful."
>
> *—Marcus Gardley*

You're also changing mediums, so you're going to have to open up the story much wider than a proscenium theatrical stage would provide. We were now moving into Steven [Spielberg's] area of storytelling. It was a fluid puzzle as we started to move through all of this, knowing that the scale of everything was going to be much, much greater. The budget was going to be exponentially larger than a Broadway show. The length of time to shoot it, the casting choices, all of those things. Once you start putting something together that is going to be a worldwide distributed film, all those creative decisions have much higher stakes in many ways.

MARCUS GARDLEY: I wanted to introduce magical realism to this world, to bring some levity to the more somber, tragic moments in the story. Even though it's a

thought magical realism would be a way for us to listen to the song of her soul. To what is in her heart. And that's how you get all of those rich moments we imagined she must be thinking that we didn't have access to when we saw the previous incarnations of the story.

I was really inspired by Zora Neale Hurston and Toni Morrison. They're two of my favorite authors. So I brought that to it. And I just kept pitching it, and it kept moving up the ladder. When I ended up meeting with Oprah and the studio, I would pitch, then I would stop and play a little bit of the music, and then I'd talk over the music. I talked about what I saw happening during these songs. Oprah cried twice during the pitch, and the studio executives said, "We don't have any questions." I kind of knew I had it then, and a couple of hours later they called me and told me I had the job. One of the best days of my life.

Left to right: Stephen Bray, Marcus Gardley, Brenda Russell, and Allee Willis in 2019, shortly after Gardley was hired as the screenwriter for the 2023 film

SHEILA WALCOTT: We were in awe. We were rapt in attention, because Marcus had brought this magical realism that never existed in the other iterations. He had his laptop, and he played the music from the Broadway show while he explained. He left, and we said, "This is the guy. We just know this is the guy."

OPRAH WINFREY (Sofia, 1985 film; producer, 2005 Broadway musical, 2015 Broadway revival, 2023 film): I thought Marcus got it in the sense that one who is of the culture understands sweet potato pie, black-eyed peas on the table, cornbread, the whole thing. I thought he understood nuance and subtlety, and he understood a head nod and a head shake and an mm-hmm, and an amen. He just got it. He understood the language; he understood the nuance of body language.

This is someone who has sat in a room and paid attention to his aunties and his mother and his cousins. He has taken all of that in, in such a deep way, that he has that vibration. That's what I loved about him. That's what comes through in the writing of it: the spirit of Black women in a way that you either have to be one or have lived with some to get it.

MARCUS GARDLEY: Once I got the job, I had lunch with Scott and the composers, Stephen Bray, Brenda Russell, and Allee Willis. I had never met them before. I was already obsessed with the musical. I'd seen it thirteen times, so I was trying to pretend like I wasn't a massive fan of all these people. I didn't speak much; I just let them talk.

Stephen Bray pulled me aside afterward. He said, "I have to tell you what Alice Walker told me when I joined the musical. And I've made it a point to pass it on to everybody else, because it can be very intimidating working on this project when you know what it means to the world." He said, "You were chosen."

I said, "Yeah, I know, Warner Bros." But he said, "No. You are being chosen by Alice Walker's ancestors. They choose everybody. Let that be something you use as a guide, not something to be intimidated by." He said, "Follow your instincts, because they picked you. Nobody else picked you." And he said, "That'll make sense later on, when you're working on it. You'll be like, 'Oh, 'tis so true.'"

I started working on the project and having the best time. It's hard to describe, because people think writers just sit in front of a computer, but there's so much joy in it when you're in the zone. It wasn't cotton candy the whole way. There were nights when I couldn't sleep and I couldn't figure things out. But there were also moments where I was feeling something moving me. It wasn't that I was listening to spirits, but I was writing things and I didn't know why I was writing them. In the first script I turned in, there was a moment where Celie walks on water. It's a heightened magical realism moment. After

Young Celie (Phylicia Pearl Mpasi) sings "She Be Mine" in one of several scenes of magical realism in the 2023 film

Alice Walker read it, she said to me, "How could you have known that this is how that character should move through the world? How did you figure that out?" And I wanted to say back to her, "It's your ancestors."

For me, that was the moment that Stephen Bray was talking about, when you have tapped into something and you are just being guided. You're being used as a vessel.

NIIJA KUYKENDALL: We had a lot of support internally for this project, especially when we got our first draft of the script in. Marcus did an amazing job. He essentially wrote a gorgeous, almost greenlightable script on the first draft. It's one of the few times in my career that that's happened. The script was proof of concept of, "Wow, this can be so ambitious. This can be its own thing, can live in its own space and still be very respectful and pay homage to everything that has existed before it."

MARCUS GARDLEY: They said they had no notes on that first script, and to me that was about those same ancestors. I know this sounds like I'm being humble, but I really mean it. Working on this project is me taking Alice

Walker's story and expressing my deep, abiding love for it. This process was just an honor, because I felt very much that this was my way of telling her how much her book saved me.

I just had to get out of the way because, working on this script, I could easily have gotten blocked if I was worried about, "Well, a million people loved this scene… Well, the studio wants X and it needs to be commercial… Well, they're going to have a really famous person play this role, so you've got to give them plenty…" Once you let all that go and say, "My responsibility is to obey the story and honor these women," then it just comes out.

VISION QUEST: FINDING THE RIGHT DIRECTOR

NIIJA KUYKENDALL: When we started looking for a director for this, we knew it had to be a Black director, and we really debated whether it should be a woman. There was real care and rigor in every single decision we made. I felt like, "I cannot be the Black female executive who messes this up. It will not happen. Not on my watch." Everybody felt that way.

We went back and forth about whether we needed it to be a Black director. There are stories that have a Black cast, that are specific because of that cast, and that dig into that culture and context. But not all of those stories need to be directed by a Black director. I made the movie *Just Mercy* with Destin Daniel Cretton, and though he is not Black, it was beautiful to work with him, and he was the perfect person for that job. And I would argue that *Just Mercy* is a singularly Black experience. But *The Color Purple* felt so specific to Black culture, to the Black female experience, and so iconic to our community today, however many years later, that it felt really hard to entrust it to someone who did not understand or was not exposed to Black women, was not raised by a Black woman.

In hindsight, if we had gotten an amazing vision and pitch by someone who wasn't Black, it would've been hard to say no to that.

SCOTT SANDERS: I kept lamenting to Oprah, "I can't believe we're going to pick a director for this important movie over Zoom." Normally, you would want to have lunch or dinner or coffee and meet and talk and talk

"The script was proof of concept of, 'Wow, this can be so ambitious.'"
—Niija Kuykendall

some more and meet again and really get into their heads and figure out how they want to do it. So we were in the middle of COVID, watching lots of movies, and I heard about *The Burial of Kojo*. This was Blitz Bazawule's first full-length movie, which he self-financed in Ghana. And it turned out that Beyoncé had seen it and asked him to help her do the South African sequences for her film *Black Is King*. So we had those two bodies of work to look at. Very limited, but *The Burial of Kojo*'s magical realism pieces are quite beautiful, particularly when you understand how few resources he had to work with. [Director] Ava DuVernay had seen *Kojo* and gotten it to Netflix. Oprah watched it. Steven watched it. And we put Blitz into the running for director.

BLITZ BAZAWULE (director, 2023 film): I got a call—it always starts with a call—and was told that the producers and Warner Bros. were looking for a director for a new iteration of *The Color Purple*. And like anybody else who got this call, the first question is, "Why?" If you read the book, saw the play, and saw the movie, you'd say, "*The Color Purple* has been done, and done incredibly well."

My first exposure to this story had been through the novel. I went to Kent State University and had a literature professor who was adamant that we read not only African American novels, but African American women writers. We read Toni Morrison, Jamaica Kincaid—several really great novelists—and we ended up with *Color Purple*, which for me was a revelation.

Of all the books we were reading, I hadn't read anything that imbued the character with such global knowledge of both diasporic and continental Africans. At the time, I was an immigrant in the U.S. I still am, but

I was new, so Ghana was still a very fresh reality for me. And here I was in America, and this character's sister had been, in a way, exiled to the continent of Africa. And then I saw the Spielberg film. I'm glad I experienced *The Color Purple* in that order, because the book is obviously an endless well of experience and direct knowledge, and then the film takes whatever rises to the top and creates a motion picture out of it.

It wasn't until I had Zoom conversations with the producing crew and studio execs that I understood what the goal was, which was to add another layer that hadn't existed, one that would combine the visual world of Spielberg's film with the musical dexterity of the musical. We had to find something that would make it very obviously ours, and that core conversation started to revolve around magical realism and imagination as the conduit. What sets our film apart is how much of it exists in Celie's mind. Our film gives the audience the opportunity to delve into the mind of the oppressed as opposed to putting the oppressed and her oppressor on the same level, which inevitably gives the oppressor more power. In actuality, there's no such thing as an equal footing between oppressed and oppressor. As it relates to Celie, we would be in her mind, and she could have more power and more agency because she was actively working her way out of her oppression. That's what really makes this its own version.

SCOTT SANDERS: In his first pitch, which was to me and two of the other executive producers, Mara [Jacobs] and Carla [Gardini], Blitz elaborated on what those magical realism scenes were going to be. They had been alluded to in the screenplay, but Blitz brought his visual sensibility to the conversation.

The next round of interviews was with Oprah and Niija. All of this happened for Blitz in a matter of two

Celie (Fantasia Barrino) dances with Shug (Taraji P. Henson), 2023 film

A photo of Shug (Taraji P. Henson) comes to life as Celie admires it, 2023 film

weeks. He went from interviewing to Round 1 to Round 2. There were five directors in the finals. Blitz was one of them. I remember Oprah and I texting each other during his pitch, saying, "Oh my God, this is the guy."

We said to Blitz, "All right. Niija, Oprah, and I think you're our choice. That's the good news. The bad news is you have to do this again for Steven Spielberg tomorrow." And he did, and Steven called us and said, "This is the guy."

Then we went to the studio, and Toby Emmerich [chairman of Warner Bros. Pictures Group at the time] was gentleman enough to say to Blitz, "I know you've

can feel it in our everyday encounters. We needed an elevated approach to how to interpret what works so well on Broadway and bring that to a new audience.

For that, Blitz was the perfect choice. I teared up when I saw his presentation, his vision for Celie. The magical realism that Marcus introduced and Blitz brought to life is a heightened, sensual approach to this material. He's a visualist, able to paint the pictures of Celie's life, and Mister's and Sofia's, in such a way that Dan [Laustsen, the director of photography] and he could bring the cinematography to life, so that you feel that you are part of it, and you're with them.

> # "Someone might have read the book, someone might have seen the movie, someone might have seen the musical. It may be the only piece of Black intellectual property that can make that claim."
> ## —Reuben Cannon

gone through the gauntlet already. If Oprah and Steven and Scott think you're the director, you're the director. Give me your pitch, but you have the job." It just took the pressure off Blitz at the top of the meeting.

OPRAH WINFREY: I really felt that this time around, it had to be a woman or a person of color. For sure. Steven's version stands as a classic forever. You can't touch it, and don't try. We're not even trying. For this space and time that we're in, for this moment that we're in, we are not trying to remake the film that Steven did. We're trying to take what was on Broadway and bring that to film in a way that it will be relatable to the world.

I thought it was best to have someone who, like Marcus, understood the textural fiber and foundation of what it meant to put that on the screen at this particular time in our culture.

Everybody's sensibilities are heightened in every area now: racially, politically, emotionally, economically. We

NIIJA KUYKENDALL: When I left Warner Bros. to go to Netflix, we had hired a writer. We had a greenlighted script. We had hired a director. We had negotiated our stars. The movie actually was one of the hardest pieces of my decision-making in leaving.

It's very hard to get a movie greenlighted. There are many a movie that we love and that we even put together with directors and actors, but they don't end up getting made. Ultimately, it's not only about your advocacy and your passion. At the end of the day, you're spending lots of money on these productions and then lots of money on the marketing of these productions. In this case, my boss at the time, Courtenay Valenti, and I had to make our colleagues see that Blitz's vision for this was not a small drama, and it was not a small African American drama. This material is iconic, it's universal. His vision for adapting the musical to screen was visceral, epic, and magical, making it a far larger aspiration than what you would normally think.

SHEILA WALCOTT: I would classify Blitz as a visionary. He's very intentional about how he shoots because he knows what he wants at the end. He's not traditional. He's not conventional, but we trusted his vision. I think that's a staple of this studio in particular. Filmmakers are our lifeblood. You can see it in our product. For example, Tim Burton's *Batman* is different than Chris Nolan's *Batman* is different than Matt Reeves's *Batman*. They're all *Batman*, they're all canon, but they're all very different. Blitz is one of those filmmakers where you felt like, "Man, his vision is so specific and singular and beautiful that I want to see that movie. What does he need to make that?"

My job became: How do I support this vision? We've still got to hit a budget, we've still got to hit a schedule, and we've still got to make sure that there's authenticity to the source material. This was his first studio movie, so in order to bring his vision to life, you get an Oscar-nominated [director of photography] like Dan Laustsen. You put Blitz in the hands of amazing filmmakers he can partner with. You give him a great crew that he trusts. You give him the days and the money he needs to render his version of this movie.

STEVEN SPIELBERG (director, 1985 film; producer, 2023 film): In my earliest conversations with Blitz about casting, I suggested to him from experience that I know in my gut who is the right choice for every role. Others may disagree, you may have intellectual doubts yourself, but that tickle in your heart means no one knows the movie you're about to make better than you. I really believe Blitz knew the movie he wanted to make from the start.

WHY THIS, WHY NOW:
THE STARS ARE ALIGNING AGAIN

REUBEN CANNON (casting director, 1985 film): You could take three generations to see *The Color Purple* because it's been around for so long in different versions. Someone might have read the book, someone might have seen the movie, someone might have seen the musical. It may be the only piece of Black intellectual property that can make that claim and that can span multiple generations. It's the only one I can think of that went from novel to screen to stage and now screen musical, too.

Cinematographer Dan Laustsen on the set of the 2023 film

STEPHEN BRAY (music and lyrics, 2005 Broadway musical, 2015 Broadway revival, 2023 film): Blitz was committed from the beginning to making it not just for the older people who grew up with *Color Purple* or experienced it in their twenties or thirties. He wanted to make sure that the new film would be relevant even to people who don't know the novel or the show or the film. He wanted to make it strong enough that you're pulled into the story, regardless of anything you know about it.

SALAMISHAH TILLET (scholar, critic, and author of *In Search of the Color Purple: The Story of an American Masterpiece*): I consider *The Color Purple* an American masterpiece in part because of the ways in which Alice Walker's novel can change. Every time Celie appears in some form, she changes the landscape. She creates new audiences. The art form in which she's represented is done at such a high standard that it's seen as something that's worthy of being rewarded. Just on paper, it is so

Celie (Fantasia Barrino) reads a letter from Nettie, 2023 film

heralded. At the same time, maybe they don't teach *The Color Purple* as much anymore, or it's not as read anymore, or it's one of the more highly censored books in the American literary tradition. That tension between it being so heralded and yet so often underappreciated is actually what happens to a lot of work created by Black women.

The fact that Walker shaped the entire novel around letters and in this Southern Black vernacular was so remarkable as an experiment in form and is also why it's a masterpiece. She broke away from what we thought the novel was supposed to be and gave us another model for what it could be. And did it with such an exquisite

MARSHA NORMAN (playwright, 2005 Broadway musical): Our entire world is rife with Celie stories, people who are born into situations where they are given no reasonable chance to survive, either through illness, or poverty, or parental abuse, or racial discrimination, or lack of education, or faith in themselves, or the views of their community, or the failure of religious and social institutions, or all of it together. This has almost always happened to girls whom no one is watching out for, but we are beginning to understand this happens to boys, and young strong men, to the elderly, to immigrants, to people besieged by drugs they sought for relief, or anyone with a sign of disability, which may be as simple as shyness or the

> ## "*The Color Purple* is Alice Walker's great gift to the world, a virtual instruction manual for how to be a good and grateful person in what precious time you have left."
> ### —Marsha Norman

story of sisterhood and trauma and redemption and forgiveness. All of that is there. The novel transfixed me as a young person and then stayed with me as I became a teacher and now a creative writer.

Walker enabled us to see these characters as fully human and familiar so long ago. That's why there are so many adaptations. A lot of what Walker anticipated in the novel resonates in new ways today.

LAWRENCE DAVIS (hair department head, 2023 film): People are always facing challenges. We want to know, in the end, that they won, that they got through it, and that they survived. Any type of survival story resonates with people, and they're always interested in seeing that person win. Any story or documentary or anything I see where somebody had a hard time, but at the end of the day overcame a lot, makes me feel good. It makes my heart happy for them, and it gives hope to situations that feel totally hopeless.

inability to read. Children are trapped in homes where they are not safe. Women are trapped in marriages where they are regularly abused. And guns and knives are everywhere! Violence is not limited to people with poor educations who have lived through violent childhoods. Violence seems to be our favorite subject on TV, even by space creatures, like we need them to get in on all the abuse down here.

The Color Purple is about how two sisters survive. It is a tribute to faith and love, without which all of us, including Celie and Nettie, would be doomed. It is a how-to book for learning to believe and how to exercise that faith in each other. With Celie and Nettie, it was letters. To us today, the musical asks the questions, "How can you help? How can you believe in yourself and show your gratitude for what you have? How can you be a part of the family of human beings?" *The Color Purple* is Alice Walker's great gift to the world, a virtual instruction manual for how to be a good and grateful person in what precious time you have left.

Sofia (Danielle Brooks) suffers in jail after her
confrontation with Miss Mille, 2023 film

Celie (Fantasia Barrino) suffers abuse from
Mister (Colman Domingo), 2023 film

BLITZ BAZAWULE: You can never create art that is void of its environment. It's impossible, or at least it is for me. While we were doing research for this film and getting into preproduction, it was right out of COVID, which had its own social, political, and economic consequences. Our film is deeply entrenched in the things that were happening then: George Floyd, Black Lives Matter, and vilification of members of the LGBTQ community. All of these things were happening simultaneously.

Sofia going to jail at the hands of Miss Millie deals with racial abuse and mass incarceration. Celie goes through domestic abuse, an issue that's still relevant today. In response to a lot of these things, young people are beginning to go, "Enough is enough."

This film is landing in the midst of these things, and it's speaking to a lot of these things. Exploration of the diaspora when Nettie goes to Africa. What does she realize that's different? Colonization, the effects of which you can still see in the legacy of the British imperial machine, the French imperial machine, whether it's in Africa or a lot of the Global South.

All of this was happening while we were making our movie. Even while I was scouting locations, it was the November [2020 U.S.] election and then the attempted coup d'état in the United States. You look at this environment and say, "This work is in response to all of these things that people are trying to sweep under carpets instead of having honest, true conversations."

Until the world arrives at the place where it takes accountability for specifically how minorities of all groups and classes have been treated, and it starts to make amends, a film like this will be necessary. I'm sure in twenty years another group is going to come and say, "Blitz and his team pushed this forward, but it wasn't forward enough. Now it's a new day, and now we want to have a conversation about it." That's what's powerful about *The Color Purple*. It is an evergreen text, and the only time this text will become obsolete is when society is at an equilibrium in terms of accountability. Until everybody sits back and says, "I've done wrong and I'm willing to atone for it in this way," this text continues to endure.

JON BATISTE (Grady, 2023 film): The new film speaks to a lot of things that are ongoing parts of the dialogue nationally and around the world. Questions of identity and women's rights, and questions of domestic hierarchy. Questions of the self-worth and importance of the African diaspora in America, and how we overcome the lineage of oppression and marginalization that has become systemic. How different regions of the country, particularly the South, have really felt the brunt of that, and what that means in the lives of everyday people.

You get a depiction of all of that in this narrative and more. But it's also not something that is just about politics or sociocultural scenarios, it's about empowerment and knowing who you are and that you have worth

Purple Rising

intrinsically as a person living on this planet. You have just as much of a place and value as anyone else, and discovering that is the most freeing and liberating experience anyone could have, even if you're dealing with all of those forms of systemic oppression or bondage, or even if your lineage comes from the struggle.

DANIELLE BROOKS (Sofia, 2015 Broadway revival, 2023 film): It's not just a remake, for sure. What sets our version apart is that we're taking all the best parts of the original, highlighting them, and then bursting it open in new ways. Things that were just sparking—whether that be exploration of sexuality or someone coming back into themselves or redemption—we give ourselves permission to go an extra mile further, which is exciting. You get to really understand these characters, how all

of us are broken and how we can come back into ourselves and discover the beauty of who we are, even in our brokenness.

MARCUS GARDLEY: The Black community has embraced the original movie in such a powerful way, and through the generations, they'll respond differently to it. When the word got out in my family that I was working on it, people would grab me at family functions and say, "Don't mess this up." My sister went to a cousin's shower, and when she came back, she said, "They wanted me to tell you, if you don't do this scene and that scene, don't ever show your face again."

I started laughing, and she said, "They're serious."

I was like, "Wow, this is intense, guys. This is very intense."

The "African Homeland" scene, 2023 film

QUINCY JONES (executive producer and composer, 1985 film; producer, 2005 Broadway musical, 2015 Broadway revival, 2023 film): As with the original film, everyone from all disciplines of the filmmaking community wanted to be a part of this iteration of *The Color Purple*. That speaks to the power of Alice's novel and the impact of the original film. I believe that there is a sense of ownership that the audience has with *The Color Purple* through the novel, the original film, and the Broadway show, and that ownership spans generations and continues to this day.

A great piece of art, whether it's a song, a story, a painting, or a sculpture, is timeless. And that is what *The Color Purple* is—a great piece of art. From the time that Alice put pen to paper to write *The Color Purple*, at

was so much that he brought to our consciousness with his movie. It was needed so that today we could get here.

SHEILA WALCOTT: I don't know who the director is that could have gotten this movie made in 1985 at Warner Bros. if it wasn't Steven Spielberg. Thank God he was drawn to this material. He's one of the greatest directors of our generation. I don't know that it gets made if he doesn't say, "I want to make it." Maybe it gets made, but nobody sees it because it's some indie film that doesn't get the marketing and distribution that Warner Bros. could put behind it. We'll never know because, thank God, Steven Spielberg said, "No, no, no, I want to do this."

"Now you have this director who is of the African diaspora, and in this movie, that diaspora is what we're dealing with."
—*Taraji P. Henson*

every turn, it has defied expectations, and this new presentation will continue that legacy. Blitz is an incredibly talented young filmmaker and musician, who by virtue of who he is and his background is inherently connected to the story. Visually, musically, and contextually, he understands exactly what *The Color Purple* is.

NIIJA KUYKENDALL: I could talk about *The Color Purple* all day. I'm so proud of everybody. It honestly makes me tear up a little bit to think about it.

TARAJI P. HENSON (Shug, 2023 film): I am very grateful for Spielberg's version, and it's always going to be a good one. But now you have this director who is of the African diaspora, and in this movie, that diaspora is what we're dealing with. That first production of *The Color Purple* is etched in cinematography history. That is the go-to. So, thank you, Mr. Spielberg, for doing that for us, for our culture, for humanity. Thank you. There

Thank God Quincy Jones found Oprah Winfrey to be in it. Thank God we introduced Whoopi to the big screen. It feels like the stars aligned on that first movie. And then thank God that forty years later, here's this movie, and Steven Spielberg lends his hand to mentor this young filmmaker. And Oprah Winfrey—I still don't know what the word is to describe her and what she means to Black culture. It's intangible and indescribable, but it's something really awesome and probably a long, profound word. She's putting the full weight of that behind the movie. And Scott Sanders is out there like a warrior—"I'm going to get this made!"—and [producers] Mara [Jacobs] and Carla [Gardini] are right there behind him. And [former Warner Bros. president of production and development] Courtenay Valenti was a warrior for this movie. And I came back to Warner Bros. and was like, "Great, where's my spear? Let's go. Let's get it done." The stars feel like they're aligning again.

Celie (Whoopi Goldberg) in the
1985 film and Celie (Fantasia Barrino)
in the 2023 film

CASTING THE LEADS: CONTINUING THE LEGACY

The Telsey Office, a casting company based in New York and Los Angeles, has been involved with *The Color Purple* three times over: first for the Broadway debut, then the revival, and, most recently, the musical film. Here, three of its casting directors—Destiny Lilly, Tiffany Little Canfield, and Bernard Telsey—weigh in on finding the right actors.

Left to right: Taraji P. Henson, Fantasia Barrino, and Danielle Brooks

FIRST ENCOUNTERS WITH
THE COLOR PURPLE

DESTINY LILLY: I grew up in the '80s, and *The Color Purple* movie was a really big part of that time and that culture for Black people in America. So it is pretty enmeshed in my upbringing, part of the cultural fabric of my youth. I was too young to see it when it came out, but I remember people—people from my family, my friends, people at church—would say quotes from the movie, quotes that I didn't realize were from the movie until I saw it when I was twelve or thirteen.

TIFFANY LITTLE CANFIELD: When I was a kid, I was a voracious reader. If I went anywhere, like to people's houses we were visiting, I would just get a book. And that happened to be a book I picked up when I was in fourth grade. I read it and read it and read it, and then the people we were visiting let me take it home. I was reading a lot of not-age-appropriate things, like *The World According to Garp*. I loved *The Color Purple* so much.

BERNARD TELSEY: I'm the older man here. I was in my twenties. I did not know the book, but I remember I couldn't wait to see the movie because I already knew who Whoopi Goldberg was, having seen her one-person show. I was working as a casting assistant for theater, so for me it was about going to see Whoopi Goldberg and then being blown away by this story. And blown away emotionally.

Even now, I remember sitting in the audience with my twenty-year-old friends, living in New York by myself, thinking, "How could that have happened? How could that be?" I didn't grow up understanding a lot of Black culture, so this was a story that stayed with me. And then getting called to do the first musical by Scott Sanders. And then to do it again with the revival. And then again for the movie. The only thing left is *The Color Purple on Ice*, but I don't know when we're going to do that.

THE CASTING
DIRECTOR'S ROLE

TIFFANY: We assemble a film's cast, working with the directors, producers, and studio. Usually we start with idea lists of actors that are known, as well as starting to search for talent that perhaps is less known. That would be through an audition process.

BERNARD: We come up with the descriptions of what we think is in the script of these characters. Clearly something like *Color Purple* is so specific. But we'd start by asking, in this case, "What is Blitz's interpretation?" Because we're here to serve the vision of the creative team. We're doing whatever we can to get a thought, an idea, or a person in front of the team.

DESTINY: When we started, Blitz had come on board. We had Marcus Gardley's script, and it brought together

> "It definitely felt like these were big shoes to fill, but also it was clear from early on in our conversations with Blitz and with Scott that we weren't trying to replicate what had come before, that this was not your grandma's *Color Purple*."
>
> —Destiny Lilly

the best things about the musical, the original movie, and the book. For example, there's a real connection to the lines, some of which are in the book, but have really had a continued life from the film. But this version also brought together the epistolary parts of the novel really well, getting inside what Celie's feeling. And many of the visuals that are in the script and then eventually in this film take a note from the 1985 film as well.

In terms of casting, it's our job to take all those elements and turn them into people, which is fun and challenging.

TIFFANY: That's always interesting because some shows, for the right actor, they'll make the magic happen. And I wonder if it's partially because Blitz is a musician himself that he strongly wanted people to be able to sing as well as act.

On our minds a lot, too, was who you really believed could age up and down. The first time you meet Celie, she's fourteen, but by her big number, she's in her fifties.

DESTINY: On film, you can't really get away with having

> ## "The entire conceit of theater is suspension of disbelief, whereas with film, people imagine that directors are taking their crews to shoot on Mars."
> ### —Tiffany Little Canfield

CASTING ACROSS PLATFORMS

DESTINY: It definitely felt like these were big shoes to fill, but also it was clear early on in our conversations with Blitz and Scott Sanders that we weren't trying to replicate what had come before, that this was not your grandma's *Color Purple*. Something we said a lot was, "Yeah, we're paying respect and homage to the past, but we're also doing something new for the twenty-first century." So we were never made to feel like we had to find a Whoopi Goldberg. It was a lot about, "How do we interpret this work today? Why tell this story again?"

BERNARD: What helps make it different from the classic film is that it's a musical. Putting the stage versions aside, we needed to find people who we knew would bring to the table what the first movie didn't.

DESTINY: All the actors are singing for themselves.

one person play from ten to fifty. There's a different expectation. The suspension of disbelief is different on film and on stage. On stage, audiences are more accustomed to seeing people playing ten roles.

TIFFANY: The entire conceit of theater is suspension of disbelief. As soon as you walk into that theater, you know that we're all in a room together. Whereas with film, people imagine that directors are taking their crews to shoot on Mars.

DESTINY: That's why we had the fun and exciting challenge of finding younger versions of Celie and Nettie, as well as adult versions. We see Nettie mostly as the young, teenage version of her. With Celie, we get to see both, and that was a big, exciting challenge for us—to find the right balance of age, type, and matching physicality, but also people who could sing the role. Someone who was young, but not too young and not too old. Just finding that balance, so it would feel seamless as you transition from Young Celie to Adult Celie.

TIFFANY: Makeup can only do so much.

DESTINY: It's the makeup, but also the life experience.

BERNARD: The gravitas.

DESTINY: You're not necessarily going to believe someone who's in their late teens or early twenties singing "I'm Here" as a fifty year old.

BERNARD: What made it easy was not feeling like we had to cast the Oprahs and the Whoopis. We had been lucky enough to have worked on casting two of the musical incarnations and the tour, so we knew there's a million people who can play these parts. We needed to find the best person for *this* movie *with Blitz* at *this* time. We know that lesson in all projects, but in this project, it gave us confidence, because you could say no one was better than LaChanze, and then you can say nobody was better than Cynthia Erivo. And so was the woman on tour who I bet you didn't see. It gives you hope that there isn't only one person.

CASTING DURING COVID

BERNARD: Our casting was during the worst time.

DESTINY: It was definitely a challenge.

TIFFANY: We did the scenes on Zoom with all the actors, but they had to tape their singing separately because Zoom distorts the sound.

DESTINY: The thing about COVID was, in non-pandemic times we would have scheduled these big sessions where we were in the room with Blitz and saw every person who could possibly be right. This time we had to do that on tape. We started out with hundreds—and eventually thousands—of tapes. Eventually, we did a few auditions in the room. When we finally got to that point, it was such a breath of fresh air. It was exciting, because you can get a little lost in so many tapes.

BERNARD: In general, when you're in a room with a director and someone comes in, whether they're it or not it, there's a conversation about, "OK, that's good, but I need this." Or, "That's not right because of so and so." What happens on these self-tapes is there's no way Blitz can talk to us about his reaction to every tape, even though Blitz was so open and so willing.

DESTINY: And he watched a lot.

BERNARD: But we were not going to ask him, "I want your exact comments about all ninety-five tapes you watched yesterday."

DESTINY: And you can't just say to the actor, "Oh, try it this way."

TIFFANY: My heart went out to Blitz that he was having a process like this for his first huge studio feature film. It was mind-numbing. When we were finally in the room together, you could feel the palpable joy and excitement.

DESTINY: Yes. Remember that session in Atlanta where Fantasia finally came in person? We'd been doing stuff on Zoom, we'd done tapes. She was there with the piano accompanist, and she did a warm-up version of "I'm Here," and it was jaw-dropping. She said, "I'm just getting warmed up." And I was like, "That's your warm-up? That's your practice?"

> "When we were finally in the room together, you could feel the palpable joy."
> —Destiny Lilly

THE CAST COMES TOGETHER

COREY HAWKINS | HARPO

I was lucky because I had gotten to work with Scott and Mara [Jacobs] on *In the Heights,* but I also didn't want to be presumptuous and think they would say, "Of course, we'll pick you."

When Scott called me, I was set to get on a plane the next day. Scott said, "Corey, we are doing this *Color Purple* movie." I said, "Yeah, I know. That's so cool." I was thinking he might ask me to audition or talk to some people, but he said, "We've spoken to Blitz. We've talked to Oprah. We've talked to Steven Spielberg. I'd like to offer you Harpo." I said, "What?!" It took my breath away. I was very grateful, very thankful. I was in shock.

We hung up. Then I called him right back and said, "Scott, I might be overstepping here, but I honestly can't imagine doing this as Harpo with anyone other than Danielle [Brooks] as my Sofia." For a moment, I thought, "Oh, gosh, what did I just do? Did I just get the offer rescinded?" I remember there was a silence, and then Scott said something like, "We all love Danielle Brooks." And I said, "Yes, we do. I know what we can do together. I know the history there. I know what we are going to bring to these roles." Scott was very diplomatic. He said all the right things. He said it was going to be a process, because they wanted the best person to be in this role. I said, "Danielle is the best person to be in the role, and I'd be remiss if I didn't call you right back and tell you that. But I'm going to let y'all do what you have to do."

TIFFANY: Corey was a no-brainer.

BERNARD: Corey was the first principal cast.

DESTINY: The first person on board.

BERNARD: He was in the *In the Heights* movie that Scott had produced and we had all worked on. So we knew how much attention he was getting when that movie came out. It was like, "If we wait till Sofia is cast, he will not be available." You could laugh at casting Harpo before Sofia, but we're like, "Yeah, but Corey can go with this age and that age."

DESTINY: He could age up or down.

BERNARD: And then the minute he met with Blitz, it was done. Corey wanted to do it so much that he just held and waited, even though we didn't even know the shooting schedule at the time. Mara wanted him from Day 1 and was always saying, "You haven't gotten Corey the offer yet." I'm like, "I know. There are five women in this script. If I call Blitz one more time, it's going to look like Corey's living in my house."

> ## "It was like watching MJ do the moonwalk, like spreading warm butter on a slice of toast. It was just easy."
> *—Danielle Brooks*

DANIELLE BROOKS | SOFIA

Now what people might not know is that Corey and I have been close friends since 2007. We were in the same graduating class at Juilliard, so we have known each other since we were teenagers. Corey was actually cast before I was and did not have to audition. I say that with a tad bit of judgment, in a lighthearted way, but he didn't have to audition. When I heard he was in the movie, I called him immediately. I said, "Corey, I want to be in this, and have you heard anything about casting Sofia yet?" He was such a champion for me and such a huge supporter, kind of casually dropping my name to producers and stuff. He was definitely in my corner. When we had the chemistry read together, it was like watching MJ do the moonwalk, like spreading warm butter on a slice of toast. It was just easy. Because of our long history as friends, there was already a built-in backstory we carried that bled into our characters so naturally.

DESTINY: Aww, Danielle's the best.

TIFFANY: I know. We love Danielle Brooks.

BERNARD: I met her back in the day at Juilliard while teaching a class. In those days, they didn't really teach people who were singers. Well, they taught them, but they didn't pursue singing within that program like they do now. It's still not a musical theater program. At our classes, we would always ask, "Who here sings?" And in that class, up went the hands of Corey Hawkins and Danielle Brooks. She made such an impression. I didn't know her personally at the time, but you could tell that she was special. You wanted to become her champion.

TIFFANY: There was a lot of pressure on this role. I almost felt like the fact that she had played the role on Broadway was looked at as a slight negative.

BERNARD: Because she did it already.

TIFFANY: Right. So I really do appreciate that she leaned into this audition process, because there might be people in that same situation who would've said, "I should get the offer for this because I already did it." And instead, she just engaged so fully and claimed the role.

BERNARD: Yeah, she really claimed it, and early on.

DESTINY: She just put her stamp on it.

BERNARD: And that's a role where there was so much more than in the stage version about that character and what made her tick.

TARAJI P. HENSON | SHUG

My father always said, "Wait until the world hears you sing." And it's not that I have such an amazing Whitney Houston voice, but he was saying, "You can also sing. Wait until they see this talent." And sure enough, you can't run from it. Whatever's destined for you is coming for you. I had no idea singing was coming my way. Right when I got [the role of Miss Hannigan in the] live *Annie*, that's when Blitz called and said, "I'm tapping you for Shug," and I was like, "Me?"

He asked me to audition. I had to check my ego, because I'm kind of a vet in the game. I said, "They want me to audition? OK."

I got that there was nothing out there that had me singing like this. I had to sing; I had to do choreography. I was warming up with Fatima [Robinson, the choreographer] and because we had worked together before, Fatima said, "Girl, you going to kill this. They don't even know."

I come from musical theater, so I'm a trained thespian. Whenever it is time to read or audition, that's like an interview. So, I show up appropriate. I did my hair in the period. I had on a Shug Avery dress that I could shimmy, shimmy, coco pop in. I had on a stole and I had a flower in my hair. I had on a red lip to die for. I had the purse, the shoes—I ordered me some Shug-ass character shoes from Amazon! That's how I do. Because Shug would. That's what she would do. Shug takes control of the room.

So, I just walked in and threw my stuff down. Blitz was like, "What?" Everybody in the room was like, "What?" Blitz said, "Do you need time to rehearse?" I said, "No. Hit it." I told the piano player the key. I said, "Let's go."

They had the studio booked for four hours. I was taillights in two. See, that's what you get. And I'm not bragging. I'm not. I'm just built that way. I was trained like that. I'm not coming here to waste your time. I know that this is a job. The boom guy over there is not trying to hold up that boom for eighteen hours. He's trying to get home. This is a job. I come to work. I'm prepared. I hit my mark. I know my lights. I know my lines and I say them. I come to work every day, ready and prepared. I get everybody home. For singers, that is their instrument. My body is my instrument. It is the actor's job to be able to push a button at any given moment and evoke whatever emotion is there. That is your job.

Something about me, when you doubt me, I'ma come in kicking the door down, and that's probably why I went in the way I did. Gonna snatch all y'all's edges so you will never, ever, ever doubt this talent again.

TIFFANY: Taraji came in and took that part.

DESTINY: She's so good. We did a lot of Zoom conversations with Scott and Blitz where we would talk about ideas and talk through lists and lists of people for hours. I will toot my own horn here because I remember saying, "What about Taraji?" As soon as we reached out to her people to consider it, we were told that she wanted it very much as well.

BERNARD: God bless Taraji's agent for taking it to her without any offer. Taraji said, "I'm coming in." She wanted it, and she owned it. I love that about actors. She was game, and willing, and just wonderful.

TIFFANY: That'll be a top audition of our lives, honestly. She just came in and claimed it. From the hair, the outfit, she went all out. When you see an actor leaning like that to come in and collaborate, it feels like you're making a movie.

COLMAN DOMINGO | MISTER

I didn't know Blitz at all. I got a call that Blitz would like to have a conversation with me about Mister. It wasn't an audition. We had a conversation, and then I didn't hear anything for a few months. I thought, "OK, well, clearly it's not for me." Then apparently it was. Oprah told me that I was always her first and only choice. She said that. She said, "You stand on

the shoulders of Danny Glover, and you have the capacity." She said that she discussed this with Blitz, and apparently she said, "He's an actor that you can always believe has some goodness in his heart, even while he's doing terrible things."

DESTINY: I'm a very big Colman Domingo fan, and have been ever since I saw him in the Broadway musical *Passing Strange* fifteen years ago. So he was always on our list, especially for a role like Mister. There's not a lot of people who are going to be able to really do it, who have the acting chops, who have the gravitas, but who are also willing to put themselves in the role of a villain. Mister is not a good person, and a lot of actors don't want to be viewed that way. They want to be the good guy, they want to save the day. And it's even more complicated as a Black man playing a character like this. So Colman Domingo was always on our list because he was someone we knew had the skill, but was also not afraid to take risks and play characters that aren't always the hero. And he's just the best and the nicest person on the planet.

BERNARD: We know him from seeing him in all these plays, but he's someone who's just getting recognized in the film world.

TIFFANY: Right, as a lead, because he's been in so many excellent films in a supporting role. And that's what happens sometimes to an actor like Colman, where they become this character actor and you don't recognize them. Their brilliant transformations actually prevent them from becoming an A-list movie star. He's such a pure artist. And I feel really grateful that Blitz got to have someone like that in this film.

BERNARD: When you have a name like Colman, you're thinking, "Will the studio or producers want someone bigger and fancier for the box office?" And one by one, as Colman was discussed, it was yes, yes, yes. From the studio to Oprah to Steven, it was so exciting that everybody was wanting him.

TIFFANY: His career is so eclectic. He got into *Fear of the Walking Dead* and *Euphoria*, sometimes shooting the same season plus features.

> ## "People overlooked Celie a lot. They said a lot of things about Celie, they laughed at Celie, but in the end she wins. And I want every young girl to see that."
>
> —*Fantasia Barrino*

DESTINY: He's also a playwright. He's really just brilliant. And from the people I've talked to who were on set, they all said he was the dad of the set or the person who made sure that everybody was OK. He was really looking out for other people and talking to all of the actors, even the people with small roles.

In *Passing Strange*, he played a number of different characters, from a youth minister to a German punk rocker. And I was like, "That guy can do anything." And he has this physical presence, but also a versatility and elasticity that just makes him so compelling to watch. From that point on, I went to see everything he was in. I was practically a stalker.

For some people, even just considering the role of Mister was not something they were going to do. To this day, there are people who still have negative feelings about Danny Glover because he played that role. Completely unwarranted. Lovely man. But they have such strong feelings about that role, and especially because in 1985, when the movie came out, there wasn't the same diversity of portrayals of Black men. But it's exciting that Colman wanted that challenge, and he handled it beautifully.

FANTASIA BARRINO | CELIE

[Playing Celie] was easier for me this time. I'm wiser now. I'm grown now. So what I felt this time were things like, "Look how smart she is. Look how wise she is. They think she's slow, but she's the smartest one in the room." And it was totally different. There were still mornings that I would up and cry. Because even though it's acting, everybody on set becomes your family. Taraji became Shug Avery, Colman became Mister, Danielle became Sofia. And Celie has to carry and take care of all of them.

Everybody has their own form of ministry. I'm a musician, so music is a healer. I'm kind of new to this. Yes, I did Broadway fourteen years ago. I did my Lifetime movie. But the people who I was going to be on set with—like how I grew up in music, they grew up acting. When they embody characters, it's a ministry for them. They are tapping out of their world, leaving their homes, leaving their kids, husbands, wives. They're zoning in on a role and giving it their all because it may bless or help somebody else or bring laughter to them, maybe even a tear. Whatever it is, it's a ministry.

For me, Celie is something that was truly destined. Her relationship with me, our bonds, what I dealt with fourteen years ago, what I got to do this time. She is special to me and I believe God [wanted me] to do it.

Times are changing right now. Our young people have so much telling them that if they don't have certain things, then they don't add up. You have a lot of young people feeling not beautiful, feeling not smart, feeling all sorts of things. For those girls, Celie is a role model. People overlooked Celie a lot. They said a lot of things about Celie, they laughed at Celie, but in the end she wins. And I want every young girl to see that.

BERNARD: We all knew Fantasia, and there was such an authenticity when she did it on Broadway. Tiffany brought up her name right away.

"It's like [Nettie is] holding Celie the whole time. That was really beautiful."

—Halle Bailey

TIFFANY: I'm a really big Fantasia fan.

BERNARD: We had not talked to her for a while, although Scott was always crazy about her. We had conversations about discovering somebody new, but we said, "Well, Fantasia is really a discovery. She doesn't have six movies or six Broadway plays."

TIFFANY: I watched her on *American Idol*. I'm not a very spiritual person—I was not raised religious at all—but there's something about when Fantasia sings. Something bigger is happening. I'm going to get emotional. I feel something when she sings. I also remember her story and how her God-given talent is what saved her from potentially a life of poverty. So she, to me, has always been a hero who has a gift from something bigger. She can connect to a spirituality when she sings that I don't know if I've seen with anyone else. I've watched and rewatched the YouTube video of her singing "I'm Here" at the Tonys. It uplifts me. To me, we just had to go through the process, bide our time, and it was going to be Fantasia. That's how I felt.

BERNARD: Once everyone actually put their energy into Fantasia, whether it was a meeting, an audition, whatever, they all had that same experience that Tiffany is talking about. That's why casting is such a crazy and wonderful process. Let's not assume we know, because that's getting in the way of the experience.

TIFFANY: We had to see everybody else we saw, because we saw some tremendous artists—artists that I could see winning awards in this part. But the process led us to the right person.

HALLE BAILEY | YOUNG NETTIE

Because of COVID, we had to self-tape our auditions, but that was cool for me because I'm very shy. I get nervous, so I'd rather do a video than be in front of you. Honestly, I did it in my bathroom and didn't think anything of it. I was thinking, "OK, I'm going to submit it just to say that I've tried." I didn't think anything would come out of it.

There was a bit of freedom in what you could put on your self-tape, so I chose this gospel song called "It Is Well With My Soul," which I've heard since I was a little girl. I can get kind of overwhelmed and nervous whenever I self-tape like this, where it's an immense, beautiful, classic story. But seeing that there was a song selection that they wanted, I'm like, "OK, at least I can get my nerves out by singing first."

The original Nettie [Akosua Busia] was amazing, astounding. It helped me to think that she was more of a guide than me trying to impersonate her performance, but I did want to mirror her emotions. I put her on a pedestal, and then let my own experiences flow through me so I could get my version of her. It's amazing how, even though she's only in the first half of the film and then gone for a long time, you can feel her love throughout. It's like she's holding Celie the whole time. That was something really beautiful, and something that I tried to play.

DESTINY: [Casting Young Nettie] came together really quickly.

BERNARD: Tiffany and I had worked on casting [the remake of] *The Little Mermaid*, so we had experience with Halle [who played Ariel]. Everybody knows who she is from her music. But we were able to bring to the table what her work was like, having seen the *Mermaid* dailies and having talked to [*Mermaid* director] Rob Marshall.

TIFFANY: She's an incredibly old soul. A really beautiful, deep, sensitive person. I was very impressed with her through the *Little Mermaid* process, which you can imagine was quite intense. And she just always radiates this depth, which we all felt for Nettie was so important because Nettie is the one who really gets out and sees the world and has that worldly point of view.

> # "Overall, [Phylicia] blew me away."
> ## —Tiffany
> ## Little Canfield

PHYLICIA PEARL MPASI | YOUNG CELIE

 My grandmother passed away in May of 2021. And when she passed, to cope with it, I said, "She's working for me. She had to go. I don't know why, but she had to go to open a door for me." And when we were in Africa for her funeral, I had only tiny gigs of data. I decided to go online and look at a website called Actors Access, where they list open calls. The first thing that popped up was Celie in *The Color Purple*. I was literally lying in a bed in Congo about to bury her the next day. And it was like, "Huh, that was fast."

I sent in a video. They loved it, but they said, "She's reading a little too young." And I let it go. I said, "OK, I made a good impression. Thank you. I receive it. And I've moved on with my life."

A few months later, my agents heard that they were opening the role of Young Celie and wanted someone over eighteen to play the part. I had just been told by someone that I couldn't play teenagers anymore, so I was thinking, "Why waste my time?" When you record self-tapes, you have a tendency to do it over and over and over till you think it's perfect. I decided, "I'm going to give it thirty minutes." And that was the key. Sent it off, didn't hear anything.

Another month goes by, and I've forgotten about it. Then I got an email from my agent saying, "The director would like to meet you and do a work session and send that off to producers." This is the point where I thought, "I'm about to book this movie. Oh my God."

I went on a Zoom with Blitz, and we did the scene when Alfonso takes the baby. We did that a couple of times, and then we did when Celie and Nettie first see Mister. Blitz made me do this scene six times, and then the hour ran out. I thought, "It's over. I'm not getting it. He's defeated."

Then, of course, I come to find out the whole thing was intentional. It was, "No, we want her. We just need to make sure that the tape we're sending off to the producers is the tape we want."

DESTINY: We had the fun and exciting task of finding both young and adult versions of Celie and Nettie. Nettie, we see mostly in the film as the young teenage version of her. And then Celie, we get to see both, and that was a big challenge for us to find the right balance of age, type, and matching people, but also people who could sing the role. Someone who was young, but not too young, but not too old. Just finding that balance, so it felt seamless as you transition from Young Celie to Adult Celie, which I felt, when I saw it on the screen, worked really, really well.

TIFFANY: I have to say that Phylicia, Young Celie, was one of my favorite people. Maybe because I had never seen her before and because she has an amazing voice. But also just overall, she blew me away.

BERNARD: She was very, very, very strong.

VI
POWER

Don't let them run over you, Nettie say.
You got to let them know who got the upper hand.
They got it, I say. But she keep on, You got to fight.
You got to fight. But I don't know how to fight.
All I know how to do is stay alive.

—from Alice Walker's
The Color Purple

Celie (Fantasia Barrino) shaves
Mister (Colman Domingo), 2023 film

WHO TELLS THE STORIES?

SALAMISHAH TILLET (scholar, critic, and author of *In Search of the Color Purple: The Story of an American Masterpiece*): The novel came out during a moment when feminist Black women writers were actually getting publishing deals and being recognized for bodies of work that dealt with violence against Black women by Black men. A whole group of these books came out starting in the 1970s, but Walker took the biggest hit with *The Color Purple* because she has queer desire and a queer love story as the ultimate love story. The response was so vitriolic against Walker, and I think it's the homophobia of a particular readership tied to sexism. The combination of those factors created a really hostile environment for the book.

If the book hadn't come out, would we be in this moment? It was so groundbreaking for so many people. I did an interview with Oprah [Winfrey] for *The New York Times*, and she said, "In everything I do, I just want to be able to tell the story of sexual violence and healing." Everything she does. Talk shows, movies, when she's acting, when she's producing something. If Oprah hadn't read this book and then acted in the movie, would she have been so liberated to tell the story? And if she wasn't, then what would that have done for a generation of activists like me or [#MeToo creator] Tarana [Burke], who grew up knowing these disclosures were possible? I was already a big fan of *The Color Purple*, but doing my book, I learned so much. I thought, "Oh my God, it made so much possible."

SHEILA WALCOTT (senior vice president of creative development, Warner Bros.): My first memory of *The Color Purple* wasn't watching the movie. It was the iconic lines and gestures from the movie. So as a kid, I didn't know what I was quoting. "You sho is ugly." "Harpo, who this woman?" We said these things in conversation. It had permeated Black culture in the same way that I would say, "Oh, he's my Obi-Wan." Or, "Man, he's such a Voldemort." "The lady doth protest too much." I'm quoting *Hamlet*, but even people who have not seen *Hamlet* understand what that means.

When I was a little kid, my parents would not let me watch things that didn't have Black people in them. I couldn't watch things or read books or play with toys or any of that. It was super. It was great. And by the way, I don't feel like I missed a thing. The way they were trying to protect me...I could get emotional thinking about it.

I'm so grateful that they did that because I was always looking for myself. Years later, I would work at the Disney Channel, but I didn't grow up on those movies because there were no Black people in them. The version of *Cinderella* [in 1997] that I saw was Brandy and Whoopi Goldberg. When I worked on this Disney movie called *Descendants*, which was about Disney heroes and Disney villains, I was on Wikipedia looking up *Sleeping Beauty*.

The point is, when I saw Rodgers and Hammerstein's *Cinderella*, the love interest was Brandy, who's brown like me and had braids. That's why I do what I do: so kids will have a lot of options if their parents say, "You can only watch things that have you in them." Even when you're looking for yourself, you still get to engage in popular culture. That's why I do my job.

SALAMISHAH TILLET: America is a country that fashions itself as rooting for the underdog, and Walker shows us that the ultimate underdog may be the Black girl who is privy to so many forms of violence, the Black girl who's growing up orphaned in the segregated South. By giving us Celie as our narrator and as our heroine, it forces us to see ourselves in her. But it also gives us a more expanded definition of what is possible for a heroine to be.

I know from my research that many different types of people could see themselves in Celie's story. For example, [producer] Scott Sanders told me Celie's notion of forgiveness reminded him of his relationship with his father. He's a white Jewish American boy growing up in the South, which is different from Danny Glover, who's growing up in northern California but spends his summers in Georgia with his grandmother, who Celie reminds him of. Those are two different places and two different identities, but they saw something in Celie that was familiar to them. And I'm seeing something in Celie that's familiar to me, and Oprah Winfrey is seeing something familiar to her.

TODD JOHNSON (producer, 2005 Broadway musical): This is a story about a woman finding her voice, and that transcends all cultural boundaries, all racial boundaries, all international boundaries. Finding your authentic voice is a story that will always speak to people, because regardless of whether one's circumstances are as tragic as Celie's beginnings, it's still not an easy thing to do in life. To me, that's what makes these reiterations so natural: They're just other ways of exploring that central journey, which on some level is one that everyone either takes or doesn't take.

OPRAH WINFREY (Sofia, 1985 film; producer, 2005 Broadway musical, 2015 Broadway revival, 2023 film): With time, I've come to recognize that there is nothing in my life that I have done or accomplished or been a part of that has meant as much to me as *The Color Purple*. It changed the trajectory of everything that followed in my life. *The Color Purple* allowed me to believe in love.

of that film, and I remember writing in my journal, "At least I've seen what love looks like. Everybody that he encounters, he makes you feel like you're the most important person to him. That's what I want to do. I want to be like that for other people. I want to be able to Quincy other people." That's the first time I had seen that and felt that. It's the first time I had been embraced in a community of creative artists whose passion and commitment to the work was so strong that it just drove everything.

I came to work every single day, whether I was on the call sheet or not. Many times, I'd be up in the tree watching or behind the set where I could see. On the days when they filmed the sisters being pulled apart, I was on

> # "This is a story about a woman finding her voice, and that transcends all cultural boundaries, all racial boundaries, all international boundaries."
> ## —Todd Johnson

It allowed me to see what love was for the first time. It allowed me to open myself up to what that was, and without the form of a romantic connotation to it.

When I watched Steven [Spielberg] and Quincy [Jones] and Alice [Walker] and Menno [Meyjes] on set [in 1985] and saw the energetic response to the work, and the overall love and passion that was going into that film every day, I made a decision then that this is what work should feel like. This is what work should feel like. From the start, I went to do my in-person audition at Amblin [Spielberg's production company], and they had Dove bars in the kitchen. I thought, "If I ever own my own business, I'm going to have Dove bars in the kitchen."

That's the first thing I did when I got Harpo Studios. I became the owner of my own business because Steven had Amblin, because I had seen that. The first thing I did was to build a kitchen and put Dove bars in the kitchen, OK? It influenced what I thought I could be. It influenced how I saw myself. It validated me in the possibilities of love: I thought I would never see Quincy again at the end

the other side of the house. They did that scene for three days. At the end of it, the crew put down their cameras and stood up and cheered. I thought, "Oh, this is what I want. I want to work in an environment where everybody who's a part of the thing feels like they had something to contribute to it."

KIMBERLEY RAMPERSAD (director, 2019 Canadian production, Neptune Theatre and Citadel Theatre/Royal Manitoba Theatre Centre): I'm always asking, "How do I get more people on the stage telling stories that come from our communities and also disrupt Western English classics by putting us in them?"

Here in Canada, Halifax has had Black residents since about 1605. There's a longstanding population of Black people in Nova Scotia, Scotian Blacks. Their presence is older than the country of Canada. I think that that is amazing. They're our trees. They are a part of this land. They were a part of this country before this country even knew who she was. I think that that is fantastic. But in this same place, we also see discrimination and racism. To see these Canadians who have been here for so long not be treated with the respect that we give "other Canadians..." Of course, we don't even give respect to our first Canadians, our Indigenous peoples. That's another thread we could pull on.

The *Color Purple* gives voice to a struggle, and it invites us to talk about what trauma is in terms of how it keeps people in place. What is generational trauma? What is it to be in a system of repeated relegation, marginalization, and discrimination? What does that do to a community that is trying to move with its life force, but the things in life that are human-made are pushing up against them? So, to see that in Celie's world, to see that in Africville [a historic Black community on the outskirts of Halifax that was razed in the 1960s], to see that in all of these different areas of Halifax and Nova Scotia, I think was prescient.

Actually, *The Color Purple* is a good old-fashioned classic in a good way. It has all the archetypes, all the structure, all those things that we lend to any classic that makes it timeless. It also is highly melanated and flavored. So it can be more than one thing, just like everything.

JON BATISTE (Grady, 2023 film): It was an important moment for me when I realized that Grady represents possibility, the upwardly mobile Black American entrepreneur from out of town. I could relate to that, having heard those stories from my grandparents, entrepreneurs from the South who moved around the country looking for opportunity.

It was really powerful to act in this way, to draw from these associations. I've acted on television in both fictional and nonfictional environments. But to be on a set like this for something that's such a part of the canon of American stories, it's like new mythology. And to learn in that environment, to hone the craft in that way, was incredible for me. I felt like I expanded so much. I went up five levels just from being on that set and watching the playback, understanding the positioning to camera and positioning within the lighting, and how little you have to do to convey certain things versus how much you have to exaggerate in other scenarios. And emotionally, it was an incredible experience because of dressing up in the costume and putting on the character of Grady and being with Celie and Shug—all the cast—and then looking at my inspiration, which was my grandparents and their

Grady (Jon Batiste), 2023 film

friends, looking at pictures of them, channeling them. It was a really deep experience for me emotionally.

STEVE SPIEGEL (CEO, Theatrical Rights Worldwide): The question I'm asked always is, "Are there good roles for women?" One of the things that's most attractive to me about *The Color Purple* is Celie's power, the story being from her perspective and her journey. Celie, to me, is the best-created character possible for a musical. I'm sure in plays, there would be a lot of characters that are as important and as well written, but in the world of musicals, it's rare that the story's central character is female and that the arc of the story is so powerful and well crafted.

Of course, when she sings those two words, "I'm here," it's the defining moment of the entire evening. Because when you say, "I'm here," it doesn't mean you're here and you're a superstar. It just means you're here and you're alive and you're important. You first have to feel that for yourself, and she does at that moment. She feels,

Celie (Cynthia Erivo) sings "I'm Here,"
Bernard B. Jacobs Theatre, New York, 2015

"I'm valuable and I deserve to have a good life." And then, of course, the reveal of her children being under her sister's care is a spectacular moment for her, but also for the other characters. There's a reveal for all of them, even Mister realizing that he's been such a dirtbag and asking for forgiveness.

In any show, you can't have something that's all light. You need to have a moment of dark. And you can't have all dark. You need a little bit of light, you need a little bit of, "Oh, I can breathe," because it needs to mirror life. No day in your life is always going to have 100 percent happy or 100 percent sad.

We now have more choices than ever for how we're going to be entertained. And if you're going to invest your time and your money, you want to walk away knowing that you had a full experience. If you're only shown silliness and light, you also want meaning. If you are only introduced to dark, you walk away saying, "I wish I had those two hours back." You have to have both.

JON BATISTE: I saw the stage show several times with my family, and the song "I'm Here" is a really powerful song to hear live. It ties so firmly to what the spine of *The Color Purple* narrative is all about. It stands on this declaration of one's own intrinsic value and one's own worth. It really is the song that speaks to the moral of the story best.

That's how music is. Beyond any specific form of notes or lyrics or rhythm, music transfers vibrations—some may call it energy, some may call it a feeling. It's an intangible transference of meaning, and it's invisible, but it's just as real as you or me. It's just as real as a chair or a desk that you can sit in front of. It's just as real as a brick of gold. It doesn't have to have any sort of explanation. If the vibrational frequency and the intention are potent and directed enough, you're going to feel it, even if you don't understand it. It's why somebody like a Bad Bunny could be one of the biggest artists in America and doesn't even sing in English. I've toured in over forty countries, and I've done things where the audience doesn't speak the language that we speak, but they feel it. Why is a Ray Charles or a Nina Simone big in Japan? Music doesn't speak to the conscious mind. It speaks to the subconscious mind, and to the soul, and to something that is deeper than logic and surface-level understanding.

HURT PEOPLE HURT PEOPLE

KIMBERLEY RAMPERSAD: The insidious nature of racism is much more about it just being in the air as opposed to some character coming on stage and dropping the N-bomb. And you're just like, "Well, yeah, understood." But what about that pressure in the world? What is the pressure to be Black without that white gaze?

I remember it being very clever in the 1985 movie, watching Mister's father come in wearing a cream suit like a plantation owner. And I was like, "Hoo. Understood. 'Adopting the manners of.' OK, I see you." Even seeing that role being cast with a fair-skinned actor [Adolph Caesar] who has a darker-skinned son [Danny Glover] who he's riding really hard, I thought, "There's a whole story in that alone, just by casting those two actors and having them occupy those parts."

TARAJI P. HENSON (Shug, 2023 film): Shug takes her trauma and flips it. She is not a victim of it. It's her workaround. It's dysfunctional how she got there, but it's her workaround. Nobody's talking about therapy back then.

We're not even close. But you see it. You see trauma being passed down. That's still going on. You think we're past the racism, but we're still here.

JON BATISTE: It's the generational trauma and the systemic oppression that leads to a person like Mister choosing the path that he chose. Obviously, that's not the only choice that could be made, but you have to have a level of empathy for someone who was born and dealt the hand that many of our ancestors were dealt.

DEON COLE (Alfonso, 2023 film): I made my Alfonso creepy without even being creepy. I remember in the original movie, Nettie was trying to walk out of the house, and Alfonso was standing in front of her. She tried to walk the other way and he went this way and that way, not letting her go, insinuating that he was flirting with her, messing with her. You knew that he was creepy just by the way he carried himself and how demanding he was. You knew that he wasn't the guy to be around. This was a tormented guy. That was a note that they gave me as well, that he isn't where he wants to be in life. He's mad at the system. The system isn't treating him fairly. He did everything honestly at one point in time, and he can't ever come up. He's always in a rut, and he takes it out on other people.

There's a scene with Alfonso and Mister going back and forth over whether he can marry Nettie. And even when Alfonso sold Celie to him for a little bit of nothing, Alfonso still felt like he got something, anything, to make it seem like he broke even. Everything had a price with him. It didn't even matter if it was a fair exchange. He just couldn't do without. And so that was the state of mind I had with him. If we had physically fought, it would've been equivalent to the way we were looking at each other. There was a part where [Mister] spit on the ground, and [Alfonso] felt like that was disrespectful: "This is my shop and you don't spit on the ground in my shop." Little things triggered Alfonso all the time.

KIMBERLEY RAMPERSAD: During slavery, men didn't stick around because no one had choices about sticking around. Families were ripped apart all the time. You found a moment of joy or happiness where you could, but families were blown up, blown up, blown up. We don't know how many hundreds of years it has been for Black families in America to even know what a family unit might look like, however it may manifest. So you see the ravages, you see Mister pull out the whip...but who showed him how to use the whip?

DEON COLE: One scene that was powerful to me was where Celie had the baby and Alfonso had to take the baby away. It was weird. I was in the scene going, "Give me your baby." And my mind was like, "Stop it, you terrible man!"

Shug (Taraji P. Henson), 2023 film

Old Mister (Adolph Caesar), 1985 film

"The process of getting into Celie and understanding who the character Celie is has been a journey of healing, incredible healing. There are a lot of things that I resonate with in Celie, in terms of having been conditioned to silence my voice as a young Black woman or just as a woman in general. Celie goes through the journey of being told that she's ugly, that she's nothing, that she'll never amount to anything, but eventually she taps into her authentic voice. She realizes her capacity to be anything and do anything that she wants. The world can tell you that you will amount to nothing, but you were made in God's image, so if God has made you in his image, it means that you have the capacity to do whatever you want to do if you acknowledge those gifts in yourself."

—DIDINTLE KHUNOU

Actress and singer who played Celie in the Joburg Theatre
production in South Africa in 2018

From "*The Color Purple* comes to Joburg" by SABC News, 2018

MEKHAI LEE (Mister, 2012 Northwest School of the Arts production): Through watching Mister's mistakes, I was able to learn how it is OK to be soft as a man, and to be loving, and to not always have that tough exterior. That was the biggest lesson for me. Obviously, Mister was extremely abusive, but it all stemmed from a place of massive, massive hurt, and so in a way he became a lesson of what not to do in order to be a good man. I was watching the effects of pain in somebody cause pain in other people as well. For me, the lesson became: How can I work through my own shortcomings, my own pain, my own insecurities in my manhood? How can I heal that sort of thing and be more generous with myself, give myself some grace so that I'm not walking around scarred and beaten and hurting other people? It's been said millions of times: "Hurt people hurt people." So for me, I think the lesson is that he is a blueprint of what not to do. Also, he is a lesson in that it's never too late to realize the error of your ways and to start again.

WHAT GOES INTO MAKING A MISTER

DANNY GLOVER (Mister, 1985 film): I had to consider the historical context of the story itself. The story takes place at a specific period in the journey of formerly enslaved Africans. These are people who function within a larger historical context that has to be explained—the behavior, the fears, the role that women play, et cetera.

I work from being inside the character. I'm investing my own memory, a much larger memory than just

> ## "Part of Mister's journey is liberating himself from his father."
> ### —Danny Glover

Danny's memory of what I've read, what I understand historically about a context in which to look at African Americans. Who I am. My grandmother who was born in 1895. She lived to be ninety-nine years old, and she was in my life. I lived on her farm. That's a part of my own memory of that context and who she was as a woman. My mother was born in 1917, and she would always tell me, "I'm eternally grateful for my mother and father because I didn't go pick cotton in September. I went to school in September." Consequently, my mother was the first to graduate from college, in 1942. From that framework, those are the tools that I've used: what I knew and what I understood historically.

Alice Walker was in a group of contemporary writers, incredible women, who left a major imprint on African American storytelling. The Color Purple film is grounded in writing that had never been seen before. In film, most depictions of us were caricatures, drawn from the perspective of a country that has never taken responsibility for its incredible diminishing of enslaved Africans. I'm not making excuses for Mister. I'm not making excuses for the choices that were made. I'm saying that his experience is real. I saw it. I may have been born in cosmopolitan San Francisco, but I lived for a time with my grandparents in rural Georgia, in Jefferson County. Mister came from nothing. Mister was about power, in a sense, but he's a product of historic forces.

I come from a very strong matriarchal line. When the overseer came to pick up my mother, her sister, and her brother in the morning and take them to work in the fields, he said to my grandmother, "Well, Reecie Mae, where them kids are? It's not raining outside." And Reecie Mae said, "My kids are in school. When they're in school, they don't work in the fields." Her kids were not going to live her life. These are the stories told.

My grandmother was a midwife. My grandfather's mother, Mary Hunley, was a midwife. My mom made sure that I understood who these people were. And she would always say about her parents, "I am who I am because of these two people."

Part of Mister's journey is liberating himself from his father. Adolph Caesar was wonderful playing my father in conveying the sense of having power over Mister's life. In that small context of that community, that's power.

You're acting out what happens in this whole process of dehumanization in the outside world. It reminds me

Old Mister (Adolph Caesar) and Mister (Danny Glover), 1985 film

of a photograph from the Civil War. It was a photograph that was taken when they stopped the battle between the South and the North to execute a formerly enslaved African who had deserted. I tried to think about this man who had been enslaved and then somebody puts a gun in his hand to fight for...well, maybe he doesn't know what he's fighting for. But later he becomes afraid. Maybe he becomes afraid of dying and runs away. And both sides, the South and the North, stop the war for this formerly enslaved African to execute him. How many times did that happen? That context is not something that goes away in a generation.

The first thing you ask as an actor is, "What does the character want? What does he need?" And Mister needed to love. And then he had to learn to love himself. It's all about love and healing. I worked from moment to moment in building a character, and I knew at the end: What purpose is it to tell the story if it's not about redemption and love? Why do you tell the story? Where do we find literature that evokes a better world and a better place if it's not imbued with love? Where does Mister resolve this healing process? That's the approach, where you see Mister evolving into that last moment where he brings Nettie home.

STEPHEN BRAY (music and lyrics, 2005 Broadway musical, 2015 Broadway revival, 2023 film): Mister is such a sad and terrible character to have to embody, because there's obviously so much pain there. With the musical film, I credit Marcus [Gardley] and Blitz [Bazawule] for doubling down on the idea that Mister's heart is broken. That's a brokenhearted man from early on. He did not have the nerve to fight for the woman he loved. What is that like inside to have your heart broken and then be living this life of anger until it snaps? That's one of my favorite scenes in the earlier movie too. When Danny Glover walks into the juke and he's drunk and says something kind for the first time in the movie. It's so good. Danny Glover's so good in that moment. It's so believable.

COLMAN DOMINGO (Mister, 2023 film): The thing I was interested in about Mister was showing that he's broken. That he's broken not only by being a Black man at the time in the system, but he's had dreams that were deferred. And what do abused people do? They abuse others. Whether he was abused by his father or the system, he sees that cycle of abuse and trauma and how Celie makes a choice to break it. He has to find that with himself to break it too. That's how we survive.

Power

Mister (Colman Domingo), 2023 film

When Oprah and Blitz met me and said that they believed this role was for me, I also understood it was for me. I thought, "Oh, I have the capacity to fill this man. Let it be wholly my own design, not based on Danny Glover's tremendous work, but based on what I understand about the script and my place in it." I had to divorce myself from the film and from the stage musical. I'd seen both iterations of the original and the revival. I have the soundtrack. But I had to divorce myself from all of it in order to look at it fresh and new, and to live inside of it. I couldn't have those traces of my friend LaChanze playing Celie in *The Color Purple*. Instead, I had this formidable woman, Fantasia, in my presence. See how we rock together. I had to look at how Mister lives in me. How does he smile? Is he charming? How does he have sex? All that stuff. So that was the exciting part, to actually look at it as something brand-new. My Mister was a hopeful blues musician. He wanted to be in a band. He had dreams, like everyone else. He wanted to move through space like these guys who have the ladies looking at them a certain way. So, I adopted that part of his culture—the way he smokes, the way he sits his hat on his head. You see that this is somebody who's actually a musician, but then the world has beat it out of him.

We made sure we made a point to say that Mister is never, ever touched, so he's constantly in need of touch in some way. He's like an animal. He doesn't know how to touch. When he wants to have sex, it's rough because nobody's been tender with him. No one's held him. No mother, nobody. What happens to a person when that happens? That's how they act out. Then we could understand it as being human.

But there are traces of charm in my Mister. Maybe this is because I'm such a feminist, but I wanted to create a formidable character that would challenge these smart, vivacious, bold, strong women to fall under his spell in some way. Whether that's with Shug Avery or Celie or any other woman, you see a boyish quality in him and something attractive that you can get caught up in and can confuse you in that way. How do you create a real challenge for the audience? A great challenge is to be charmed by someone who's doing terrible things. It makes you ask: How well do you know him? How well do you know yourself? What are you susceptible to?

SCOTT SANDERS (producer, 2005 Broadway musical, 2015 Broadway revival, 2023 film): Heading into the musical film project, it felt really important that we dig deeper

"It felt really important that we dig deeper in the exploration of Mister's character."
—Scott Sanders

than the 1985 film or the stage musical had in the exploration of Mister's character—to give more validity to the forgiveness that happens at the end of the novel. I knew that it was going to be delicate, because on one hand you may have some people who say, "He's unredeemable. He should have a restraining order against him and you should never see him again."

As I've gotten older, I've realized that many families are messed up, and the world is more gray than black-and-white. People are complicated and behave in unacceptable ways sometimes. Why do they? What was their trauma? Again, not to excuse it, but to perhaps further enlighten as to why. I got the sense that in the book Mister is forgiven, and it's not just because he went to the immigration office. That's just too simple and too easy, quite frankly.

SHEILA WALCOTT: One challenge that all of us wanted to address was the critique that Black men were not portrayed well in the Spielberg movie. How do you humanize the character journeys that the men in this movie are going through so that there's more understanding about where they were coming from? With Alfonso, there's kind of nothing you can do. He's a villain and it is what it is. Every movie needs a villain. But with Mister's character, how do you shade him in a way that he's not one-dimensional? He had more layers to him than just being this guy who's mean and abusive to Celie throughout the entire movie. It was important to us in terms of representation to address that in how the characters were drawn, and I think Marcus and Blitz did a great job of that. And then Colman finds levels in this character that you never thought could exist. In Danny Glover's version, Mister is stoic. He's hard. And he's iconic. The new film is a different iteration, but man, Colman found some levels in Mister's character that I just didn't know were there.

MISTER MEETS MISTER

Two actors, Colman Domingo and Mekhai Lee, talk to each other
about taking on the role made famously infamous by Danny Glover.
They played Mister at different stages in their careers, but both
strove to manifest their character's humanity.

Mister (Colman Domingo), 2023 film

Mister (Mekhai Lee), 2012 high school production,
Northwest School of the Arts, Charlotte, North Carolina

MEKHAI LEE: I played Mister when I was sixteen years old.

COLMAN DOMINGO: Wow.

MEKHAI: I know, it's crazy. But my high school was actually one of the first high schools in the country to do *The Color Purple*. And my teacher, Corey Mitchell, surprised everybody in our school with this show. He changed my life. I didn't grow up with a positive male figure in my life—the same old story—but Corey kind of stepped in with all of us, especially with this show, and really changed who and what I became.

COLMAN: Yes. What was your experience with not only the musical but the source material? You were sixteen. Did you read the book? Did you see the movie?

MEKHAI: I had seen the movie as a kid.

COLMAN: How old were you when you saw the movie?

MEKHAI: Not old enough to understand. It was very much just on as background noise. I knew who Whoopi Goldberg was, I knew who Danny Glover was, but I wasn't paying too much attention. And then I read the book in high school a couple of months before we announced we were doing the show. I can't even tell you how I found it. It was in the library or something. I was reading it, and Mr. Mitchell looked at me reading it. He was like, "You're going to need that one day." And I was like, "OK, whatever. Sure, Mr. Mitchell." And then we were doing the show. Now it's one of my favorite books of all time.

COLMAN: Why does it speak to you?

MEKHAI: I think because as I reread it as I get older, it's just that constant lesson of gratitude for me. And in the musical, Shug really alludes to the message and the theme of the book for me with, "God not some gloomy old man in the sky. The pictures you've seen of him. God not a man at all." And just the idea that God—not to get too spiritual here—God constantly surrounds us.

COLMAN: "God lives inside me."

MEKHAI: Exactly.

COLMAN: "And everyone else."

MEKHAI: Every*thing* else. Even when I'm walking to the damn gym and I see purple poppies, it reminds me to be grateful I'm alive, grateful that I can even go to the gym, grateful that I have the opportunities that I have. Every time *The Color Purple* is in my life, blessings follow. So I'm extremely grateful for the story. I'm extremely grateful for the magic it brings to who I am and how I live my life.

COLMAN: Something you just said is something that Oprah actually said to us on set. She said there's something about *The Color Purple*, about Alice Walker's ancestors, that being associated with this will change your life. She said, "It's changed mine." I feel the same way. It's funny because I've watched the movie many times—it's one of my favorite movies—and when it first came out, it was like, "Oh, Danny Glover's so horrible." I think people personally started to hate Danny Glover—he was the most hated actor in America because of that. How could he do Whoopi like that?

And then when the musical came out, I first saw it with LaChanze [as Celie], and then I saw the revival with Cynthia Erivo. When I saw the revival, it was my birthday. I went as a birthday gift, and I had an incredible seat. And I felt like it was just telling the story and singing it right to me. When they get to the end and they go, "I don't think us feel old at all." I don't even know what happened to me, but I said, "Not at all!" Loud.

MEKHAI: Yes, you did.

COLMAN: I was in my own space.

"I'm extremely grateful for the magic it brings to who I am and how I live my life."
—Mekhai Lee

MEKHAI: I love it.

COLMAN: In the Broadway musical theater community, even though I've done musicals like *Passing Strange* and *Scottsboro Boys* and was nominated for a Tony Award and an Olivier Award, I feel like I was this odd thing. No one knew where to put me because I'm a character actor who does weird stuff. Honestly, I felt like this when the idea of me getting cast as Mister in the *Color Purple* musical feature film came up. No one thought that would happen, not even me, because I started to think something like that was impossible for me.

So the idea that when Ms. Winfrey said I was her first choice and [director] Blitz [Bazawule] agreed, I understood it was a great challenge for me, because I didn't set myself up to play Mister at all. I didn't know that that was part of my trajectory, but I knew I had all the things that I could operate from and bring to and explore this character. I knew where it lived in me. And that's what I want to ask you about: your take on this character, what you know about this character, the way people perceive this character. Like I said, Danny Glover was the most hated man in America because, wow, [Mister] is so vicious and horrible. How did you approach your Mister?

MEKHAI: Well, I want to comment on you not feeling like people really understood how you fit into the musical theater canon. I felt that way graduating from college. I was like, "No one's really going to see what I do." I present extremely masc, and we've never met in person, but I'm a bit shorter than you, and I'm broad-shouldered. I don't really dress like traditionally queer people dress. But I'm an extremely out and comfortable person. And if you were to ask me, it's no issue for me to talk about what it is to live a queer experience. But when agents and managers and casting directors were coming to visit us our senior year, they always struggled with where to place me.

COLMAN: Yeah, because you're very comfortable with who you are.

MEKHAI: Exactly.

COLMAN: It almost messes with their mind. They're like, "Well, what—"

MEKHAI: "Why are you not confused? *I'm* confused." And I'm like, "This is who I am." So it felt extremely right that the first job that I did after school was the *Color Purple* tour. Again, it brought a new set of blessings into my life. So this show has always felt sort of home, for lack of a better word. It was very true to me and true to my history, true to being Southern. So it always felt like home.

COLMAN: You just touched on something that I think is interesting, because I didn't think of it until this conversation. Like, "Oh, we're both queer men of color playing a very hyper-masculine man." And the idea that people outside of our experience sometimes think that it's almost foreign to our experience. No. That's a man. I can play this man who does these things, complicated things with women. I'm like, "No, I understand that because it's human." Do you feel the same way?

MEKHAI: I think that's exactly right. That's how I approached playing Mister in high school. Granted, we were in high school, so there's only so much life experience I could bring to it. But that's how I approached it back then, just understanding the men in my life, my uncles and those who had raised me, and feeling at times in my own experience like a Celie because they put a lot more attention into the various Shugs of my life: my cousins, the men who were good at basketball, the guys who loved being in the barbershop. And here I was a queer kid who liked to read and play video games. My uncles didn't really know how to relate to me, didn't really understand me in that capacity. I brought that knowledge to Mister.

> # "We're both queer men of color playing a very hyper-masculine man."
> ## —Colman Domingo

Mister (Colman Domingo) in his fields, 2023 film

Now, Mister behaves differently, and he takes his anger and misunderstanding out on Celie in a very different way than I received. I was not abused by the men in my life, but I could understand misdirected anger. I could understand having learned a behavior from the men you were raised by and repeating that cycle, that generational trauma. It's something that is very prevalent, I feel, in a lot of Black families. Very prevalent in my family. And I watched as men tried to learn out of it but still struggled with it. I watched as the women in my family tried to learn out of it. So that's how I approached it then. And Corey is really open as a teacher, as an educator. He was very much unafraid of these conversations, which is not orthodox for high schoolers. Most people wouldn't even touch this show. The queer themes, the abuse—

COLMAN: It's heavy-duty for high school.

MEKHAI: It is, but we were in an underprivileged neighborhood at an underprivileged arts high school with a huge Black student population. We knew this story in the South. We just knew it. It was innate. It was almost ancestral because there was not a lot of thinking. The music would start, we'd start singing, "It's Sunday morning…" that whole part, and next thing we're just coming alive because that music brought it out of us. It was spiritual in a lot of ways. And again, like Oprah said, like everybody says, it changes your life. So I think that's why it felt like home again.

COLMAN: That's beautiful.

MARCUS GARDLEY (screenwriter, 2023 film): Think about why the first movie was received the way it was, in terms of both praise and protest. This was one of the first major Black films from a major studio that had a lot of buzz around it. It was epic and based on a Pulitzer Prize–winning book. Because of all that, for a lot of people it was a first. When you're a first, and I notice this even in queer communities, audiences want to see themselves reflected in the best of lights. So the original movie had all this responsibility that was unfair, and that's why the response was the way it was.

When we're talking about the portrayal of masculinity and the male characters for this current iteration, it was important to me that I didn't rewrite them. I still wanted to see the Mister that we all know, but what are the other colors that we didn't get a chance to experience? A lot of times when people respond negatively to a character, it's because there's repetition happening. I already know that guy, but what else? What's underneath it? The director was really excited about this idea of Mister's inner life as a musician. Did he want to join Shug's band but never had that opportunity? And then this was the real challenge: Some people argued that he was actually in love with Celie, which was a hard one for me to get around—that he actually falls in love with her or realizes what he had.

I always felt that this was a man whose father is really important. In that time period, for Old Mister to have owned land and a house in the South? That right there should stop everybody. It should make people say, "Wait, how is that possible?" There's no way Mister as a boy and his parents weren't harassed by white supremacists. Let's be honest, they probably had a lynching here or there. Probably somebody got shot. Probably some people fled north. But Old Mister—this is a man who stayed. What kind of men are these? These men are super-strong.

In my screenplay, because Old Mister sacrificed so much to keep the land and keep the house, he feels the son has to do this, too. This is about legacy. The son didn't know he had a choice.

My great-grandmother tells the story about her own father having been a slave as a boy. As a boy, he would have to sleep under the bed of the master because his responsibility was to shift the coals under the bed to keep the bed warm. Well, he was a boy, and he would fall asleep and be burned.

That was my great-grandmother's father. All this stuff gets passed down. All that pain gets passed down. I wanted to see those layers in Mister, even though some of it's going to be implied and subtle. And where are the moments where he breaks, where he can no longer hold together these private moments?

We have this moment in our film that I'm really proud of where he has this break. It's not in the book, it's not in the musical, and it's not in the Spielberg film. He has this break, and it's still Mister, but it's just a little shadow. That little shade that you never got to see. Alice cried when she saw it.

HARPO BREAKS THE CYCLE

SCOTT SANDERS: We really went out of our way in the musical to expand on Harpo. In the 1985 movie, Harpo was sort of a comic foil. He falls through the roof of the Juke Joint, and there's not a whole lot going on with him. I always thought Harpo was a really remarkable character, because if you come from that lineage and suddenly decide to marry Sofia and not be your father and grandfather, what does that say about Harpo?

TARAJI P. HENSON: Old Mister is continuing to pass the trauma down, but it stops at Harpo. What you're seeing is a generational awakening. Harpo's not necessarily conscious of breaking a cycle, but in the same breath he's doing it.

WILLARD E. PUGH (Harpo, 1985 film): Mister is like his father, and his father was abusive. That's why Celie spits in Old Mister's glass. Harpo is trying to be better than his daddy was. Some great scenes that showed this got cut out of the final film. Funny scenes between Harpo and Sofia where we fought, we made love, we fought, we made love. Then there was a scene in the Juke Joint, when the fight breaks out and Sofia hits Squeak. I stop the fight. For the first time in this movie, you see Harpo being a man. You see Mister looking at his son and watching him stop this fight, watching his son be a man and take control of the situation. You saw Sofia looking at her ex and realizing that she'd made a mistake: Look

Harpo (Willard E. Pugh), 1985 film

Left to right: Harpo, as played by Ahmed Hamad, Birmingham Hippodrome, England, 2019; Brandon Victor Dixon, The Broadway Theatre, New York, 2005; Corey Hawkins, 2023 film

at this man controlling this whole room and telling everybody that this is his juke joint and you are not going to destroy it!

My other big scene that didn't make the cut was one with Mister after Sofia and I have gotten back together. Mister's in the Juke Joint, and it's raining, and me and Mister, who's drunk, walk back to the house. Back at the house, he's looking at a coat rack. And on that coat rack, all these faces are coming up. He sees the faces of all the people that he abused. I'm walking close to him, and when he reaches out to grab one of the faces, the face he grabs is actually mine. And he realizes at that moment, that me and him, we ain't got nobody but each other. I'm holding Danny in my arms at that point, like I'm now the daddy and he's the baby. It's the best love scene between a father and a son, with no dialogue.

Steven [Spielberg] had to shut the set down for an hour or two and let everybody get over it. Because if you've got a father and you ever loved your father or another family member, you're going to cry and feel something.

That scene got cut. Steven said he cut it because they would have to use special effects to show the faces Mister was seeing on the coat rack, and he didn't want any special effects in the movie. He wanted everything to be as close to real as it could be.

One night, a storm came up while we were on location. In North Carolina, they had some crazy lightning storms. Steven made the crew get up out of bed, get their cameras, and start shooting. And I'm thinking—this is at, like, two or three in the morning—"Are you kidding?" Steven was yelling, "Everybody up, up, up!" I got up, too, because I didn't want to miss *nothing*. And so when you see the movie, the lightning you see in the background, that was real.

My favorite scene that did make it in is when Oprah comes back home from jail. When she was with Dana Ivey, who's driving the car. The best moment for me in the whole movie is when Oprah comes home for the first time and she's walking up the stairs. My girlfriend [Rae Dawn Chong as Squeak] is standing next to me, and here's my wife coming. And there's a moment when my hand touches her hand. Just our fingertips. It's a really small touch, but it's a very powerful touch. People who really paid attention to the movie tell me, "Oh my goodness. That scene, when y'all touched each other's hands, it was like electricity went through the screen." He still loved her, and she still loved him, and then to see his wife beat up with her eye half-closed… It was hard to see. But she was home. That was more important than anything. So that, for me, was my best scene that stayed in the movie. Everybody else's best scene is me falling through the roof and the line, "It's going to rain on your head."

Purple Rising

That's what most people remember as soon as they see me.

TINUKE CRAIG (director, 2019 U.K. production, Leicester Curve and Birmingham Hippodrome): It is super-radical what Harpo does. Yes, he does beat Sofia in that moment, but overall, he's open and generous with his love, and excited to elevate and amplify Black women's voices. And his mother died in his arms. He's seen such shit. He should be a hot mess. You would understand why Harpo is being a bastard in the same way that you'd understand why Mister's a bastard. And yet there's something in Harpo that he manages to hold on to. Despite the lineage and legacy that has befallen him, he manages to break cycles. And because he breaks cycles, women respond to him.

grandfather doesn't get to do it. Harpo's father gets to start late in life. But Harpo is the one who gets the opportunity to live a life as the kind of man he can feel proud of in the world. As the kind of husband he would like to be. As the devoted lover—not even husband, but lover in our version of this show. He's able to accept the sensitivities that come along with being a fully formed, mature man in ways that the novel reaches for but the theater piece manages to do very successfully.

Harpo's also a product of the strong female influence in his world. Sofia, Celie, Shug. Celie's beat down, but she's not weak. She's a strong figure. And Harpo has respect for her—until he starts to learn that maybe he shouldn't. Then he falls in love with a woman who's not going to take it. Certain men would deal with that in one way, but Harpo eventually deals with it in the way that he

"For our production, what was really useful was to think about the fact that the father ends up being inspired by the son."
—Tinuke Craig

For our production, what was really useful was to think about the fact that the father ends up being inspired by the son. The father sees what can really be done. During that pivot to "Mister's Song," Harpo manages to show his father a better way. This is in the novel. It's in the film to a lesser extent, but it's quite explicit in the stage show. It can be done. Look, he did it. And then look who else was able to do it because Harpo did it. It felt really useful.

And also, Harpo's funny in the show, but within that, there's a humanity that maybe isn't quite as exposed in the [1985] film.

BRANDON VICTOR DIXON (Harpo, 2005 Broadway musical): A lot of the men in *The Color Purple* are forced into roles that are not necessarily their nature, and they're too proud to recognize that soon enough to create a positive effect in the lives of themselves and others—at least not until later in their lives. Harpo's

should, by accepting the person he's in love with and also accepting that this is part of why he's in love with her. These things happen early enough for Harpo to affect the course of his life.

Harpo also has a lower tolerance for having a difficult relationship with his father. Mister and Old Mister have a difficult relationship, but despite the difficulty, despite the anger Mister feels for his father, Mister still strives to be like him, to honor him. Harpo, on the other hand, begins to recognize this might not be who he is, and it might not be what it means to be a man.

COREY HAWKINS (Harpo, 2023 film): What it is for me is bringing Harpo to a new generation. For a lot of my family members as I was growing up, Harpo was seen as a weak man. For the men in my family, Harpo was the butt of the joke. In the world of *The Color Purple* and in the world of so many of our ancestors, he didn't represent what masculinity is.

Coming in, I said that Harpo is here in support of. This is not Harpo's story. Harpo is not the star. This is an opportunity for the women to shine and to show who they are outside of the narrative of these men. And within that, I have an opportunity to bring to this generation a new idea of what masculinity is. That was one of the first things I talked to Scott [Sanders] about when he called to offer me the role. I was so eager and excited to finally be like, "How do I change this?"

A whole generation of young men who don't know *The Color Purple* are going to see this new film. And yeah, they're going to see Harpo, and he is funny, and he's a bit of a butt of the jokes. But they're also going to see his transition, how you can love and play different roles in a relationship.

In one of the songs Mister sings, he's saying, "Wash my shirts, scrub my pants," just telling Celie the things she is supposed to be doing. But we live in a generation now where we are redefining the roles of what a man is supposed to do, what a woman is supposed to do. In this movie, Blitz [Bazawule] gave me a work song, a way for Harpo to strut his stuff a little bit as he's building the house with his fellas. At the end of it, Harpo turns, and Sofia and her sisters are coming in. He is like, "Yeah, you see what I did?" And she grabs the hammer and she's like, "Get the heck out the way." I think Harpo loves that about her. I love that about Sofia.

Mister (Danny Glover) gets kicked out by Harpo (Willard E. Pugh), 1985 film

We live in a generation now where it's possible for the roles to be more fluid and less rigid. We live in a generation where women are really stepping into that power. There have been women doing that along the way, but now, as a society, I feel like we as men are realizing and relearning how to be a man and what that means. What does it mean to be a man? You think it's puffing up your chest, but sometimes it's puffing up your woman. It's lifting your woman up. And there's being a man in that. So I wanted to really explore that shift in Harpo, and I wanted to make sure that we saw the love.

COLMAN DOMINGO: One scene that really stands out for me is with Corey Hawkins, who plays my son. We found this moment in rehearsal, and I'll be honest, it was because I wasn't satisfied with a moment on the page. It's the moment where I'm being kicked out of the Juke Joint and my son takes me out of there. Then he says, "You OK, Pop?" Then I say, "Oh, just stop touching me. I can get on by myself." In rehearsal, I said, "Can we try something? I think there's an opportunity here that we're not taking."

Blitz said, "Try it. Show me what it is."

I laid my head on Corey's chest for a moment out of pure exhaustion. Taking in all that was boiling inside of Mister.

Then Corey stops and says, "You all right, Pop?" Harpo's line was only supposed to be in relation to his father stumbling around drunk. But Mister stays there for a beat, a brief moment of vulnerability, and then suddenly notices what's happening and thrusts away from it. For that split second, though, you can see what could have been possible between this father and son. It was that one moment of tenderness that you can see between two Black men that I think is necessary to move through the world. That brotherhood that will keep their souls alive. We can recognize that they need to sift through generational trauma and toxic masculinity if they are to be whole and healed.

Alice Walker and Marcus Gardley gave us the language, but it's for us as actors to know what we need to bring into it. To interpret with our souls. I know that the attempt, especially with this *Color Purple*, is to continue to humanize these Black men, and to show the complexity of us, and not for us to be villains of our own story. Everyone's complex. Everyone has the capacity for love. Everyone has the capacity for redemption. In that

Mister (Colman Domingo) gets kicked out by Harpo (Corey Hawkins), 2023 film

moment, I wanted to show he has space for tenderness like anyone else, but he makes the wrong choice. He makes the choice to not accept it.

We've gone through so much since 1985, when the first film came out. We as a country are still going through so much. I think if we're going to reinvigorate the story of *The Color Purple* with this new language of a musical hybrid film, it's very important for everyone on the team to reexamine the characters and really show our dimensionality so that we're not just a trope. It was on everyone's mind while we were making the film. We wanted to make sure that we laughed, that we cried, that we sang, that we danced, that we laid down, that we were human in every single way. So people can see their mothers, fathers, sisters, brothers, uncles, aunts, and their grandparents. You can see everyone—white, Black, or other. We wanted to make sure that they were fully rounded characters.

COREY HAWKINS: That was one of my favorite scenes as well. I remember being on set with Colman and Blitz that day and talking about allowing that moment to be what it needed to be.

There were many days of Mister falling asleep drunk and Harpo having to get him up and walk him back. But the thing is, love will still win out. Harpo has to ask if he's OK because this isn't the father that he knows or the guy he saw inside. And then in that moment, he pushes me off of him and walks up the gangplank. Mister realizes, "Oh, I might have revealed a little too much to my son. Uh-oh, there may be too much love here. That's not OK. If I love on him, that means I'm weak. And if I show weakness, what does that mean for my son?"

When Mister leans in, that split second for me is the generational curse being broken. It doesn't matter if Mister goes back to his ornery self after that. Harpo now knows there was a moment when his father showed just a little bit of love. He reciprocated it after years of Harpo having to be the caretaker. I remember that moment being so emotional and Harpo being a mix of emotions. Confused, proud that his father's proud, but also wondering where that love was growing up and missing that. There are so many young Black men who grow up with that kind of tough love.

Mister goes off after that and has a talk with his ancestors in the fields. It's only after that moment that things change for him, because he allows himself to love. Just that little bit. Like my grandma used to say, you got to leave a window cracked to let God in.

BLITZ BAZAWULE (director, 2023 film): Harpo, for me, was the possibility. We can look at this generational evolution in our own families. How I was with my father is not how I am with my son, and that's probably not how he will be with his son or daughter. It's a constant

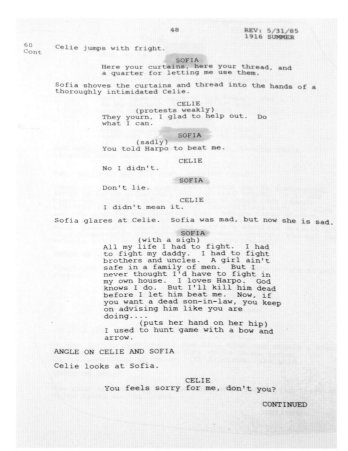

Oprah Winfrey's script from the 1985 film

"I think 'All my life, I had to fight' resonates for so many people in this world."
—Oprah Winfrey

evolution. I wanted for people to sit in a theater and look and choose. They can go, "You know what? I see Old Mister, I see Mister, and I see Harpo, and I see an evolution, and I see there's a path to building oneself better."

MARCUS GARDLEY: I think the producers in this version really wanted to show Harpo as charting the new territory on his own. One thing I always try to do in my work is equip audiences with the idea that you don't have to grow up in a certain environment or have a wise person tell you certain things for you to decide you're going to be different. And Harpo does that. He's not learning it from Mister; he doesn't even see it from Shug. He just decides, "I am going to do things differently." I love that about his character.

OPRAH WINFREY: People have come up to me for years and said that line, "You told Harpo to beat me." Now it has become a meme, which puts it into a whole other category, one I don't even understand. But the time it touched me the most was when I was on trial for saying something bad about a burger down in Texas, and we were doing shows from Texas in order for me to be able to appear in court every day. This white guy, probably late twenties, early thirties, stands up in the audience and says, "I love this movie, and I've seen it fifty-five times," and he starts quoting, "You told Harpo to beat me..." Knows the whole monologue.

I think it resonates because there are many people in this world for whom "all my life, I had to fight. I had to fight my uncles. I had to fight my brothers, but I never thought I'd have to fight in my own house." The fights are different, but the bottom line is, they are identifying with the self-proclaimed victory Sofia allows herself to have: "I ain't going to fight in my own house; I now can

Sofia (Oprah Winfrey) confronts Celie, 1985 film

control what happens to me." It's the sense of, "I've taken some shit in my day, but I ain't going to do it no more."

Along those same lines, Sofia's song from the Broadway show "Hell No" is what resonated the most in all of the preview screenings we did for the musical film. It's the song that everybody came away humming to themselves.

TARAJI P. HENSON: Harpo isn't the only one who breaks the cycle. Women break the cycle too. Sofia says, "You don't get to tell me what to do with my body. You don't get to put your hands on my body." It's a fight we still to this day are having: Men telling us what to do with our fucking bodies. It goes on and on. Every woman in this film is dealing with it.

the human spirit and our divine ability to make diamonds out of coal is something I find so life-affirming. It was gratifying to bring that story to multiple communities, especially to Nova Scotia, which has such a longstanding and still-marginalized Black community. This was a chance to use this story to shine some light on their divinity, which might be clouded at times because of how they are marginalized and continually and systemically relegated. We were able to spotlight, literally, and use center stage as a way to illuminate the whole community. I thought, "This is where my art meets my politics."

MARCUS GARDLEY: It's definitely a universal story. You could go to any country, and most people have heard of it or know of it in some way and are deeply moved by it. I remember as a child, when the first movie came out,

"It's a fight we still to this day are having: Men telling us what to do with our fucking bodies."
—Taraji P. Henson

COLMAN DOMINGO: Many aspects of the 1985 film made a strong impression on me, but especially the Sofia character. "You told Harpo to beat me." Watching this formidable woman who bucked all the conventions of what being a woman was like back then. Somebody who was really being her own woman outside of her husband. This was a character I'm not quite sure I'd seen in a film, so maybe that's why it resonated. I know these women, I grew up with these women, but I hadn't seen these women fully featured in a major motion picture.

BREAKING THE CHAINS

KIMBERLEY RAMPERSAD: For me, the triumph of the human spirit is the most beautiful thing we could ever speak about. It's not just Celie; there are many spirits that triumph in this, which is what's amazing. The triumph of

my parents said, "Number one, you cannot watch it." I heard the adults talking about it and talking about how hard it was to watch. I remember my great-grandmother, who was 104, saying to me when I became a writer, "I'm going to let you tell my story, but don't tell it like it's *The Color Purple*."

On the other hand, in the African American community, you'd better not say anything bad about *The Color Purple*. You'd better not. They will yell at you. It's interesting: The movie revealed intimate things about Black culture that a lot of people knew but were always told not to talk about, and now, the world could see it. Yet it was very healing for the community—extremely healing. It's like, "We don't want to air our dirty laundry, and we don't like the depiction of Black men in this particular story, and yet, thank you. We are having these conversations that we never had before, and now we can see this healing take place that would not have existed had the movie not come out."

HELL NO!

[Sofia] (spoken)
You told Harpo to
beat me?

[Sofia] (spoken)
I'm sorry

[Sofia] (spoken)
I love Harpo
God knows I do
But I kill him dead before
I let him or anybody
beat me

[Sofia]
All my life I've had
to fight
I had to fight my daddy
I had to fight my brothers
My cousins, my uncles too
But I never, never, never,
never, never, never
thought
I'd have to fight in my
own house

I feel sorry for you
To tell you the truth
You remind me of
my momma
Under your husband's
thumb
Naw, under your
husband's foot!
What he say goes
Why you so scared,
I never know
But if a man raise
his hand
Hell no
Hell no!

Girl child ain't safe in a
family of mens
Sick and tired old woman
still live like a slave
Oh, you better learn how
to fight back

While you still alive
You show them girl, and
beat back that jive
'Cause when a man just
don't give a damn
Hell no
Hell no!

[Celie] (spoken)
Well, what'chu gonna
do now?

[Sofia] (spoken)
My sister's comin' to
get me
I think I need a vacation
on up and away
from here

[Celie] (spoken)
But Harpo's your
husband
You gotta stay with him
I know you love him

[Sofia] (sung)
When that man used to
touch me
He'd climb on top and
start to rock me away
Lord knows I still love him
But he tried to make
me mind
And I just ain't that kind
Hell no

[Celie] (spoken)
Sometime my husband
get on me so hard it
hurt me all over
But he's my husband,
so I just talk to my
old maker
This life will soon be over,
heaven last always

[Sofia] (spoken)
Well, what you oughta
do is bash Mister's
head open
And think on heaven later
You can't stay here, girl

Sisters!

[Sister 1] Hell no!

[Sister 2] Hell no!

[Sister 3] Hell no!

[Sister 4] Hell no!

[Sofia] Hell No!

[All Sisters]
Hell no!
Let's go!

[Sister 5]
Gonna be your rock
Gonna be your tree

[Sister 6]
Somethin' to hold onto in
your time of need

[Sister 1]
Girl, you too good for
that man

[All Sisters]
Damn that man

[Sister 2]
Gonna take you away

[All Sisters]
Take my hand
Sister, you got to go

[Sister 3]
Don't be no fool
Don't waste your time

[Sister 4]
Any man who hurts you
Ain't worth a dime

[Sister 1]
But he won't know
Till you're gone

[All Sisters]
She be gone

[Sister 2]
What he's throwin' away

[All Sisters]
He be wrong
Sister, you got to go

[Sofia (to Celie)
and Sisters]
Girl, you too
good for that
man (Sister)
Let me take you
away (Sister)
Come on go
away (Sister)
You got to,
you got to leave
today (Sister)

[Sisters]
Sister you got to say

[Sofia]
You got to say
You need to say
You better say
You oughta say

[Sofia and Sisters]
Hell...

[Sofia]
Hell, hell, hell, hell,
hell, hell

[Sofia and Sisters]
No!

Cast of the Broadway musical
revival, Bernard B. Jacobs Theatre,
New York, 2015

"I don't care what the critics say. I watch what people do."
—Willard E. Pugh

WILLARD E. PUGH: I've seen *The Color Purple* on screens all across the country with every race of people you can think of. I would go to theaters in different cities and sit in the back and watch the audience, 'cause that's what tells me how well I did. I don't care what the critics say. I watch what people do. White, Black, and purple in a theater, crying husbands and wives. Some people almost got into altercations with their spouses because the person had done them so wrong. And now they felt, "I've got the strength to walk out and leave you after seeing this movie." A man came up to me and told me I ruined his marriage. I didn't ruin your marriage. You beat your wife. I never touched your wife. She saw this movie and it empowered her. And now she's sick of you.

I had a big football player come at me one time. I thought he was actually going to take my head off. But the next thing I knew, my feet were up off the ground and he was hugging me. He told me this was the greatest thing he'd ever seen. He had brought his mother to the theater. He said to me, "This is my mama, and my mama ain't been to a movie in fifty years, man. She said this is her life story."

MARCUS GARDLEY: There's a very complicated relationship with this story, which is so interesting. Because it's been passed down through the generations, for younger people, my generation and younger, it's our favorite movie of all time, because we've seen the healing. We saw how the movie was changing people. The generation before me were told, "We are not going to tell you the history of our family." Or, "They're secrets and we're never going to tell you." Or, "Be ashamed, because this is what happened." We knew that existed anyway, even though we didn't know the nuances. We knew, "Uncle Willie never leaves his room. Something happened to Uncle Willie."

When the [1985] movie came out, and Uncle Willie saw the movie—that's my own Uncle Willie, by the way—he came out of his room. That was great. And then he started talking about stuff that he never talked about before. How he had Agent Orange sprayed on him in the war. All of a sudden, people are having these conversations.

COREY HAWKINS: I remember talking with Lou Gossett Jr. [who plays Old Mister] at the Easter dinner scene. We were exploring father-son relationships: how the way he treats his son and the way he treats his grandson are two different things. When I come in with Sofia at the beginning of the movie, Mister pushes her out and basically tells Harpo to get on. But then his grandfather gives him money for his family. So there's something interesting about that trauma. You pass it down, and you determine that the mistakes you might have made with your child, you're not going to make with your grandson. "My child, he didn't get it. But my grandson, he's going to be OK because he gets it."

MARCUS GARDLEY: In the screenplay for this version, there's a moment you never saw in the previous adaptations, where Old Mister stands up for Harpo. It's that fine line of how you keep the integrity of the character but also show a little bit of his humanity.

ALICE WALKER (author of *The Color Purple*, 1982): The whole point about having male characters anywhere, at this point, is to help them see that they can transform, that they don't have to stay stuck as batterers and deserters and drunkards and whatever my grandfather was. They just don't have to. The love relationship between Celie and Shug also offers them permission to be whoever they are. That's the other reality about all these people back in the day, before I was born and you were born and all that. They were still who they were, but they were never permitted to be that. I mean, they got to marry somebody, have all the children, the fiddy-'leven chirrun. People often pretend that they think gayness started last week. It's ridiculous. It's just tragic. I mean, it boggles the mind, and my heart just goes out to anybody who can't, for whatever reason, live who they are. This is the only time you're going to be here, as far as I can tell. I see *The Color Purple* as liberatory for men and women, for everyone. You live your life. You go out there and you find who you are, you live who you are, and then come home and tell everybody about it.

EACH ONE TEACH ONE:
THE COLOR PURPLE GOES TO SCHOOL

In 2015, Corey Mitchell won the inaugural Tony Award for Excellence in Theatre Education. At Northwest School of the Arts, in Charlotte, North Carolina, Mitchell directed more than fifty shows, but a standout example is his 2012 production of *The Color Purple*, which was featured in a documentary film called *Purple Dreams*. Here, Mitchell and three of the cast members reflect on their experience.

The cast of the Northwest School of the Arts production of *The Color Purple*, Charlotte, North Carolina, 2012

BRINGING THE SHOW TO SCHOOL

COREY MITCHELL: I grew up in rural North Carolina. I remember in tenth grade, sitting in Anatomy-Physiology and hiding *The Color Purple* behind my textbook. Reading that novel shifted my DNA. There was the recognition of the way Black families hold their secrets. There was being this little country kid who didn't quite understand what gay was. There was, of course, the Blackness. I couldn't have said that in tenth grade, but with hindsight I know, "Yeah, this was why."

Purple was one of the few almost all-Black shows ever produced at Northwest, even though it's majority minority. Shows mostly looked white with some sprinklings, so when I flipped the narrative, I got pushback. What helped beat the resistance was that I was fundraising for *The Color Purple* but spent money on things that helped the whole school, including a new soundboard, fifteen body mics, and new speakers.

DANIELLE HOPKINS (Shug): When it came time to do *The Color Purple*, it was polarizing. There were white people at school who weren't invited into that space, and they were mad about it. We're like, "This is what we do every day. When we finally get the opportunity to shine, we're going to take it."

MEKHAI LEE (Mister): Doing *Color Purple* so young was crazy for us—with Mister and Celie's tumultuous relationship, the representation of lesbian love, and such adult themes—but also exciting. We all knew the story; we knew a lot of the music. It felt like *Fame*. Everybody was auditioning.

COREY: If you look at recordings of the show, you'll notice one white dude. His name is Hank Santos. For *Purple*, he served a couple of functions. First, he was the jailer. When Celie goes to see Sofia in jail, I made sure he said "Miss Celie," because it shows how much respect Celie garnered. Hank's second function was that when people said, "You can't do this all-Black show," I could say, "We have diversity. Don't you see Hank?"

HANK SANTOS (Ensemble, Jailer): They opened auditions up to the entire student body, but to be honest, I wasn't familiar with the show. I remember auditioning

Corey Mitchell, director, Northwest School of the Arts, Charlotte, North Carolina, 2012

and then hearing about how it was not a show for someone like me. For me, though, I was just a member of the community. I was at church with everybody waving my hat around. I was in the fields in "Big Dog," working alongside everybody.

DANIELLE: My name was brought up as somebody that Mr. Mitchell was interested in for Shug. As a seventeen-year-old who was very religious, to embody sexuality and undertones of homosexuality was going to be a challenge: I didn't know what that would look like for me as far as my relationship with God.

I worked hard and got the role. The next day, I almost turned it down. I'd been advised by spiritual leaders that it probably wasn't the best idea. I sat down with Mr. Mitchell and said, "I don't know if I can take this." He looked at me and said, "Danielle, you are Shug, and this is for you. You know what the scripture says about who God is." I said, "What?" He said, "God is love. If you want to represent God and do it well, you do it in love, and this is the perfect opportunity to do so."

I said, "You know what? You're right."

Shug (Danielle Hopkins) and Mister (Mekhai Lee) dance at Harpo's Juke Joint,
Northwest School of the Arts, Charlotte, North Carolina, 2012

Shug helped me find my sexuality. My partner today is a woman. Back then, it wasn't like, "I have to hide this part of me." I didn't even understand it. Ten years later, it makes me laugh that it was this major concern for me. But that was the first time I gave myself permission to own my sensuality.

HANK: That was my junior year. Sophomore year was the first year I'd ever done musical theater. Truth be told, I had been getting in trouble at my old high school; I was just a punk kid misbehaving. And because I had done a play as a kid, my parents said, "Well, you have a background, sort of, in acting and theater. There's this art school in Charlotte, and maybe you'll fit in better with this crowd."

DANIELLE: Mr. Mitchell saw us in ways we didn't see ourselves. He pushed us to do more, to go deeper, to do the work that actors have to do.

It wasn't just about doing a good show, but about having a life experience and sharing that with other people. The energy in that [rehearsal] room was intense. It was sweaty. There were tears. Literally blood, sweat, and tears. And we did it in two weeks, which was an experience you don't usually get in high school. It was *Color Purple* bootcamp every day, all day.

MEKHAI: Mr. Mitchell was almost a father figure in my life. I became close with Phillip [Johnson-Richardson], who played Harpo, and we both didn't have fathers at home. We did both have very hardworking mothers, amazing mothers. I don't feel like I went without at all, but having Mr. Mitchell be this out loud, rambunctious man who unabashedly loved theater shaped how I relate to authority figures. He combined love and incredibly high expectations, but nothing we couldn't achieve.

DANIELLE: Mr. Mitchell was there for all of us, not only as a Black male, but also a queer Black male for queer people, showing you not only that he could understand the life you're living, but how things can be better. That's the perspective he brought. He understood church culture, he understood Black culture, so that when we were met with challenges in our lives, he was able to say, "Look, I see you. I get it. This is what you can do." He was able to level with us in a way that I don't think anybody else would've been able to.

HANK: Corey pulled everybody into a room one day and said, "I want to speak to you and address you as a Black man addressing Black students." Those weren't his actual words, but that was the tone of what was about to happen. He looked at me and said, "Hank, you can sit in on this."

And then he addressed everybody about what it means to be a Black person telling the story; how it's not about that, it's about people. The fact that he allowed me in that space is something I cherish, because I don't think a lot of people who look like me have been able to experience these conversations and see the impact.

TAKING THE SHOW ON THE ROAD

COREY: The International Thespian Festival in Nebraska is like the Honor Society for theater kids. As the years went by, I never saw an all-Black show on the festival stage. My kids kept saying, "Mr. Mitchell, our shows are just as good. When can we bring a show to Festival?"

They select eight shows to showcase on their main stage each night, and not only did we get selected, we got unanimous "Superior" ratings. To get to Nebraska, the budget was about $135,000. I ended up raising $171,000.

MEKHAI: The festival was cool; everybody was there for the same reason. We were all high schoolers, and it was awesome to meet other arts-loving kids from all over the country. You go there to perform, but it's also how a lot of us heard about schools, specifically art schools. We had no idea.

We went to Northwest because it seemed more fun than going to our regular high school and better than doing the sports route. At Northwest, the musical theater kids were the popular kids, and if you booked a show, you were the star quarterback. We had been bitten by the theater bug but had no idea what happened after Northwest. Nebraska was an opportunity to see college as a reality. Meeting professors and college recruiters made the idea of going to school for theater tangible. I knew students older than me, students of color, who hadn't gone to school because they just had no idea.

Joneke Percentie (Nettie, center) talks to director Corey Mitchell and other cast members on set, Northwest School of the Arts, Charlotte, North Carolina, 2012

HANK: For me, the festival was eye-opening. People were wowed that I was in the show, and that would overshadow the amazing other performers. I mean, I danced in the background, and I had fun, but I was treated by other white people as the main event because it was so shocking, like, "Here's this white kid who's doing a Black show."

I was being treated like a freaking star, and at the time ate it up because I didn't understand what was going on. People were coming up to me and going, "Oh my God, you were this guy," and this was while I'm standing next to my castmates, and they're being cold-shouldered. When that happened, kids from my show weren't so mad at me as they were, like, "Again with this thing. You're getting the attention and the praise over us. It's our story, and yet here you go." Once I heard their perspective, I felt horrible that I didn't say anything.

and able to do it, they got pigeonholed, like, "Oh, you're going to be the Black character."

My experience at Northwest has stuck with me, and now that I do theater professionally, it affects how I move about. In the theater world, we're seeing more opportunities open up for people like my classmates, who were not able to get those opportunities solely because of the color of their skin. I'm learning how to navigate myself in a way that I'm making space for them. I'm not wearing it as a badge of honor, but I'm trying to have more perspective of how privileged I am as a white person in this industry, how much of a leg up I get because of that.

DANIELLE: *The Color Purple* sparked this curiosity in me to know more about myself. It sent me on this jour-

"*The Color Purple* sparked this curiosity in me to know more about myself."
—Danielle Hopkins

The cast was so talented; I'd never seen talent like that in my life. It's not like I was going to see a Broadway show; I was in one. It was incredible. Honestly, it's still one of the better shows I've ever done.

CARRYING IT FORWARD IN LIFE

MEKHAI: After high school, I went straight to college, to North Carolina School of the Arts. It was a straight acting program, and I had a great time there. After graduating in '18, my first job was *The Color Purple* tour, so that show seems to follow me.

HANK: The college I went to after high school was full of white kids who could do theater to their hearts' content. For the people I was exposed to at Northwest, it wasn't that easy. They had really tough battles that they fought outside of school, and even when they were supported

ney of, "I want anything that I believe in to be authentic and not just because someone said so." I related that to Shug. She grew up in the church and then left it and found herself, found her sexuality, found her power. It didn't come without its hardship, but it helped make her who she was.

HANK: Corey was very patient with me because I was a very misguided kid. I was getting in trouble and my grades sucked. But Corey made me care about what I was doing for the first time in my life. I've never had a teacher who expressed passion and understanding the way he did.

DANIELLE: The night of the Tony Awards, a lot of us gathered in Charlotte to watch the live stream. It was so validating of our experience as these poor kids in the middle of the hood in Charlotte who had produced something globally recognized. The Tonys were telling us that we really did have an incredible teacher. We really did have a special experience.

Nettie (Joneke Percentie) and Mister (Mekhai Lee), Northwest School of the Arts, Charlotte, North Carolina, 2012

VII
SPIRIT

Dear Nettie,
I don't write to God no more. I write to you.
What happen to God? ast Shug.
Who that? I say.
She look at me serious.
Big a devil as you is, I say, you not worried
bout no God, surely.
She say, Wait a minute. Hold on just a
minute here. Just because I don't harass
it like some peoples us know don't mean
I ain't got religion.
What God do for me? I ast.
She say, Celie! like she shock. He gave you
life, good health, and a good woman that
love you to death.

—from Alice Walker's
The Color Purple

Reverend Avery (David Alan Grier) and the choir, 2023 film

A PERSONAL PATH TO FAITH

SALAMISHAH TILLET (scholar, critic, and author of *In Search of The Color Purple: The Story of an American Masterpiece*): In terms of key themes in this story, Alice Walker would certainly identify spirituality and the relationship of Celie and this community to their natural surroundings. At one point, Walker said it was her most Buddhist novel, but at the core of this book is really Celie's relationship to God and her redefining her relationship to Christianity and to the divine in all things.

This book is sacrosanct to Black America, despite this dissonance between the moment of publication [in 1982] and when the movie came out [in 1985], and how we relate to *The Color Purple* now, whether it's through memes or GIFs or quotes. These characters of Celie and Nettie and Sofia are so loved by Black people.

It's fascinating that you have this novel in which Walker is critiquing Christianity both as a missionary presence in West Africa and also as an oppressive organized institution in the South for characters like Shug and Celie. But it's not an anti-Christian novel. It's a critique of Christianity as a way of showing that these characters are confined by these systems, and they need to redefine these systems in order to be free.

If you go to where Walker grew up, you can understand *The Color Purple*. You see the church, her family cemetery, and then down the street where she was born and raised. You see these beautiful trees and nature in full bloom. To me, that configuration means that even though she's critiquing Christianity, it's not an opposition. They're all part of the foundation of Celie's coming of age. And maybe Black people can understand the complexity of all that.

LACHANZE (Celie, 2005 Broadway musical): The novel was a part of my education in high school, and then I read it again as a woman in college. I remember being extremely connected to Celie because I, too, experienced childhood trauma, physical abuse. And I, too, witnessed a lot of physical abuse. Being the oldest of several children—and both my parents were teenagers, so they weren't really nurturing folks—I just identified with Celie's relationship to God, to being able to have someone to talk to other than people in her life, because I spent a lot of my childhood doing that. I didn't know who this external power was, but I spent a lot of my time talking to and trusting in this supreme companion.

KIMBERLEY RAMPERSAD (director, 2019 Canadian production, Neptune Theatre and Citadel Theatre/Royal Manitoba Theatre Centre): I grew up in this little suburb called North Kildonan in a city called Winnipeg in the province of Manitoba in Canada. It was a beautiful place to grow up. My parents immigrated to Canada in '69 from Trinidad and Tobago. My father is South Asian, my mom is African, and they raised our family there. It's a great community, but it's incredibly homogenous, and there weren't many people of the global majority there.

My first exposure to *The Color Purple* was Steven Spielberg's movie. I remember the first times I caught it on TV, it was always mid-story. I was always fascinated because there were people who looked like me telling this story. I was just like, "Oh, it's beautiful." The first time I caught it from beginning to end, I realized I'd had no idea what it was that I was dropping into intermittently. But for me, it's still that thing that anytime it's playing I will stop what I am doing, and I will watch it until the end. Wherever I drop in, I'm like, "Well, then, that's where we're meeting this story today."

It was the kind of piece that changed me, that made me feel more comfortable being who I am, that explained a little more about the mystical things that were inside of me that I couldn't quite get a grasp on. It helped me make sense of my world and my place in it, because somebody else was telling this story of another Black girl who grew into a Black woman who was trying to find her place in the world. There was something just so human about that.

Then I was introduced to the novel and especially to the way that Celie speaks to God and has such a conversation with God. I found that really beautiful, because as I struggled with my spirituality, I really thought that God was much more of that friend than something on a pedestal. To see this young character, to watch the letters be a conversation and watch it not be disrespectful, but a questioning relationship, a curious relationship, a really push-and-pull relationship with what the nature of God was, was just profound. I was like, "I think that's who God is to me."

MARCUS GARDLEY (screenwriter, 2023 film): I was sixteen when I read the novel. We weren't supposed to read it. In class, the teacher said it had too many adult themes. That's why I went and got it. I checked it out of the library and read it in one sitting, and it's been my favorite book of all time ever since.

"Celie was a woman who was placed on this earth by the creator, whatever people believe that is."

—Francine Jamison-Tanchuck

First of all, I was amazed by this idea of the structure of a protagonist writing diary entries to God. I thought that was so clever and interesting. Then, the more I read it, the more the book had this profound effect on me, because I started to realize that it wasn't always "Dear God" like "Dear John." It was "dear God" as in God is dear. Then, when the book tells you that God is not necessarily masculine or male, and that God is in nature, you really realize the power of God. It just opened my eyes.

I grew up in a very Christian, evangelical environment, Church of God in Christ. I'm a preacher's kid, and my mother has two brothers who are pastors. My father has a brother who's a pastor. Our cousins are all pastors. The family is very, very, very religious.

Once I read *The Color Purple*, I started to see the world in new ways. It felt like I was reading something that was found. Discovered. It felt like I was reading something I wasn't supposed to read. Well, I literally wasn't supposed to read it, but I mean more something that was found that had magic to it, somebody's secret diary. And yet it managed to tell you about continents. It managed to tell you about hundreds of years and generations of a family. Nothing's ever had that impact on me since.

BRENDA RUSSELL (music and lyrics, 2005 Broadway musical, 2015 Broadway revival, 2023 film): One of the messages in *The Color Purple* was that God is not necessarily some old white man in the sky. It could be an energy that's so huge that we can't even understand it. It's bigger than that, and that's a good message, along with Alice's message about the color purple—don't miss out on the beauty that's happening all around you. Open up your eyes and look at it.

I always say when I'm writing songs that my co-writer is God, because that's where all my inspiration comes from. I never feel alone. I even call on old masters who are no longer on the planet. I call on different people: Gershwin and Joe Sample, Al Jarreau. I say, "Come on, help me with this song."

FRANCINE JAMISON-TANCHUCK (costume supervisor, 1985 film; costume designer, 2023 film): I love how Alice Walker was able to take us into this journey of Celie and use those flowers in the field as a metaphor. I like how she put it that God gets pissed off if you go by the color purple and don't acknowledge it or admire it.

In many ways, that's what was happening with Celie. Celie was a woman who was placed on this earth by the creator, whatever people believe that is. She was meant to be loved and admired. Instead, she came across abuse and was trampled on, just like people trample through the field. This is why this story connects with so many people. Whether you are in the United States, Europe, Africa, wherever you are, young or old, whatever nationality, men or women, it doesn't matter. I have several friends in the gay community, and they just totally get it. For anyone who has experienced any type of meanness, which every last person has experienced, it just resonates. People know what that feels like. I think Alice Walker is trying to say, "This is what we are all on this earth for, people, to care for each other, to love and admire each other, and not to trample each other underfoot."

For me, other than the character arcs in this story, the most important thing outside of love and family is faith. The new movie starts with a church parade. There's this big boisterous number where they're walking, singing "Mysterious Ways." It's a celebration of faith, but also we have them walking through nature, and they don't even realize how in touch with nature they are. But nature is essential in this opening moment, responding to them and the joy they have about their faith and the joy they have for each other. It's interwoven throughout the film.

TIMOTHY DOUGLAS (director, 2018 Portland Center Stage, 2022 Signature Theatre in Arlington, Virginia, 2023 Denver Center productions): I read the book in

1983. I had just started graduate school. I was at Yale Drama School studying acting, and it was so intense. That was the book I picked up to take myself away from my studies. I was in my first semester, and the novel just did me in. The world that Alice Walker created was immediately familiar to me. I recognized the characters, the trauma, the resilience, the Blackness. I guess looking back now, I remember the feeling of it. I hadn't yet embarked on my spiritual journey, but there was something about Celie talking to God and telling God everything that sparked my willingness to lean in the direction of accepting, trusting in this higher power. Yeah, it did all of that.

As a director, I have the privilege of getting to interpret the story. And one of the things that was most important for me—that I feel is probably an impossible exercise, for me included, and which continues to trouble me about the movie and every stage version I've seen—is this: That book had such an impact. But the instant you change the medium, the challenge for the director is enormous. And the more I work on the stage version, I realize it is the intimacy and the power of Celie speaking to God. For me, it was most important to get back to the center of that intimacy, so that was my instruction to the creative team. That was going to influence everything that I did in the name of staging. In the most basic sense, keeping Celie at the center. The actor playing Celie rarely leaves the stage in my production, and that presence—really leaning into the several times that Celie actually utters the words "Dear God"—I really make a moment of that for those in the audience who know the book to remind them, and for those who don't know the book to subliminally keep putting Celie at the center with her conversation with God.

GARY GRIFFIN (director, 2005 Broadway musical): In preparing to direct the show, I went to a lot of churches, because I was interested in the theatricality of the Black church. When I attended the churches, there was this celebration and freedom. I think both things applied in the story. The show needed to start in the church. It needed to reflect the church as essential to the way of life.

Nettie (Akosua Busia) and Young Celie (Desreta Jackson) among the iconic purple flowers, 1985 film

The church ladies (including First Lady, center, played by Tamela Mann) sing "Mysterious Ways," 2023 film

Celie (Felicia Boswell), Portland Center
Stage, Portland, Oregon, 2018

Shug (Margaret Avery) leads a crowd from the Juke Joint to her father's church, 1985 film

MARCUS GARDLEY: One of the things I was really adamant about—and I know that they thought I'm coming from this point of view because I'm a preacher's kid—but I was like, "How do you track faith through the whole show?" You start with this church, and then you arrive with these two girls, and one girl is briefly talking about faith a little bit with her sister, but there is some knowledge that one of the babies has gone to a minister and his wife.

Then she loses her sister, and in that moment she questions God. She doesn't talk to any other characters. She talks directly to God. She says, "God, why?" And then when she has her other spiritual awakening—that moment when Shug tells her that God is in everything, and essentially God is in you—that's when you see the first fleck of Celie coming into her own. So this story is very much about a person coming into their faith.

ALICE WALKER (author of *The Color Purple*, 1982): Shug is bringing a new gospel, and we definitely need one. People get so beaten down by the religion that's basically forced on them as babies. They grew up in it and they think, "OK, this is true," but they can't quite see that there's a whole other way of relating to the divinity of the natural life. Shug does this; she has a whole religion.

TARAJI P. HENSON (Shug, 2023 film): What I love about Shug is her attitude of, "You don't get to tell me what a Christian looks like or what a woman of God looks like." Because that woman, she preached. She preached. And she was the daughter of a preacher. God is in her. It may not look like what you want it to look like, but it's God nonetheless. In my opinion, God is love. That is the gift that he gave us. And it is absolutely free. So to call yourself a Christian if you're not tapped into that kind of love, watch your tongue. Because God's love is blind. It's unconditional. So, that's what made Shug. Even though everyone in town considered her to be the bottom of the barrel, I felt like she was kind of angelic.

It was angelic, the timing of when she would come in and out of town. It was like she was tapped in beyond what you could see. She was a preacher because she had fallen. Something about Shug wanted to save. Once you save yourself, almost like once you beat an addiction, you want to go and help other people. Yes, she had an odd way of doing it. She was very sexual. But even in that sexuality, that's just the way she knew nurturing. I likened her a little bit to [my character] Shug from *Hustle & Flow*, another woman who used sexuality. It's interesting that they're both named Shug.

"My favorite section of this book to record was a letter in the book where Celie is shunning God. She's been writing letters to God for pretty much this whole book, and she gets to a point where she feels that she's been hoodwinked. She's questioning God's existence, questioning how much God cares about her. She has a conversation with a woman named Shug, who she is deeply in love with, in more ways than one. Shug challenges Celie to think about God in a very different way, and to think about God as not external, but internal. That is a real turning point in the book for Celie, and in my own relationship with whatever God is."

— **SAMIRA WILEY**
Actress and narrator of the 2020 audiobook
version of *The Color Purple*

From the video "Behind the Scenes with Samira Wiley, Narrator of *The Color Purple*" by Audible, 2020

Celie (Fantasia Barrino) and
Shug (Taraji P. Henson), 2023 film

Sexuality is Shug Avery's love language. Unfortunately, trauma drove her there, probably molestation. But that's where she is with it. Now, she could have chosen a dark path with her sensuality, but she didn't. This woman is trying to make it work the best way she can out of the trauma that has been handed down to her. Some people call it flawed. But she could have been a murderer. She could have turned around and become a molester. There are different ways to do it. But that just happened to be her love language, and she didn't apologize for it.

OPRAH WINFREY (Sofia, 1985 film; producer, 2005 Broadway musical, 2015 Broadway revival, 2023 film): There's an energy connected to what Alice first intended. When intention and energy combine, and then you have all of that ancestral stuff mixed in there, it's a holy moment for everybody involved.

FINDING COURAGE

OPRAH WINFREY: The ultimate question that *The Color Purple* answers for everybody, for every woman in particular, that everybody has within themselves is: "Am I enough?" *The Color Purple* fulfills the answer that yes, you are enough. It's the reason why it will go on and it will go on and it will go on. We have this new musical film iteration of it, and it will continue either in this form or another form. The story continues to live in the hearts of generations because it fulfills the answer that, number one, you're enough. Number two, you're still here. You survived all that you've faced because you are enough, and you're still here. If you peel back the layers of everybody's therapy, that's what they're in therapy to figure out: "Am I enough?"

Celie (Whoopi Goldberg), 1985 film

> # "When intention and energy combine, and then you have all of that ancestral stuff mixed in there, it's a holy movement for everybody involved."
> ## —*Oprah Winfrey*

LACHANZE: My training has always been to start from the outside in when it comes to age on stage, because age shows up not only in your knowledge and your experience on the planet, but also in your body. The wariness, the fatigue, the inability to walk and do all the things that you used to do easily. And so I started my aging process with every trauma that I experienced as Celie. Each trauma bent my back just a little bit more and lowered my voice and got me to be a little bit more afraid of those around me. It's just like when you see an abused person or an abused animal—they're sort of in themselves because they're in a protective state. So I worked outside in physically. In terms of the acting journey from teen all the way up to sixty, internally I was mostly thinking about my relationship with God and the maturity of that, because that was Celie's focus.

Internally, I would work on how that relationship would've grown. In the beginning, my conversations with God were very innocent, nuanced, young. But by the time I got older, God had been with me for so many years that I felt more of a familiarity in that way you do as you age. You know how it's said that if you don't learn a lesson, it'll just get louder until you learn it? I think that's what was happening with Celie. She didn't learn that no one's going to love you like yourself until much later in life. When she did, everything locked in. Her spine, her chest, her heart, her mind, her spirit.

Everything opened up. I think that was the point that Alice Walker was trying to illustrate: that you're going to keep getting beaten down until you stand up.

FANTASIA BARRINO (Celie, 2005 Broadway musical, 2023 film): Celie didn't really believe in God at a certain point because everything, including her children, was being taken away from her. Then Nettie. So it's almost like, "What is this God I keep hearing y'all talk about? Because from how y'all speak of Him, it's not supposed to be this hard. It's not supposed to go like this. I don't see any light. All I see is dark. I want no part of it."

As Celie gets older, she starts to realize that all those things that are happening in her life are necessary things, and we don't always like how things go. When we want something, we want it. My husband always says, "Patience is what you do when you wait." But we live in a world where everything is microwavable. We want a quick relationship, a quick business—we want it quick, right?

But how does that word *faith* even come about? When you want something or you can't see something, you've got to have faith the size of a mustard seed—just the size of a mustard seed. You've got to hold onto that in order for God to say, "See, now I can show you some things. You stood, you believed, you didn't give up, you didn't give in."

Celie (LaChanze), The Broadway Theatre, New York, 2005

THE
CURSE

Any more letters come? I ast.
He say, What?
You heard me, I say.
Any more letters from Nettie come?
If they did, he say, I wouldn't give 'em to you.
You two of a kind, he say. A man try to
be nice to you, you fly in his face.
I curse you, I say.
What that mean? he say.
I say, Until you do right by me,
everything you touch will crumble.
He laugh. Who you think you is? he say.
You can't curse nobody. Look at you.
You black, you pore, you ugly, you a woman.
Goddam, he say, you nothing at all.
Until you do right by me, I say,
everything you even dream about will fail.
I give it to him straight, just like it come to me.
And it seem to come to me from the trees.

—from Alice Walker's *The Color Purple*

1. Fantasia Barrino, Warner Bros. Feature Film, 2023
2. Cynthia Erivo, Bernard B. Jacobs Theatre, New York, 2015
3. Didintle Khunou, Joburg Theatre, South Africa, 2018
4. Jessica M. Johnson, Theatre Horizon, Norristown, Pennsylvania, 2018
5. Keston Steele, Northwest School of the Arts, Charlotte, North Carolina, 2012
6. Mariah Lyttle, U.S. National Tour, 2020

1

2

3

4

5

6

That's what my life has been like since I was a kid. You're going to go through some things and you're going to have those moments of, "This can't be God, this just can't." But in the end of the new film, when Celie sits at that round table and she looks and sees all these generations, she looks and sees Mister, she sees Shug—trust me, she remembers all these stories like they were yesterday—and it's, "Look what God has done."

All of that stuff is necessary. We won't have testimonies if we don't go through tests. So this whole story is just a big testimony of all the tests that she went through. Everybody in the Bible, everyone who was called, all were tested. Celie was not perfect. She didn't look quite like

get through anything if this woman Celie can. That's what it says. This story is about the triumph, not only of Celie and the human spirit, but about Black people in America, knowing that we were given the scraps and we've made magic. That we're still here, that we still love, that we still laugh, that we create culture from nothing.

TARAJI P. HENSON: Scraps? Pig feet! Chitlins! Whenever they say, "Did you know a Black person invented that?" I go, "I know." Because we didn't have anything. So we had to get creative. We took care of everybody. When it was time to do and make and think, it was: "What can help me get through this fast so I

"Celie was not perfect. She didn't look quite like Nettie, she wasn't glamorous, but she was special to God."
—Fantasia Barrino

Nettie, she wasn't glamorous, but she was special to God. And He called her for such a time as this, and she was able to pull every last person in the end back together and build a community and build a family. And that's what God looks like in the end, if you just stand still. And that's what Celie did.

COLMAN DOMINGO (Mister, 2023 film): This book tells people that you, wherever you are, if you feel marginalized in any way, with fortitude you can overcome. You can create out of nothing. Look at us, at Black people. We've done it for generations upon generations. We continue to do so, through such immeasurable hardship. That's why people always go to this book. When you discover the book, discover the film, discover the musical, it speaks to something inside of every human being.

The world gave Celie rough times, and she still survived. She was a devout believer in God, or whatever people want to call it: Buddha, magic, whatever. She's still a deep, faithful believer. She's still trying. So you can

can go home and be with my kids?" Especially if it's anything domestic, I will put all my money that a Black person invented it. We had to invent everything.

BRANDON VICTOR DIXON (Harpo, 2005 Broadway musical): I think the story has become more relevant to the mainstream as time has gone on: the nature of the relationships Celie has and figuring out who she is and where she is in the world. Those conversations—that kind of examination of a girl coming of age in the world—have been given a lot more space to come forward in the last ten, fifteen, twenty years, which is a good thing.

COREY HAWKINS (Harpo, 2023 film): Danielle [Brooks] and I were at Juilliard together, along with Joaquina Kalukango [who played Nettie in the 2015 Broadway revival] and two other brothers, so we were five Black people in that class out of eighteen, which was a lot, actually, for Juilliard. I remember in our singing class with Deb Lapidus, we would sing *The Color Purple*. We would

Celie (Fantasia Barrino) celebrates after being reunited with her famiily, 2023 film

sing these songs. We would talk about "I'm Here," and for me, back then, it was like we were breaking through these walls. By all accounts in our lives, and the things that we'd made it through, we should not be here right now. But we were here, we were beautiful, we were Black. "I may be poor"—we was poor —"I may be Black, I may be ugly, but I'm here." I'm here. And we celebrated that. This music kept us going while we were in school because we were dreaming of what would come after, where our careers were going to go. It was all this possibility. So *The Color Purple* was part of the formative years of our lives.

Did the artists who made *The Color Purple* know that they'd be planting the seeds for young Corey Hawkins, young Danielle Brooks, and young Joaquina Kalukango, who played Nettie with Danielle? And now Danielle and I get to play Harpo and Sofia.

BERNARD JAY (producer, 2018 South African production): Producing the musical *The Color Purple* in South Africa in 2018 was a highlight of my sixty-year career as a theater producer. I was fortunate enough to hold the position of chief executive officer at Joburg Theatre, previously known as the Johannesburg Civic Theatre, from 2000 to 2014. Part of my responsibility as CEO in this period was to identify, negotiate the rights for, and then executive produce non-replica, original stage productions of major Broadway and/or West End musicals. The most important aspect of my job, however, was to gradually find ways of building a new theater audience from the Black communities of South Africa—communities previously denied the possibilities of such by the apartheid government.

With this challenge in mind, I had been eager to stage the musical *The Color Purple* since its Broadway debut in 2005, believing that the classic Alice Walker story now musicalized for new generations would attract a crossover audience in South Africa, both white and Black. However, with its large cast and orchestra, it would not have been financially viable. The scaled-down London Menier theater production in 2013—followed by the Broadway revival in 2015—opened the doors for a run at Joburg Theatre. By this time, I was serving as an independent theater producer and partnered with Joburg Theatre for the production.

Our production coincided beautifully with the rise and global importance of the #MeToo movement, when victims of sexual harassment and assault were urged to share their stories on social media. Gender-based violence is an epidemic of frightening proportions in South Africa, an infamously patriarchal society. With its overarching message of female independence and empowerment, *The Color Purple* on stage lit a spark of release for many South African women long suffering from male dominance and abuse. The #MeToo movement was the facilitator, the instigator: *The Color Purple* provided for our audiences a participatory method of self-identification.

At every single performance, without fail, women in the audience would stand with Sofia's insistent "Hell No!" and with Celie's declamatory "I'm Here," arms raised

Celie (Didintle Khunou), Joburg Theatre, South Africa, 2018

Purple Rising

and fists pumped, screaming back at the actor with "I'm with you there, sister," or a similarly supportive outburst. What was even more wonderful, though, was to watch the women's male partners gradually rise with them and join in the celebratory moment. Blacks and whites together. Females and males together. In one with Alice Walker, with Sofia and Celie. With female empowerment. How joyous was that experience?

REDEMPTION AND FORGIVENESS

KIMBERLEY RAMPERSAD: The redemption of Mister is there, but it's not easy. Yes, he has done the right thing at the end. Yes, he can be a part of the community, but don't put a tie or bow on it. People see what you are. We can coexist now, but sir, you will have to stand in your truth. And your truth leaves you alone still. Yes, you're in our community, but you're still isolated because you have to make peace with it. He hasn't let himself off the hook even though he's done this good thing. And that's what I wanted people to feel at the end of the show, to see him still have to do work and imagine what happens when that curtain comes down, or the work that he will die with because there hasn't been enough time.

COLMAN DOMINGO: What resonates to me the most about *The Color Purple* is the power of redemption, of love, of grace. Having grace for even those who abused you. I think if Alice Walker was writing about anything, she's writing about love, and what love is, and what God's love is, and the power of that.

SALAMISHAH TILLET: Something about the #MeToo era created a different lens for me. For my book, I interviewed people in high school who were reading *The Color Purple* at the same age as I had. This was maybe in 2019, right after #MeToo came to the fore. One girl said to me, "Mister is such an interesting character—his redemption and his atonement." In the early phase of #MeToo, there were a lot of attempts to hold people accountable outside of the law, in their workspace or in the court of public opinion or on social media.

What do we do with a figure like Mister? Well, there's a restorative justice model, and Mister isn't exiled from the community. That was really important for Alice with the musical, for him to remain part of the community, as opposed to the [1985] movie, where he watches the reunion of Celie and her sister and her children from afar.

What I find interesting about Mister is that he really wanted redemption. You can see in real time as you're watching the play or you're reading the novel, and somewhat in the 1985 movie, this character who has to acknowledge his harm and then go through really important steps to redress the harm that he has caused Celie and, to a certain degree, Harpo. That's such a remarkable figure. You actually don't see that path within a lot of stories. He's an elusive figure in terms of a character who's caused so much violence in his home. So I find him to be remarkable as part of Alice's imagination, because [Mister] is based on her grandfather, and her grandfather did not necessarily have that redemptive arc with his wife. So he's a complete figure of fiction. His ending, anyway, is all [Alice's] imagination.

HALLE BAILEY (Young Nettie, 2023 film): The hopefulness in this story was something that shocked me. Celie has so much trauma, but the fact that she's able to get through that and forgive Mister and forgive Alfonso and move on with her life, it's like, "How?" That's so much strength.

STEPHEN BRAY (music and lyrics, 2005 Broadway musical, 2015 Broadway revival, 2023 film): This story says to people that anything is possible. No matter what you may have encountered or done, or what has been done to you, there's a way through it and out of it. It is a statement of an unlimited capacity for love and forgiveness. That's what I think. But then, I like Frank Capra movies.

> "The hopefulness in this story was something that shocked me."
> —*Halle Bailey*

THE COLOR PURPLE (REPRISE)

[Celie]
Dear God
Dear stars
Dear trees
Dear sky
Dear people
Dear everything
Dear God

God is inside me and everyone else
That was or ever will be
I came into this world with God
And when I finally looked inside I found it
Just as close as my breath is to me

[Celie, Nettie, Sofia]
Rising

[Adam and Olivia]
Rising

[Shug and Mister]
Rising

[Ensemble]
Like the sun
Is the hope that sets us free

[Celie]
Your heartbeat make my heartbeat

Celie's family gathers under the branches
of a centuries-old oak tree, 2023 film

[Ensemble]
When we share love

Like a blade of corn like a honeybee
Like a waterfall all a part of me
Like the color purple, where do it come from
Now my eyes are open look what God has done

It takes a grain of love to make a mighty tree
Even the smallest voice can make a harmony
Like a drop of water keep the river high
There are miracles for you and I

Like a blade of corn like a honeybee
Like a waterfall all a part of me
Like the color purple where do it come from
Now my eyes are open look what God has done

[Celie]
I don't think us feel old at all
I think this is the youngest us ever felt

[Ensemble]
Amen!

Mister (Colman Domingo) embraces
Celie (Fantasia Barrino), 2023 film

BLITZ BAZAWULE (director, 2023 film): Coming into this film, there was that baggage of Black men feeling vilified, specifically by the Spielberg version, and having reservations about it. I didn't make choices in response to any of that. I was working in response to my lived experience as a Black man on this planet. That's all. There is no one-dimensional Black man. It doesn't exist. There are people who feel life has cheated them out of opportunities, and they lash out at the world. They're in everybody's family; we know this character.

One thing about our film is that everybody is fallible, even Celie. When we end up at that table in the final scene and everybody's together, we are not looking at a picture of perfection. It's people who have accepted each other as flawed beings and are willing to be forgiving of each other. Sofia forgives Celie. Celie forgives Mister. I've always said that this film is about radical forgiveness. It is a core tenet that I really believe exists deeply, specifically in the African American community, based on what they've endured in this country, and the fact that the country is still standing. They would be justified in exacting a similar or worse abuse than they have endured in this country, but they've chosen love, empathy and forgiveness, radical forgiveness, and all that is asked is accountability—and accountability is the reason people are still protesting in the streets. [The movie] is a microcosm of the larger existence of Black people in this country. All they ask is for you to take responsibility and be accountable for what was done. And until that day, there's going to be a reason to be in the streets.

SCOTT SANDERS (producer, 2005 Broadway musical, 2015 Broadway revival, 2023 film): Making a movie in 2022 gave us the opportunity to revisit the character arcs in this film and to think about how we could make this story continue to feel relevant. Were there any nuances to the storytelling that we wanted to give a different level of emphasis? Clearly, forgiveness is a very important theme in Alice's book, and probably the most talked-about character in relation to forgiveness is Mister. And then part of Celie's growth as a human being, as a woman, is finding her own full self-love, but also her ability not to be a victim. We see Celie being incredibly generous and kind and compassionate, particularly to Sofia when she's put in prison. Many of us look at Shug Avery as the person who opens up Celie's heart. But it was reciprocal. In Shug Avery you have

someone who also had a hole in her heart that Celie was able to fill. In addition, Celie's generosity and compassion toward Harpo helped him grow into the man that he became, which was a very different man than his father and grandfather. All of these themes and character arcs intertwine.

We watched Celie grow to the point where she found compassion for herself as well as for others, and then ultimately found forgiveness for Mister. We really wanted to explore how she is able to rise above everything at the end of the story and realize that people are complicated, families are complicated, relationships are complicated, and how it is that she finds peace in her own spirit.

EVELYN C. WHITE (journalist and author of *Alice Walker: A Life*): I think Alice is able to lift up people out of pain, anguish, and despair because she's done it in her own life. The cosmic forces around her have given her faith that people can get better, that things can get better. She's very, very blunt and focused on the fact that we're in a horrible situation, but she has infinite belief in the power of human beings to be better. The book conveys this notion of transforming pain and hurt into understanding and forgiveness. I think that Alice has had a very pained life in many regards, but she has always, in my experience, been able to transform the anguish and the abuse into healing and self-love and forgiveness.

In the novel, Mister is transformed. That concept—that people can move toward their best self—is very much a part of Alice Walker's personal and professional lives, if you look deeply at her work. And Alice apologizes. She has forgiven people. You read her journals, and there's the pain, but eventually, she will bring people back in. She will say, "I'm sorry" to people. She has these reconciliations.

She is always about possibilities, which is why, in my view, we are forty years later still having another iteration of *The Color Purple*. I think cynics would probably say, "Oh, it's all about money." But I think Alice has wanted to give this work of hers the fullest life and breath possible. She said somewhere recently, "I took care of them," meaning the characters in *The Color Purple*, which we know are directly related to real-life people in her family. She said, "I took care of them, and they have taken care of me."

A WAY FORWARD

Actress Gabrielle Union and scholar, critic, and author Salamishah
Tillet both model fierce courage as outspoken survivors of sexual assault.
They work to bring the experience of survivors out of the shadows,
and for both women, *The Color Purple* was instrumental in their healing.
They speak with each other here for the first time.

Gabrielle Union, 2018

Salamishah Tillet, 2013

SALAMISHAH TILLET: I'm a big fan of yours and also a fellow sexual assault survivor. I started an organization with my sister that's based in Chicago called The Long Walk Home. She documented my healing process for ten years, and then we turned it into this nonprofit where we empower young, mostly Black girls and gender-expansive youth to use art to end violence against girls and women. Maybe we could start with when we first encountered *The Color Purple*, whether it was a film or book?

GABRIELLE UNION: I encountered the film first. Seventh grade—1986. My mom took us to a theater a few towns over, because where we lived, there were no Black people and they refused to show Black movies out of a fear of what might happen if the Blacks gathered.

I could literally go frame by frame of everything that landed. When Shug says, "You sho is ugly," I felt that because that was my inner dialogue moving through life as The Black in Pleasanton, California, constantly feeling like that's how I was being received.

God, there were so many moments. It was one of my first times really seeing chocolate girls and being so struck by the beauty of their sisterhood. And then there was that moment when Sofia makes the decision to fight back, that point where she was like, "Fuck it." Even at twelve or thirteen, I recognized the constraint of always flying under the radar. But it took me a long time to understand why I felt such joy when Oprah's character finally fought back. At the end, when Celie's wearing pants, I thought about what it is to be free. What is it to be a free Black girl? A free Black person? A lot of things came together sitting in that movie theater.

To say I felt seen by this work feels basic. I felt understood on a level that it is hard to articulate in the moment when, as a survivor, you're trying to put words to your trauma and your pain. Somebody got me and reached inside of my body and could feel the terror and put words to the terror, put words to the confusion. Time does a lot of shit, but it never goes away. It's those moments when you don't acknowledge that it kicks your ass. And with *The Color Purple*, they always acknowledge it.

SALAMISHAH: I read the book first when I was fifteen years old. It was the summer of 1991, and I went to this independent school in New Jersey where I was one of three Black kids in my grade. I visited my dad and his family for the summer in Boston, where I think my older cousin's girlfriend thought of me as a confused Black child who needed some guidance. She gave me three books to read that summer: Toni Morrison's *The Bluest Eye*, Malcolm X's autobiography, and Alice Walker's *The Color Purple*. These books helped me start developing a Black feminist consciousness, but I remember falling in love with the novel and with Celie in particular, probably because of how vividly Alice was able to capture her voice and her story. I also identified with this Black girl who, like you, Gab, was an outsider. I, too, was a Black girl in a private school who didn't fit the standard of beauty that was valued and overly desired. I always felt there was something wrong with my skin and my hair. I identified with Celie feeling unloved and underappreciated.

I wasn't reading this for class, and I wasn't talking about it with anyone, so it was a very pleasurable private experience. That fall when I went back to school, the nation exploded with Anita Hill coming forward with her testimony of sexual harassment allegations against Clarence Thomas. For me, *The Color Purple* and *The Bluest Eye* helped me understand what was happening with Anita Hill—the pushback that Anita Hill was experiencing from the country, but also from Black people.

Then I went to the University of Pennsylvania. I was sexually assaulted twice in college. The first year, first semester, I was sexually assaulted by an African American man who was in a fraternity and was a senior. And that created a different relationship to the novel, because now I am not only identifying with Celie as someone who's feeling unloved and underappreciated, but also I'm identifying with Celie as a survivor. I think my need to constantly go back to the book since then comes from this place of championing her journey as a way of celebrating all our journeys as survivors, but also willing my own survival into existence.

After I experienced sexual assault my first semester, I told few people. And then I was in a class on Blacks and film and television and we watched *The Color Purple*. We got into this heated debate about whether this is a movie that reinforces stereotypes about Black men as being hyper-violent or whether this is a film that liberates Black women. It was 1993, and we were still repeating the debates that Alice Walker herself experienced when the film came out in 1985. It was intense. I remember trying to defend the film and watching other people say that the way that Pa [Alfonso] and Mister are represented is offensive, that it's feeding into white stereotypes about Black people. And I'm still dealing with my own experiences on a predominantly white campus being sexually assaulted by a Black man. All of that made my relationship to the book, and now the movie, even stronger, me seeing myself even more in Celie's story.

GABRIELLE: There's the before—who you were before being assaulted—and then who you are after. And how your reception of the film and the book changes. Years ago, my professor of African American Studies at UCLA told us to reread *The Autobiography of Malcolm X* every year—that we'd be surprised by what we relate to as we evolved over time. That has been dead-ass. Every year I reread it.

SALAMISHAH: That's so interesting. I haven't gone back to it since I first read it.

GABRIELLE: There's something else, *always*. I read *The Color Purple* as a survivor. I'd been a survivor at that point, maybe fifteen, twenty years, and it made me think about everything we do to excuse the very real behavior of some Black men.

I remember when the police showed up after I was raped, feeling hesitant about saying it was a Black man. When he first walked in the store where I was working, everything in my body said to run out the back. But because he was Black and my coworker was white, I didn't want to lean into the negative stereotypes about Black men, so I stayed. Then when I'm telling the police, there's that moment of, "Do I protect this man?" Because we're so conditioned to it.

We can't even honestly and openly discuss this text without that acknowledgment that this is true for many people. Not true for all, that would be ridiculous, but it's one fucking movie. It's one book. It shouldn't have that responsibility.

I'm glad you brought up Anita Hill, because there was this Black man [Clarence Thomas] who had finally made it. Even though he has not ever been for us, there was this sense of, "We need to protect him and she needs to stand down with all those pesky abuse allegations. How dare she besmirch this Black man?" We're never able to fully own our own pain, nor dare ask for justice.

I was raped at my job at gunpoint by a stranger and they still asked what I had on. They make you complicit in your own abuse and completely decenter you from your narrative. That's *The Color Purple*. Never getting to own any part of that.

I loved how you coupled it with the other books, because I think there's just a point when some lovely person will give a young Black woman *Tar Baby*, *The Bluest Eye*, *Sula*, *The Color Purple*—these gifts where they're like, "You've suffered enough, girl, here you go." And it's interesting the before and after—how you receive the words and the visuals once you intimately understand her pain.

SALAMISHAH: I kept on coming back to it as a reader, as a young person, as a teacher. One of the best experiences I've had teaching the film was in my early twenties. I was teaching at a school for adjudicated youth. Instead of being incarcerated, these young people, predominantly Black and brown boys, would opt to go to the school run by the Archdiocese. There were two films they knew all the words to: *Belly* and *The Color Purple*.

I was amazed to see these teenage Black boys knowing the words to *The Color Purple*. I remember one of them had a tear in his eye with Nettie and Celie's [separation] scene. For me, that was a really important moment, because as a feminist and as a Black woman and as a teacher, I realized, "Oh, they're identifying with Celie." It's not just me, but Black people who've experienced trauma—there's something about this story that taps into that. Black women can be the way in for all Black people to understand the stuff we experience in this country.

I interviewed Quincy Jones and Danny Glover because we associate Spielberg with the movie, but I wondered, "Why did these Black men choose to do this?" Quincy Jones did so much to make this movie possible. He found the director, he became a producer for the first time, he did the score. His love of this story is partly why it became the film that we saw. That was interesting to me, these Black men at the time who loved *The Color Purple* and wanted to give it a different life. Danny Glover is from Northern California but would spend the summers in Georgia with his grandparents. He saw his grandmother in Celie's story. He was committed to doing this because it was a story that he felt was important. I'm always wanting to convert people to the cause of Black feminism, so I'm asking, "Who are the Black men who actually understood the value of the story that Alice Walker was giving us?"

Now, we obviously have reached a different moment where we have a Black man directing the film. Now, young people would probably find it less controversial, the depictions of sexual violence and domestic violence and then this love between Shug and Celie. That combination was such a catastrophic thing for so many people initially. Alice Walker got attacked for it, but decades later, our relationship to it is so different as a country and as a people. Now it feels like, "Oh, of course that's normal, and of course that love is healthy." So it's an interesting evolution of a story, too.

I always thought Black people loved *The Color Purple*, but when I was doing my book tour, I saw that, "OK, if you go to a Black household, it's Jesus, Obama, and Martin Luther King, and then the Bible, and then there's *The Color Purple*." I think that's amazing.

I'm curious, Gab, why you think there's something about it for Black people that feels as though it's our kin?

GABRIELLE: Because we live it. When you look at the totality of Black life, it is familiar. As much as we like to reject certain darker parts of ourselves and our personal histories, it's true that every part of it happens and has happened in every family at some point. It feels personal, it feels familiar. It's something we can own. Many of us have owned it the whole time, and there are others who were slower to say, "This is mine, and I'm OK with that. It is in no way an indictment of me." People reveal so much by their reactions; hit dogs straight up hollering.

As more men become more evolved, they can separate and acknowledge poor behavior and not internalize it, or perhaps sit within their own bad behavior without projecting. Our community is evolving. There's also so much more content. This isn't our one story anymore.

SALAMISHAH: Most of the criticism back then came from Black men. Not to say there weren't Black women who were anti–*Color Purple*. But it's an interesting divide that Black women who saw themselves in this story the way you and I did were really trying to push back against the loud criticism. So much of who represented Black people on television were Black men. There's a famous video of Louis Farrakhan doing a whole seminar. He has a blackboard and everything, and he is schooling people on why this is a problematic movie. What's interesting, though, is it was not the incest that clearly is acknowledged as a problem. It was Steven Spielberg, and Shug and Celie's relationship.

Our generation has had our own versions of these controversies, whether with Anita Hill and Clarence Thomas or now with Megan Thee Stallion. There's an ongoing inability to believe Black women's stories when

Anita Hill testifies before the United States Senate Judiciary Committee on the Supreme Court confirmation of Clarence Thomas, 1991

they say that they've been hurt by people who look like us. In my case, I was sexually assaulted my freshman year in college. Then I went on a study abroad program to Kenya, and one of the weirdest things that happened was on the border of Tanzania and Kenya. These Kenyan men were talking to me and asked, "Do you believe Desiree Washington?" [Washington's rape accusation against boxer Mike Tyson resulted in the heavyweight champion's conviction and prison sentence.] I'm millions of miles away from the United States, and this is the question they're asking me as an African American woman.

Speed up to my actual really brutal experience with sexual assault there. I'm in a room, and I'm trapped by this Kenyan man, and I flash back to, "Oh, this is how Desiree Washington must have felt." There are these national crises in which people are forced to choose between race and gender, and then there also are private ways in which we're told we've got to pick one, and we suffer as a result. Literally, you and I have suffered as a result of the violence that people have enacted on us.

GABRIELLE: It's as if we've decided that collateral damage is reasonable as long as we do not speak ill of Black men, certainly not in a way that white people can hear or see. Those cases that made the news just show the enormity of what a girl like Celie is up against. She's chocolate, she has heavy trauma, she's in poverty. The only person who gave her an ounce of

Shug Kisses Celie by Mickalene Thomas. Silkscreen, ink, and acrylic on acrylic mirror mounted on wood panel, 2016

anything—kindness, grace, compassion, love—was Shug. In the book, it's clear there is a mutual, consensual love and passion and desire between the women. It's mutual, whereas in the [1985] movie, what should have been a beautiful queer love story is conflated and vague.

SALAMISHAH: Alice writes in her journal about that love story falling under the censor's knife. When she sees that kiss between Celie and Shug, it seems like a response to the controversy and the campaigns when they flatten Shug and Celie's relationship to that moment. The song "Sister" does more than the kiss does. But what was exciting for me in looking at how *The Color Purple* has shaped so many people's lives, I think of the artist Mickalene Thomas, who has a series on Celie. Like you, Mickalene went to see the movie with her mom, who was in a very violent, abusive relationship. The young Mickalene Thomas sees in that kiss possibilities of who she is. As young girls, you and I are identifying with Celie, and Mickalene is looking at Shug and Celie's relationship as a path forward. So even with the censor's knife, it's still doing the work it's supposed to be doing. There's something about these characters and the way they defy the genre that they're in—whether it's the novel or the film or the stage and now the screen again—they just are so vibrant, so beautiful, so full that even when they're being contained, they can't be fully contained. I just love that about these characters.

The book is healing, and the world is a different place. We're in the midst of #MeToo. I was interviewing young people, and a high school student said to me, "Mister really wants to be forgiven." That's such a hard conversation to have in this moment when we're trying to hold people accountable, because a lot of the people we're trying to hold accountable don't want to be held accountable. Right after the whole insurrection debacle

Celie (Naomi Van Der Linden) and Shug (Ana Milva Gomes) kiss, NDSM Wharf, the Netherlands, 2018

on January 6th [2021], I wrote a piece about how there were quick demands for forgiving those people. How was that possible? How could we go from people lying about an election, taking over the Capitol, and trying to lynch the vice president to thinking that they should be forgiven?

I wanted to reflect on Mister, and I thought: It's not that they forgive Mister easily, it's that he goes through a whole process of trying to be held accountable for his bad actions. I wrote about how the people who raped me have not asked for my forgiveness. I long for that as a rape survivor, but that's something that I have to take out of my realm of possibility.

As a figure who can represent a way forward, I think Alice was ahead of her time with Shug and Celie, and she was definitely ahead of her time with Celie. The times have kind of caught up with those characters. But with Mister, we still don't see people trying to redeem themselves in public. We see people saying that they haven't done this bad thing, or we see people being removed from their posts. We haven't seen lots of people have the courage, the desire, or the fortitude to say, "I've done this wrong, and here's how I want to repair that." So I think it's still very much a wish fulfillment in the way he tries to rejoin the community. As much as we see Celie's growth, there is this other character who's also growing in the novel, which goes back to Alice's deep capacity to forgive her characters.

> ## "The young Mickalene Thomas sees in that kiss the possibilities of who she is."
> —*Salamishah Tillet*

> # "Recently, I've been thinking about who has the luxury of being dysfunctional and who has the luxury of forgiveness. It's rarely Black women, certainly not publicly."
> ## —Gabrielle Union

GABRIELLE: When you're on the other side and you're on the receiving end, it never feels tidy. It always feels like it's our job to make our abusers more comfortable and to grease the wheels of return. You just forgive, you forgive, you forgive. As long as they come home, you forget whatever it is. Then I was like, "Or no. I want something akin to truth and reconciliation. I need you to acknowledge all of it and to truly understand the gravity of your actions and the lifetime sentence you gave me." I need that, and that never happens for us.

The idea that we would want that is seen as absurd, and that's why we keep repeating the same fucking cycles. We don't acknowledge the bad behavior. We don't demand any proof of growth or sincerity. We don't require anything. You showed up, I guess you're back. There's no grace or consideration for those who are abused. The onus of forgiveness is always on our shoulders. Recently, I've been thinking about who has the luxury of being dysfunctional and who has the luxury of forgiveness. It's rarely Black women, certainly not publicly. In the [1985] movie, it just felt easy for Mister, and it didn't add up to the trauma that he caused. No accounting for the years, the decades of poor behavior. Celie being reunited with her family is supposed to be enough. We force our characters and people back into the game quickly. Dust it off, you've sat down long enough.

SALAMISHAH: The movie does that. I think the musical tries to course correct.

GABRIELLE: I saw the musical with LaChanze, I saw Cynthia [Erivo], and I saw Fantasia. It felt dramatically different each time. Cynthia's anger was more visceral, so that performance felt like the one I'd like to wear. That's the depiction that feels right to me. What are we allowed to want? Are we allowed to hate people forever? Because I do.

There's that notion to be protective of Blackness, to always put Blackness in the best light. But what does that mean to people who are suffering at the hands of their own people, the intragroup conflict? What do we say? What do we do? What can be expected?

SALAMISHAH: I agree. And I think maybe Black children even more than Black women pay the price for that. Forgiveness without accountability. That's where a cycle of abuse gets to keep on going because it's not interrupted by creating different behaviors. It's just forcing people to say sorry because we all want to move on. That's why it's so hard to talk about childhood sexual trauma, which is obviously what Celie was experiencing, and why, when the novel came out, it broke families and communities apart. It's such a clear-eyed and unvarnished and unfiltered truth. You either have to believe Celie or you don't believe her. Walker doesn't give us an out, because she opens the book with Celie's point of view and we can't escape it. As a survivor, I think that's the brilliance of the book. We are invited into Celie's world, and we have to stay with her through the worst moments of her life, and then we can be on this journey with her. But we have to believe her to continue reading.

I'm just really grateful to Alice Walker. And to you for having this conversation. This is so meaningful, and I've long wanted to talk to you as a survivor, outside of all of the great things you've done in the world; on this level it's very intimate and very important to me. So thank you. This was beautiful. This is such an honor.

GABRIELLE: The honor is all mine. Thank you.

Celie (Cynthia Erivo), Bernard B. Jacobs
Theatre, New York, 2015

VIII
CONNECTION

Everything want to be loved.
Us sing and dance and holler make
faces and give flower bouquets,
trying to be loved.

—from Alice Walker's
The Color Purple

Young Celie (Phylicia Pearl Mpasi)
and Young Nettie (Halle Bailey)
play patty-cake, 2023 film

SISTERHOOD

HALLE BAILEY (Young Nettie, 2023 film): I'm twenty-two, so I still feel very new when it comes to this acting world. I'm most comfortable when I'm singing. That's what I've grown up knowing that I'm good at, and that's my comfort zone. So with this new creative outlet of acting I've discovered, it's this kind of beautiful therapy lesson. Every project I'm taking on is teaching me more and more about myself. The only other big film I've done is *The Little Mermaid*. I actually sent in my audition tape for *The Color Purple* while I was filming that movie.

I remember thinking to myself, "Wow, that's beautiful that they're going to do a remake. That's really cool that

Celie. That's where I got the inspiration from for Nettie, because I felt very much myself and like I could connect to her.

It was a heartbreaking dialogue to do because I thought about my sister, who is my angel. Chloe's my hero. She always has been. It's so funny, seeing little baby pictures of us. Chloe is always, always, without a doubt standing over me or protecting me or holding my hand. She thinks she's my mom sometimes. That's how it feels. It was interesting, playing this relationship between Celie and Nettie, because Nettie, to me, acted more like how my sister acts. She knows the path. She knows the way. Even though Celie's the older sister, Nettie was kind of showing her the ropes. I just pulled from that experience.

"There are these constellations of sisterhoods that are created as a way of working through."
—Salamishah Tillet

Oprah [Winfrey] and Steven [Spielberg] are involved. And it would be beautiful to take on a role like Nettie because it's a way more mature version of this girl that I am in this other film." Ariel [in *The Little Mermaid*] is young and lighthearted. She's still very deep, but Nettie is a whole other level of me I hadn't discovered yet.

Long story short, I wanted to take on this role because I felt like Nettie would teach me things about myself that I need to know [in life]. There were so many things Nettie knew about herself from such a young age that I would like to take with me and take on: a sense of pride, a sense of purpose. I was excited to play something that has a bit more depth than what I could show with Ariel. With Nettie, I could really show the pain that I've experienced.

The dialogue I had to learn for my audition was from two scenes between Celie and Nettie: when they were taking away the baby from Celie, and then when Nettie was getting thrown out. I have two sisters, Chloe and Sky. We're all close, but Chloe is my best friend. She's like my

FATIMA ROBINSON (choreographer, 2023 film): My mom came home from seeing *The Color Purple* in the theater. She said to my sisters and me, "I have to take you to see this." I was thirteen. My sisters were eleven and ten. I remember how passionate my mom was about us seeing it; I think she wanted us to see what was possible out in the world.

My mom was always cautious; she wouldn't let us have play dates or spend the night at other people's houses. She was just very protective of us in that way. I'm sure she wanted us to see Celie's journey and what she persevered through. The cinematic scope and the sisterhood was so beautiful. She wanted us to see that onscreen. Also, she knew that I loved singing and dancing. The music in it was amazing.

I catch the original film once every few years or so. I cry at the end every time. My sister and I text hand emojis to each other. If I'm having a day, I send the hand and she'll text it back. We know it means patty-cake. Just as they did in the movie.

HALLE BAILEY: Chloe and I would always sing to each other when we were little, "Sister, you've been on my mind." Even before I understood the full context of the lyrics, I knew that song and sang it.

What's beautiful about what they show of sisterhood in this new film is their relationship from the beginning and their innocence. I really admired doing the scenes with Phylicia [Mpasi, Young Celie] where we're learning patty-cake and having fun in the tree, and how little things like that just filled my heart with so much joy, to the point where I felt like I was five years old again. Those moments were the most special to me. Also, the story of healing. When I was playing Nettie, especially when I was doing her voiceover for her letters when she's gone, I was trying to put myself in her state

Celie (Fantasia Barrino) reads a letter from Nettie, 2023 film

of mind of what she could be feeling. What amazed me about Nettie was how she held onto such hope, even after all those years. That was one thing that never deteriorated between Nettie and Celie. They both had this hope they would see each other again. The strength in that was just so honorable and some of the most beautiful work I've ever had to play.

JOHN LATENSER (supervising location manager, 2023 film): When we first started filming on Jekyll Island [in Georgia] and the sisters are running off to go play on these weathered, washed-up dead trees on the beach, it made you remember what it was like to be a child and to be so excited about running off to your magical little place away from home with your sibling and just enjoying that aspect of life. It brought back a lot of memories of me playing with my siblings when I saw that. Just that love and that happiness and that escapism from whatever might be going on at home. You're going to this other place where you can get away from it all and just be yourself and enjoy. That's a theme I could relate to.

MARCUS GARDLEY (screenwriter, 2023 film): This book saved me. I grew up with so many family members because my dad has ten sisters and four brothers. My mother was raised with cousins who we consider aunts and uncles. That's eleven. That's already twenty-four people. Then, all those people had kids, and a lot of them lived on my street. In that environment, you have to stand out. You have to be loud. You have to make yourself known. I'm not that guy. I'm quiet. I like to keep to myself. So people forgot me. It happened all the time. I had an uncle who went to Ghana. He came back with gifts, and he forgot that I was a child of my parents. Everybody got a gift but me. So I really responded to Celie because she was passed over. People didn't notice her.

Just as Celie had a sibling who loved her and always said, "You matter," my brother was that for me. He was my protector. I didn't get bullied in school because he would literally declare to the whole school, "If you mess with this kid, I'm going to try to kill you." My brother was intense like that so I could walk through the world being myself. He gave me that. I knew at the time, even while he was doing it, that that was a rare gift. I just knew it. But reading the book confirmed it for me.

Young Nettie (Halle Bailey) and Young Celie
(Phylicia Pearl Mpasi), 2023 film

Young Celie (Desreta Jackson) and
Nettie (Akosua Busia), 1985 film

I felt devastated when Celie separated from her sister, because I couldn't imagine living without my brother, us being separated. I didn't think I would survive. I really didn't.

When I was sixteen, my brother, who was two years older, went off to high school. It was the first time I experienced that little separation. All of those people who knew not to mess with me had been waiting. They knew my brother wasn't going to come from the high school, which was far away, to the junior high.

Keeping to myself made me a target. I was a nerd. I was into books. I will never forget, this group of guys told me that I was going to get it after school. They did this thing where every time they saw me, they punched a fist into the other hand, and they all did it all day long. I realized, "Oh, it's going to be six or seven of them. There's no way I can defend myself. I'm just going to take it."

So they jumped me, and they started pounding. And this kid named Terrence swooped in and grabbed me and said, "Start running." And he held them off. He was the guy that my brother assigned if something happened to me. Didn't even know there was a guy assigned.

I just thought, "My brother is an angel. He's got to be." Who would've thought of that? But he has always been that for me in my life. So when I read *The Color*

Purple, I felt like I was reading my life, just in a different period. Parallel sibling stories.

SALAMISHAH TILLET (scholar, critic, and author of *In Search of the Color Purple: The Story of an American Masterpiece*): There's the sisterhood between Nettie and Celie being a biological sisterhood, but then there's also the community of women with Celie's relationship with Sofia or Shug's relationship with Squeak. There are these relationships, these constellations of sisterhoods, that are created as a way of working through: How do you survive patriarchy and segregation? How do you try to be as free as possible within these really, really oppressive structures? Alice Walker gives us the sense of community, but also the center within that is sisterhood.

KIMBERLEY RAMPERSAD (director, 2019 Canadian production, Neptune Theatre and Citadel Theatre/ Royal Manitoba Theatre Centre): One of the things I love most is how matriarchal the story is, because my mother's family is incredibly matriarchal. It's a string of the most badass women you've ever seen. The men are great, love them all, but it's about women. We are trees. So, we had a tree in our production, and that's a metaphor that is for Black women in particular. This tree is Celie.

Shug (Taraji P. Henson) and Celie
(Fantasia Barrino) kiss, 2023 film

QUEER LOVE IS LOVE

AISHA HARRIS (co-host/reporter, National Public Radio's "Pop Culture Happy Hour"): The strengths of the 1985 film definitely lie in the performances, and Spielberg obviously had a hand in that. When I think about the scene between Celie and Shug—even though, yes, the movie definitely did not go as far in terms of depicting their relationship from a romantic point of view—that scene between them where they kiss is so beautiful. Even if it's not sexually explicit in any way, it is very sensual. The way it's shot, and just the time that's taken with it… It's maybe three minutes, but it's three minutes you have the phonograph in the background playing some old-timey music, and you have them sitting on the bed, and the looks that they give each other. Shug's going from playfully teasing to affectionate and loving. That scene is so beautiful and so wonderfully done.

The movie is about women bonding—not just Celie and Shug, but also Sofia and Squeak to some extent—bonding and forging their own family away from the typical, traditional family. That's such a thing that queer people can latch on to, of being rejected or mistreated by your biological family, or in this case the family that Celie was forced to start with Mister. Lots of queer people, especially of previous generations, can absolutely relate to that, of having to create your own family and that idea of family being what you make it.

SHEILA WALCOTT (senior vice president of creative development, Warner Bros.): In the first movie, there was a beautiful rendering of the love story between Celie and Shug. In the new interation, Marcus and Blitz leaned into it even more. In terms of representation, no one's going, "Oh my God, they're lesbians!" It is what it is. They are falling in love, and it is what it is. Our film harkens back to the source material, which takes up chapters and chapters of the book. It's a lot of story to be able to get right and give justice to. Spielberg's movie is the gold standard. It's iconic. It's legendary. Blitz and Marcus's iteration of it just feels like now in terms of representation.

NIIJA KUYKENDALL (former production executive, Warner Bros.): What's so cool about this version is that Celie gets to be in love. She gets to have love sequences and have that experience and that relationship. That's not something we see on the screen much. We don't see fully complex, comprehensive, Black womanhood onscreen from the perspective of a dark-skinned woman who wouldn't traditionally be the star of a movie.

Celie (LaChanze) and Shug (Elisabeth Withers), The Broadway Theatre, New York, 2005

Celie (Whoopi Goldberg) and Shug (Margaret Avery), 1985 film

WHAT ABOUT LOVE?

[Celie]
Is that me who's floating away
Lifted up to the clouds by a kiss
Never felt nothing like this

[Shug]
Is that me I don't recognize
'Cause the one thing I knew all about
I had it all figured out

[Celie]
What about trust?
[Shug]
What about trust?
[Celie]
What about tenderness?
[Shug]
What about tenderness?

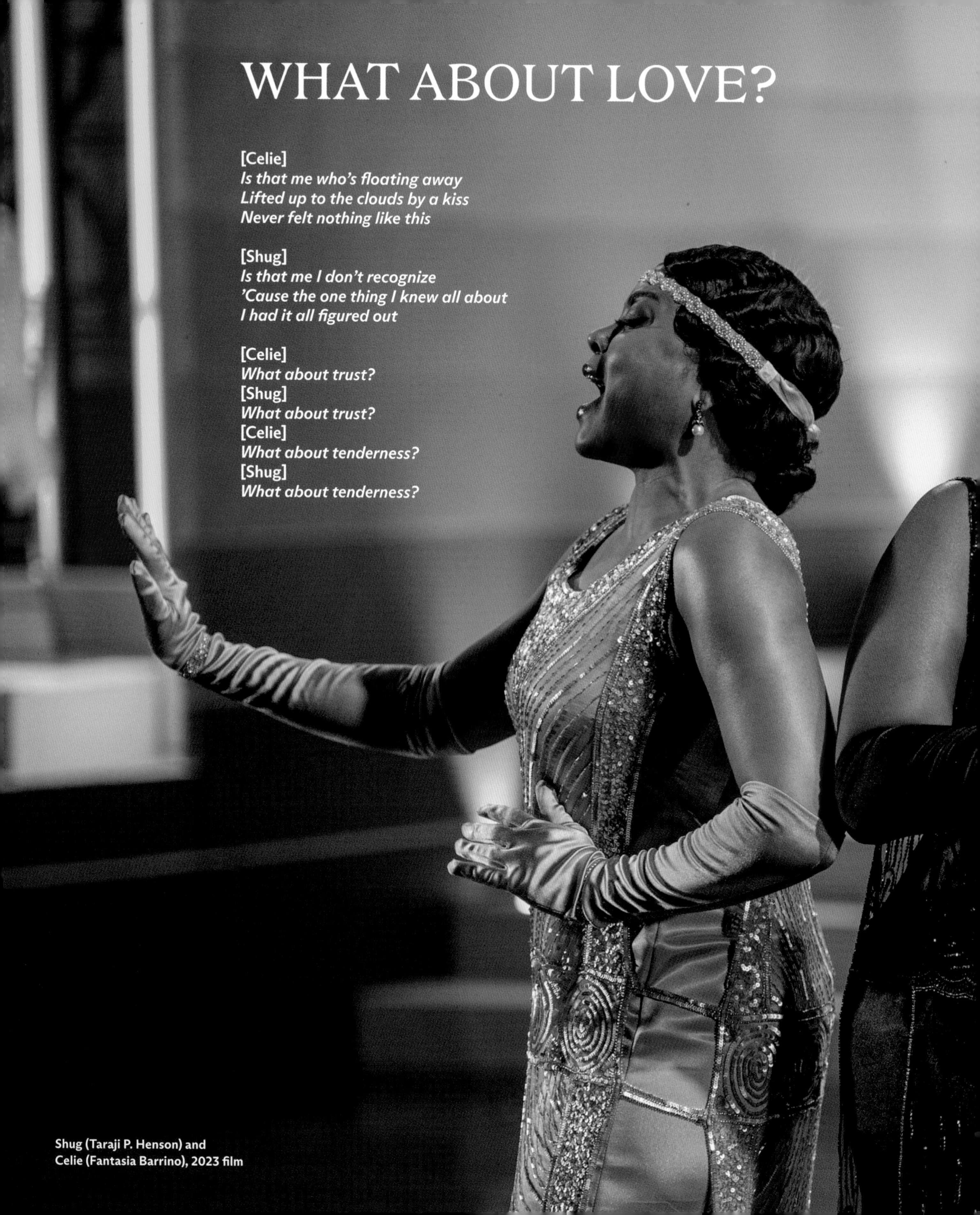

Shug (Taraji P. Henson) and
Celie (Fantasia Barrino), 2023 film

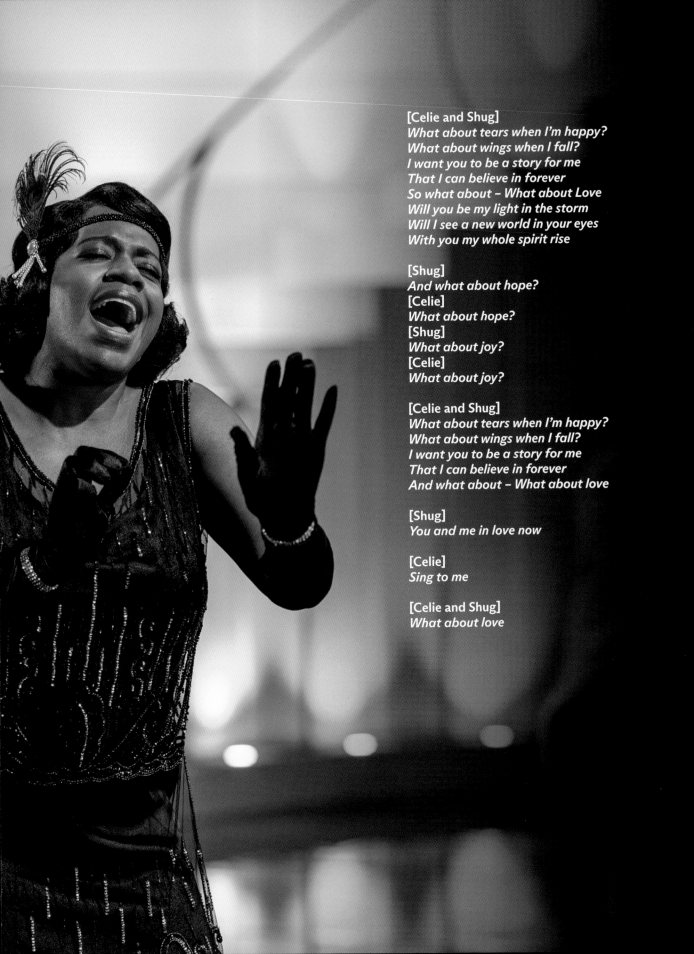

[Celie and Shug]
What about tears when I'm happy?
What about wings when I fall?
I want you to be a story for me
That I can believe in forever
So what about – What about Love
Will you be my light in the storm
Will I see a new world in your eyes
With you my whole spirit rise

[Shug]
And what about hope?
[Celie]
What about hope?
[Shug]
What about joy?
[Celie]
What about joy?

[Celie and Shug]
What about tears when I'm happy?
What about wings when I fall?
I want you to be a story for me
That I can believe in forever
And what about – What about love

[Shug]
You and me in love now

[Celie]
Sing to me

[Celie and Shug]
What about love

LACHANZE (Celie, 2005 Broadway musical): One of my favorite moments on stage was in the "What About Love?" scene with Elisabeth Withers [who played Shug]. I thought she was brilliant. As an actor, I was able to sense a sincere and genuine, beautiful chemistry with Elisabeth that I've never had with another woman on stage before. I happen to be heterosexual, not that I can't play that I'm in love with a woman, because you can love anyone. I never thought of Celie as being a lesbian. I thought of Celie as finally having love.

People ask me, "Have you ever played a lesbian on stage? And I say, "Celie." And they say, "Oh my God, you're right." People don't think of it. And that's the brilliance of Alice Walker. Some of my favorite moments were working opposite Elisabeth, and our chemistry, and how we together were able to focus on the love. That came from the words and not the lust. People today sexualize everything, but I didn't feel sexualized with her. It felt like it was about love—I mean, it *was* "What About Love?" When we kissed, it was so tender and so beautiful. Everyone in the audience is so happy that someone actually loves Celie that you're not thinking, "Oh my God, Celie's a lesbian. She's going to have sex with a woman." That's what I mean. It wasn't written to be about sex. It was written to be about love.

TARAJI P. HENSON (Shug, 2023 film): One thing I wanted to explore through Shug was love. Unconditional love. "Take me as I am" love. Shug saw so much of herself in Celie. She saw who she could have been if she hadn't gotten out of that town. Nobody in that town ever took care of her the way Celie had. In the beginning, she started going back to town for her father's love and acceptance, but it shifted once she was cared for and nurtured in the way she was with Celie. She was going to Mister's house for that from him, but it was empty 'cause that man ain't shit. And she knew it, but it was her excuse to come home.

She never told anybody she was coming home for the acceptance of her father, but think about how she came to town: She's got big news, and the first person she sees is her father, and he shuns her again. So what does she do? Drink. She goes right to her numb-out. But then, Shug's reasons for going back to town after that shifted when that woman touched her and bathed her and took care of her. That is something Shug had been longing for with all of those men that she'd been with. So love got a hold of her—true love. It didn't matter that it was a woman. It was a feeling that we all long for as humans. And she found it. Shug saw herself in Celie and didn't want this woman to go to ruin. She fought for Celie because Celie couldn't. She became her voice.

MARCUS GARDLEY: In her book *The Same River Twice*, Alice mentioned that the lesbian love story was not as present in the 1985 film as she would've liked. So, when I was pitching the movie, that was one of the things I was adamant about. Not only because she said it, but just because it's important. I thought we needed to really talk about this beautiful love story between these two women. Everybody was gung-ho and excited about doing that. But oftentimes in queer stories, and I mostly do tell queer stories, what I find is people get really excited about it at the beginning of the project, and then you find them petering away. It's become such a sore subject for me that I'm a little paranoid about it now. I've watched so many programs where the queer love stories start to be taken apart consciously or subconsciously. So I held onto it the whole time: "We are not changing that; we are not changing that."

SALAMISHAH TILLET: Celie has to understand the possibility of sexual pleasure as part of her healing process. I think that's such a key part of the story and continues to resonate with people, but particularly with women and girls and maybe gender-nonconforming youth, and then women who are trying to understand pleasure in a patriarchal society.

> "We have been chosen to keep these characters, and their stories, and what they can teach us as a society, alive."
> —*Scott Sanders*

Left to right: Jennifer Hudson, Cynthia Erivo, Whoopi Goldberg, and Danielle Brooks, 2015

Felicia P. Fields and Brandon Victor Dixon, 2005

FINDING FAMILY

OPRAH WINFREY (Sofia, 1985 film; producer, 2005 Broadway musical, 2015 Broadway revival, 2023 film): When Gayle [King] and I saw the cast perform the finale in the musical film, we couldn't help but give a standing ovation. We nearly ruined the scene with our clapping and screaming, but they were so incredible, it felt like we were at a concert. There were so many fantastic day players to help support that scene. In the final scene of the day, everybody broke out into dancing the electric slide and singing. Every person I spoke to, from the camera crew to the hair and makeup team, was delighted to be there.

JOHN LATENSER: I grew up in the Midwest in a very, very white area. Until they introduced busing, I hadn't met very many African Americans. To this day, most film crews are dominated by white men. I've always made an effort since I got into this business to have a diverse crew. Oftentimes, you'll be on a film and there are a few Black people, but they're not properly represented. This [2023] film offered an opportunity for a lot of aspiring African American filmmakers to get into the business and see how a film was really made, a big film. Every African American person on my crew just saw this as the biggest

privilege ever. They had all seen The Color Purple at least twenty times. This was a really big deal for them. I thought, "Maybe I can't appreciate it the way they can, but I can at least give them the opportunity to have that experience."

The good thing about making a project or a movie is, if you don't like someone, you only have to put up with them for so long, and then you get to move on to another project. With this project, it was more like you're going to miss these people because you don't know if you're going to get to work with them again anytime soon. It was a big family, and there was a lot of inspiration. There was magic happening on this film. I've made a lot of movies in my career. You know when you're making something special, and this was something you just knew was going to be really special.

SCOTT SANDERS (producer, 2005 Broadway musical, 2015 Broadway revival, 2023 film): If you talk to Broadway companies or film or television casts, many feel a sense of camaraderie, particularly if something runs for a very long time. But I've been producing now for nearly forty years, in all different media, and The Color Purple stands alone in that regard. Alice's story represents something that feels bigger than all of us. We have been chosen to keep these characters, and their stories, and what they can teach us as a society, alive.

Left to right: Phylicia Pearl Mpasi, Halle Bailey,
Oprah Winfrey, and Deon Cole on the set of the 2023 film

There is a thread that you hear from people, and it's not made up. It's not scripted. They may be alumni of thirty-five years if you're talking to someone who worked on Steven's movie. They may be alumni of the first Broadway show, like Brandon Victor Dixon or LaChanze. Or they may be somebody like Halle Bailey, who just did the movie.

The Color Purple family continues to grow. It's always wonderful to hear how artists outside of the American South relate to the characters and the storytelling—and also relate to their responsibility for telling it correctly and doing it the right way. So there is a very large *Color Purple* family now—multi-national, multi-generational, multi-racial, multi-gender—who have had their fingerprints on some part of this story being told somewhere, somehow, someway in the world. We may not even know all of each other's names, but there's definitely a connection, and I'm not just being all New Agey when I say it. It's a genuine feeling that I have every day.

BRANDON VICTOR DIXON (Harpo, 2005 Broadway musical): The bonds that we formed in that show among one another were very real. We were very connected to the material, and we were very connected to our collective endeavor to bring that material to life in a way that honored how it had come into our lives originally. Felicia P. Fields [who played Sofia] is not only an extraordinary actress, singer, and performer, but she is a wonderful human being. I came to know her daughters and her sons—I know her family very well. We all became close: me, Felicia, and Krisha Marcano, who played Squeak. Our trio in the show became very much a trio outside of the show.

LAWRENCE DAVIS (hair department head, 2023 film): When everybody would come in the door, they were just glad to be part of something that's so historically embedded in us. I was so grateful to be a part of that team, and to bring that team together, and have everybody give their all. So, having a wonderful team behind me, and a team that wanted to be there, made my day.

When the original film came out, it spoke volumes to the African American community: It's a survival story, and it's an overcoming story. People know the history of *The Color Purple*: the book itself, and the movie itself, and the Broadway musical. They want to tell that story and they want to be a part of it, whether set dressing or costumes or just helping build the characters, everybody wants a hand in it.

CYNTHIA ERIVO (Celie, 2015 Broadway revival): Even though I came from another country, the thing I experienced with the Broadway *Color Purple* is that I didn't feel like an outsider in that cast. I didn't feel like my Blackness was less than, or more than, the other Black members of that cast. Rema [Webb, who played a church lady] still calls me Niecy, her niece. I still talk to Angela [Birchett, who played a church lady], and we still eff and blind [swear a lot] together. Danielle [Brooks, who played Sofia] and I still call each other and commiserate or talk. I gained family there. I think the thing that I learned the most is that what is not helping us is us separating ourselves and putting ourselves into different factions when really we're long-lost family members. Once we allow ourselves to experience each other as individuals, we realize how close we are and how familiar we are.

When someone was leaving the Broadway show, something we started doing was to send them off at the end of the performance. On Heather Headley's [Shug's] last show, our music director asked us to sing a gospel song called "I Won't Complain." And I don't know why, but the memory of that just keeps coming back to me. I loved that performance. It felt really good, and I think it's because when you know you are leaving something behind, you leave it behind. So you give everything so you don't regret that. And then we sent her off with this song—we sang the song to her. While I was singing the first verse, I realized at that moment that I had truly fallen in love with this person who was playing Shug. The thing that Celie dreamed of happening had happened.

This doesn't happen between actors all the time, but it happens if a pairing is right and both of you are being as truthful and as open as possible. And Heather was just a massive open book, so you can't help but fall in love. First, second, third performance, and that was kind of it.

That was it. I'm really glad that we had that experience. It was really special.

I was genuinely sad to lose this person, and I just thought to myself: what a wonderful thing that we connected in this way, that I had actually fallen for this person. And I needed to. So I sang this verse, and I was deeply, deeply sad singing it. I still remember feeling that, and I don't know why, but that's one of my favorite moments.

CAROL RASHEED (makeup department head, 2023 film): I'm kind of like a mother figure. People often confide in me. Even if they're not saying anything, I can feel their spirit. Sometimes I'm that person that they're going to cry to. Part of my job and my responsibility is to help them get through that moment so that they can perform.

I think that's why I was chosen for this project. When my agent brought it to me, I was like, "Oh, this would be great." The more I got into it, and when I met with Blitz, I was like, "Oh, this would be amazing."

It was definitely divinely ordered, not just for me to be there to do the makeup, but also to help with the process of people being able to get through that. They're at their most vulnerable when they come in. You know if somebody's had a fight with their wife or their husband. You know if somebody's died in their family. That's why I always tell the people that are coming up behind me that makeup is more than just putting products on somebody's face. The bond that you get with the person when you're there, sometimes it's a bond that's there because they've relied on you, they've trusted in you, they've shared so much of who they truly are with you. The space

> ## "I realized at that moment that I had truly fallen in love with this person who was playing Shug."
> —*Cynthia Erivo*

with us is their safe haven. And I make sure I hire people who fit in that mold of thinking because I know how difficult it is sometimes to have to pull out a character like a Mister or a Celie.

LACHANZE: Every live performance I've ever done, it's based on the audience. The audience has a personality. I've said this before in interviews, but if the audience is drunk, it's going to be a silly show. If the audience is stubborn or bored or tired, it's going to be a hard show. A lot of the audiences for *The Color Purple* were ready and attentive and leaning forward. That gave us license to really immerse ourselves into these characters and into this story. So it was like confirmation. When you hear a bunch of audience members react and respond audibly, in the Black culture that's how we communicate anyway. We acknowledge our approval or disapproval audibly, so that is something that I personally, culturally, am used to. When it happens on stage, I know that they are listening. It's like being at a family barbecue, where you can say, "I don't like whoever made the potato salad," and someone else goes, "Mm-hmm." You know that what you've said has been not only heard but digested, agreed about, and they want you to acknowledge it. That is call and response. That is very Black. And that's something that, when you're telling a story about Black people, is really wonderful. It's pretty much a cosigning of everything that's being done on stage.

THE BELOVED COMMUNITY

FATIMA ROBINSON: When I heard that Blitz was a part of the film, I got really excited. I was excited because he's a Black man from Ghana, Africa. For me, that was like, "Whoa." It really resonated with me because so much of the wrong committed in the movie, particularly the ways they treated each other, was—and still is—so deeply rooted in us because of slavery and the atrocities that happened. I knew this film would be deeper than just a remake, just by having someone like Blitz.

TARAJI P. HENSON: I love the way Blitz had Shug floating into town on a barge through the swamp. Even Harpo building the Juke Joint in the middle of the fucking swamp, us taking the scraps and making something incredible. Come on, now. This whole movie is church,

and we felt it on set. We felt it. I can't explain it. The hairs on the back of my neck are standing up. Just these places that Blitz chose to film. You could hear the ancestors. I literally could not breathe.

The first day I filmed, we filmed the end of the movie, the big Easter dinner where all the generations come together. We're around this big tree with Spanish moss hanging down. And I'm telling you, this tree was something massive. I just remember sitting there one day and thinking, "If those branches, if these roots, could talk." Then just beyond us in the back, I don't know if it was set pieces or actual real slave shacks, but they were there.

I remember sitting there really, really quiet and thinking, "This piece that we're doing is special. Why are we here? Why was it this tree? Why was it this land?" Even the place he chose to film was spiritual. So with us in these ancient places came the ancestors, came the spirits. I'm telling you it was there. I experienced it. And we were in Savannah! There were certain places I wouldn't go. I was like, "Yeah, no. They ain't going to throw no root on me. Mm-mm. Mm-mm." But I'm just saying you could feel it. That's something we wouldn't have been able to accomplish on a set.

LACHANZE: *Color Purple* is a universal story. Yes, it's centered on a Black family, but we as human beings want to see the underdog—the one that people are down on, that they beat on—win. And in this case, you're dealing with the abuse of a young woman. There's a race factor. Then there's the trauma of the family. All of those ideas and storylines are American. They're not just Black. As human beings, we all align with that. And all of us have a little Celie in us somewhere; it's how that part of us is expressed and how we want so badly to feel like we're loved and seen.

CYNTHIA ERIVO: In our [Menier Chocolate Factory] production, there was nothing to hide behind. There were no sets, no anything. We had wooden walls, wooden floors, wooden chairs, a couple of blankets, a couple of baskets, and some glasses. That was it. And everything else had to come from us. That's not to say that every other cast didn't have to create the story and tell it, but we really had nothing else to rely on. It was just us and the story. We had to create the world around you so that when you were watching, you saw the trees, you saw the house, you saw all of those things.

Celie (Fantasia Barrino) and her family celebrate in the closing scene of the 2023 film

"Do I ever find myself overwhelmed? What! It always gets us, me and my castmates. We laugh about it when we get off stage, but usually it's during the ballads and during the last number where we sing the 'Color Purple' reprise at the end. You're singing to the audience and they're looking at you, and they're a part of it. It's overwhelming, the amount of love you receive from audience members. It's crazy."

—JOAQUINA KALUKANGO
Actress and singer who played Nettie in the 2015 Broadway revival

From a video interview with Paul Wontorek for Broadway.com, 2016

Director John Doyle on the deliberately spare set of the Menier Chocolate Factory production, London, 2015

Because we were doing it in that way, we're immediately asking the audience to come with us, to suspend disbelief, to open your eyes and see what we're showing you. So that you all have your own picture painted. Imagine if we ask each of those people to paint a picture about what they saw. Every single one would be very, very different—and the same. And that's what we're asking of the audience. I think that creates a really immersive experience. I can't even begin to explain how many people came to me and said, "I came with so and so, and we wept and really didn't know why we were weeping." What I think was happening is that we aren't giving you your emotional cues. You are feeling it as we are feeling it. So in real time, we're all feeling something together. You are getting from us the information you need to feel how you need to feel. That was a really special thing to watch happen.

TODD JOHNSON (producer, 2005 Broadway musical): How can I even talk about this without talking about Alice Walker? There was one time that doesn't have to do with the show itself as much as the life around the show. I was introducing Alice to a group of about 300 teachers who had come to see *The Color Purple* musical on a special night that was honoring educators. I have

never forgotten one thing she said that night. Basically, she said, "The only good reason that we are here on this planet is to heal each other."

I remember thinking, "That's *The Color Purple*." It's the healing that comes to Celie, the healing that Celie's growth and voice bring to everyone around her. A life is transfigured, a community is transfigured. And Alice said it in that one line.

BONDING BEYOND BORDERS

YUMIKO YANAGISAWA (Japanese literary translator, 1982 novel): In the Japanese language, there are hierarchies in how you speak to people, depending on class and sex and position and age. How you speak shows where you belong. For example, if I want to ask the question, "Are you going?" I would say to a child or my husband, "Iku?" And if I say it to my equals or friends, I say, "Ikimasuka?" But if I say it to my elders or older people, I'd say, "Irasshaimasuka?" You would never say, "Iku?" to upper-status people. So in my translation, I used this "Iku" type—a simple, non-gendered, equal way of speaking—when Celie was talking.

Connection

BRINGING *PURPLE* TO BRAZIL

In Brazil, a country that prides itself as being diverse, Afro-Brazilians face discrimination and systemic inequities. In large-scale theatrical productions there, Black people were entirely absent until shows like *The Color Purple* inspired producers and directors like Tadeu Aguiar to break tradition.

Shug (Flávia Santana) and other patrons dance at Harpo's Juke Joint, Cidade das Artes, Brazil, 2019

TADEU AGUIAR (producer/director, 2019 Cidade das Artes production, Rio de Janeiro, 2019–2022 Brazilian tour): A couple of times a year, I go to New York to see shows and friends there who are directors and actors. One time, my friend Charles Randolph-Wright asked me whether I would like to see *The Color Purple* and gave me four tickets to the revival production with Cynthia Erivo. At the end of the first act, I couldn't stand up. I was completely devastated by the emotion of the story. Right then I thought, "My God, I would like to produce a play like this in Brazil."

CHARLES RANDOLPH-WRIGHT (American director and playwright; colleague and friend of Aguiar): There's a small group of people who produce Broadway-caliber work in Brazil, and Tadeu is one of them. I met Tadeu years ago on one of my first trips to Brazil, and we just instantly became brothers, friends. He kept wanting to

TADEU: I've been in this career for forty-two years, and until ten or twelve years ago, we didn't think about putting Black people in our shows. The first time I thought about this was in 2009, when I invited Charles and Ken Roberson to Brazil to direct and choreograph *They're Playing Our Song*. We had no Black actors in the cast, and they were very, very surprised. Some time after that, we bought the rights to produce the *Love Story* musical. A friend called and said, "I have a boyfriend, but he is Black. Do you have any roles for Black people in your cast?" That made me think. That same day, Eduardo [my husband and producing partner] and I decided to make a change, and our *Love Story* had ten Black people in the cast. It was the first time in Brazil that we had Black actors in a show that wasn't connected to Africa. No one in the audience questioned this choice, and Eduardo and I decided that every show we produce, we have to put Black people in the spaces that they deserve.

"At the end of the first act, I couldn't stand up."
—Tadeu Aguiar

do something, so I actually directed a musical in Rio, in Portuguese, which I don't speak. I love Brazil so much, but I was surprised by the lack of representation and diversity in the arts, the lack of color. Still, as an artist of color in the United States, you always have to prove yourself. In Brazil, I didn't have to do that. So even though the country has its issues, I had an acceptance immediately that I don't have at home.

TADEU: Even though 56 percent of the people in Brazil are Black, it's a very prejudiced country, and it's very, very difficult to live here as a Black person. I thought this show would help dissolve some of the prejudices.

CHARLES: I've always been pushing projects that had people of color, and I felt that *Color Purple* was something that would resonate with him. I didn't know it would completely blow him away.

CHARLES: Tadeu went out on a limb to do *The Color Purple*. It had not been done, and it's not an easy task to make that happen there. For these Black artists in Brazil to tell this story on this scale, on a Broadway type of scale, was amazing.

TADEU: When we decided to do *The Color Purple*, putting together an all-Black cast was a challenge. So many Black people here can't afford to study dance or voice, so they had not been trained for the theater. Things are changing, and as more Black actors and singers get roles, they've started going to classes because now they have the chance to work, to have a job as an artist.

LETÍCIA SOARES (Celie): The theater came into my life really, really late. I'm from Magé, Rio de Janeiro. It's a very poor city, so it's strange to even think of being a professional actress or singer there. Even nowadays, we don't have any theater or cultural life in my city.

I started singing in my bathroom as a child, performing shows during bath time, but I didn't study music growing up. Instead, I became a social worker, but the desire to perform ate away at my heart. As an adult, I decided to study samba, and when a Brazilian musical play started, I auditioned for it and got a small role. That's when I started to work professionally. *The Lion King* was my first big play, and after that, I did almost everything that came to Brazil.

Almost eight years later, I auditioned for *The Color Purple*. As I was leaving the house, I told my husband, "I'm only going to play Celie. That's it." The Celie story is the story of how society keeps telling so many of us that we're not good enough, that we're not beautiful, and that we don't deserve love. This resilience and hope she keeps in her heart is amazing: Celie is one of the most important characters in musical theater history, in my opinion. No matter what language you speak, it touches you, it catches you.

CHARLES: I remember being on a beach one day in Rio. There are these cliffs that go out into the ocean, and when the sun set, everyone applauded. I realized why I appreciate Brazil; they're grateful for what they have. I thought, "Well, it's like the color purple. God gets mad when you don't notice." People of color all over the world

Celie (Letícia Soares), Shug (Flávia Santana), and Nettie (Ester Freitas) in the scene where Nettie's trove of letters is discovered, Cidade das Artes, Brazil, 2019

are unseen and unheard, and this musical is about a woman who is unseen and unheard.

And here's my friend Tadeu, who didn't realize the inequities on the stage because he did not have to. If he looked Black, like me, he would've been aware of it, but because he looks white, he lived in a world where his look is the norm, it was not an issue for him until the veil was lifted. I don't mind taking credit for that.

LETÍCIA: I chose two songs for my audition: "I'm Here" and "Colored Woman" from *Memphis*. I showed my list to the music director, and he wrote on my sheet, "We don't have any Celie yet. Sing 'I'm Here.'" I was sick that day—sick, sick, sick. I didn't even know if I could sing. But I thought, "Oh my God, I'll give everything. It's now or never." And afterward, when I looked at the director and his crew, they were all crying.

TADEU: We opened the show in Rio de Janeiro and then went to São Paulo. Both runs were so successful that our sponsor, Banco Bradesco, said, "Let's make a tour." We started in the south, which was once colonized by European people and still has cities where the population is almost entirely white. One of the actresses said that in Florianópolis, at first the people who worked in the theater wouldn't even make eye contact with the cast. They were absolutely ignored because they were Black. But after the first performance, everything changed. This is the reason that I fight so much for this show.

LETÍCIA: During our warm-up, once we started to sing, they started to sit down and watch us. By the end of the weekend, they were our biggest fans. It happens. *The Color Purple* is not just a good play. It touches. It goes deep. No one can fight against it.

TADEU: I never saw this before in Brazil, but when Letícia sang "I'm Here," in 99 percent of the performances the entire audience stood up and applauded. It was incredible. In the middle of the show! At the end, of course, everybody was crying a lot, even me. I cried every time because I know the performers and I'm the director and the producer, but mostly it's that I was seeing seventeen Black people being stars in my country. This touched me more than the story. Bradesco said *The Color Purple* was the first time people asked for more comp tickets than they had for *Phantom of the Opera*.

We also went to Salvador, which is the capital of Bahia. Outside of Africa, Bahia has the largest population of Black people in the world. We were scheduled for only three performances, because the theater was very big—1,700 seats. We were sold out in three days. So, we had to add three more shows. It was the most incredible feeling that I ever had in my entire life. Those audiences cried a lot, and I think that they cried more about being represented than about the story.

LETÍCIA: The way that we face racism is different from the way Americans do because we were never separated by law. There was this thought that we are a racial paradise where everybody loves each other, but we still know where we stand as Black people.

Slavery didn't end in Brazil until 1888. Most of us, after the end of slavery, remained at the margins of society, facing discrimination and limited employment opportunities. We keep living the consequences of that history today, that denial of membership in the society. Every twenty-three minutes in Brazil, a young Black man gets killed. Twenty-three minutes, every day. That's the statistic. To have the luxury to be an actress in this country, looking like me, is a really, really big deal. I'm not half white. I'm Black, dark-skinned. It's a big deal. Even though *The Color Purple* is not exactly the history of our country, sometimes we have to take these stories from outside to reflect our reality.

Back in the '80s, everybody kept saying, "There's no prejudice here. It's in your head. You're crazy." And you start to think, "OK, maybe I am crazy." But young people today are more aware of the signs, and they're really fighting against it. We are walking, but we need to run. We need to run because we're dying. They're killing us, so we have to run against this brutal society that keeps trying to deny us our place in it. I heard a quote that says, "There is a story of the Black people without Brazil. But there isn't a story of Brazil without the Black people." We cannot talk about Brazil without talking about our contribution. Our music, our culture, our food, our way of life is marked by the African heritage and the Indian heritage. So, we have this mixed-up country that has to understand how beautiful it is to be so diverse. It's not easy, but we keep trying. *The Color Purple* helps.

CHARLES: I think it's no accident that this story is having the success it's having at a time where there is, I hope, an

Celie (Letícia Soares), Cidade das Artes, Brazil, 2019

awakening in the world. The [COVID-19] pandemic shifted things in a monumental way. I say there was a health pandemic and a race pandemic, and both pandemics fed upon each other. The murder of George Floyd especially happened at a time when the world watched, the world saw. So like the color purple, George Floyd was noticed, and that was something that happened all over the world.

LETÍCIA: This was my first protagonist role, and I grabbed it. I won every prize you could win. I am part of *The Color Purple* story, and nobody can deny that. I'm a girl from Magé. I started to sing in my bathroom and now I am part of one of the most important stories of all time.

To me, the most powerful part of the show is when Celie finds self-love. Sometimes it's hard to know that as a Black woman in this world. When we start to see our real self in the mirror, we realize, "I always looked like this, but I let society make me believe that I wasn't beautiful, that I wasn't worthy. I let that happen." It's really empowering when she decides to love herself. And that's the real point of change in Celie's life, when she says, "I'm beautiful, and I'm here. If I'm here, I can change the world. I can change the world around me. I can change the relationships I have. I'm the owner of my path. I'm God."

Left to right: Shug (Lelo Ramasimong), Celie (Didintle Khunou), and Nettie (Sebe Leotlela), Joburg Theatre, South Africa, 2018

TADEU AGUIAR (producer/director, 2019 Cidade das Artes production, Rio de Janeiro, 2019–2022 Brazilian tour): It's difficult to translate a show to Portuguese because the English language is very monosyllabic. It's very short, the words. For instance, "I do," which is two syllables, to speak this in Portuguese, I would say "Eu tenho que fazer," six syllables, or "Eu faço," and that's three.

Look at the song "Push Da Button." The syllable break is: push / da / but / ton. Four syllables. In Portuguese, just the verb is a single word: a / ce / le / ra.

What we have to do is to take the idea and put it in Portuguese using an image or word that we can recognize. It's very, very difficult work. And this show was even more difficult because the characters speak in slang. We couldn't use an accent, because we have many accents in Brazil. It's a big country. It's a continental country. So, the translator changed little things to show the audience that people speak in a wrong way. It was very difficult, but it was perfect.

BERNARD JAY (producer, 2018 South African production): In preparing our production, our director, Janice Honeyman, suggested we get a genuine African language interpretation of the imaginary "Olinka" chants [in "African Homeland"] because she felt that South African audiences would not easily accept the lyrics provided in the script. The musical director consulted with a professor of African languages at Cape Town University, who then provided the translation into Swahili that we used. Swahili is not one of South Africa's eleven official languages; Janice was intentionally eliminating any suggestion that the opening scene of Act II was set in South Africa itself.

KOEN VAN DIJK (translator/director, 2018 Netherlands production): The real difficulties in translating *The Color Purple* lay in the technical aspect of choosing the right Dutch words that would allow the actors to sing this specific gospel-style music.

Dutch is a *hard* language. It has sharp consonants. I had to be very specific not to choose any words at the end of a line that ended with a sharp consonant. Because the style of the music is freestyle gospel, the singers must have the opportunity to elaborate on the sound, just the way American singers do. This was not a question of finding [a similar] idiom, but actually avoiding certain words in the Dutch language. The first song I translated was "I'm Here," and I found that the song works excellently in Dutch. "I am here" translates so easily and naturally to "Ik ben hier." Also, a technical aspect I faced was that the Dutch audience expects rhyme in a song, so that was a little adjustment I made: I used more rhyme.

I felt a special commitment and obligation to translate "Mister's Song/Celie's Curse" correctly. This song is, in my view, a key song to a Dutch audience. In the Netherlands, we have to deal with the consequences of slavery. The pain is felt everywhere in our society, even today. In the old days, Suriname and Indonesia were colonies of the Netherlands, and Curaçao [once a center of slave trade] is still like a province of the Netherlands. There are a lot of people who daily experience the consequences of centuries of slavery. I had to explain the backstory of Mister correctly.

Celie (Naomi Van Der Linden) sings "I'm Here," NDSM Wharf, the Netherlands, 2018

DIRECTING ACROSS THE DIASPORA

How does *Purple* play in other countries? The first women—
and women of color—to direct the stage show in the United Kingdom and
Canada, Tinuke Craig and Kimberley Rampersad, talk to each
other about what translates and what does not.

**Kimberley Rampersad, director, 2019 Canadian production,
Neptune Theatre and Citadel Theatre/Royal Manitoba Theatre Centre**

**Tinuke Craig, director, 2019 U.K. production,
Leicester Curve and Birmingham Hippodrome**

TINUKE CRAIG: As with so many books, I read it when I was slightly too young to read it. At that time, I connected to it as a historical document. Then I read it again at university, and suddenly it felt very personal, and I could connect to it on a level where it's about people like me—which I don't think I'd quite gotten as a child, but that's probably because I shouldn't have read it when I was eleven years old.

At university, I did part of my dissertation on it, comparing postcolonial women's writing with writing of the African American experience. It was a seminal text in terms of my education. Then I saw the [1985] movie years later, only about a year before it turned out I was going to direct the musical.

I know it's a lot of people's favorite film, but one thing that had really struck me as a child reading it was the queerness of it. Maybe that wouldn't be how Celie might have described herself then. And it felt that in the film, that part had been slightly erased in a way that I found annoying more than anything else. Like, what an open goal to just miss. I do understand, though, why people love that film. When we were holding auditions, I'd ask people what their relationship was with it. Almost everyone would say, "Oh, it's my mom's favorite film" or "It's my gran's favorite" or "I watch it all the time."

KIMBERLEY RAMPERSAD: My first interaction was the [1985] movie, and it made me run to the book, which captured my imagination. And then the movie was especially disappointing when I was prepping to do the musical, especially the lack of representation of what Black queer love is and its holiness. In the productions I did, I was able to center that and to show how liberating that can be and how it can be an essential part of Black communities, and that it's a good thing. I wanted to make sure we spoke about how sometimes spirituality and sexual orientation collide, as opposed to intersect.

What I found so beautiful in the story was the constancy of women and how these three archetypes of women come and relight Celie's candle when Nettie is pulled away from her. By meeting Shug, by meeting Sofia, and by holding on to the idea that her sister's there, they light Celie's candle again so that she can keep going. And then she shines light everywhere, especially the darkest places, and even to people who are so unkind.

"I wanted to make sure we spoke about how sometimes spirituality and sexual orientation collide."
—Kimberley Rampersad

TINUKE: So much of what you say, Kimberley, resonates with conversations we had in rehearsals as well. Particularly about the intersections of faith and race and sexuality, and how those sometimes feel in conflict. That felt so personal to a lot of people—a good three-quarters of our cast had been raised in the church. I think the musical holds the holiness better than the queerness. As a director, because the story had come into my life via the novel, I wanted to find ways of holding onto that beating heart of the original text without undermining the script we had in front of us.

We also had to have conversations about archetype versus stereotype. We had Americans in our company, but it was mostly Black British actors. Working out how you stay authentic, what an American audience might take for granted that the British audience wouldn't. We talked a lot about how the racism wound shot through the U.K. is mostly a colonialism wound as opposed to a slavery wound. That's not entirely true, because a lot of the Black population in the U.K. is West Indian. I'm West Indian, and therefore I'm a Jamaican. That is a country scarred by slavery, and in the U.K., that's a huge portion of the Black community.

Because we're diasporic as a nation, a privilege we have as Black people in the U.K. is invariably we know "where we're from." I put that in massive quotations because of course it's much messier than that. But if you're Black in the U.K., chances are you've got a granny with an accent, and you can say, "I am Senegalese," or "I am Jamaican," with some confidence. That meant that we had very specific relationships in the church. Nigerian churches are a very specific thing. Ghanaian churches are a very specific thing. The temptation is to go, "I go to church every week, I know the deal." You know *a* church. We need to know *this* church. You couldn't ever be lazy.

A lot of what's in the story is our experience; we are Black. But coming from lots of different cultures made for big conversations about what Blackness is and why we all connect to it, and why we're all crying at the end if it doesn't connect. One thing that was specific to our experience of doing it in the U.K. was that because we have this huge diaspora, when it came to looking at the Africa section, suddenly we were like, "Oh, we fucking know what we're doing here." There were places where we suddenly were on solid ground about where it was and why they were wearing what they were wearing, and what the dancing was, and what the lyrics were. In the end we used the Swahili lyrics from the Johannesburg production; it was one of the conditions of doing the production. I might not have been bothered if I was in the States, but I could not put *this* work in *this* country with the African diaspora that we have. I've got Swahili

speakers in my company. I've got Yoruba speakers. If we're thinking about diasporic reach, the place you are in and the people you have will always shine lights on different parts of the show.

KIMBERLEY: We had a very mixed group in the productions that I did, too. And because most of us are from West Indian background, myself included—my parents were from Trinidad and Tobago—the relationships we had with church weren't *this* church. The cast members from Nova Scotia have long-standing Black Canadian roots, and that is closer to the lineage of the churches we were trying to create on the stage.

Having Canadians in the cast who were originally from America was an incredible check in terms of giving us authenticity so that we're not mimicking and we're not misinterpreting. To make sure that it didn't feel too shiny, too jazz hands. So it doesn't feel like, "Here's the musicale!" Music can illuminate and deepen, but it can also diminish.

TINUKE: Yeah, it can wash things out, can't it?

KIMBERLEY: It can. When you have something that's so tender as this piece of work, that is just sitting on the precipice, I'm like, "We're not going to miss. We are going to hit all of those things that I know are there, because we have the opportunity to do it with all this knowledge of the novel and the movie." And the opportunity to do it as Black women of our generation right now. You want that music to support it all, and you don't want it to let the audience off the hook. Because sometimes music can let them off the hook, and that's not what this gig is. That's not the assignment.

TINUKE: The music should transport you, but it shouldn't slip you away. Trying to find a space in between that to tell the story—that's our gig, right? But it's complicated. We just did a tour of the production, and depending on where we were, we could vaguely predict what percentage of the audience could be Black. We were in Birmingham—that's a very Black city. Coventry was very different. If we were in places where people have turned up because they just want to watch the lovely Black people doing their lovely singing and dancing, we had to protect ourselves against that as much as possible, and that any kind of fripperousness—or, in the worst circle of hell, minstrelsy—was at least insured

Squeak (Jimand Allotey) and Harpo (Ahmed Hamad), Birmingham Hippodrome, England, 2019

Nettie (Allison Edwards-Crewe) and Celie (Tara Jackson),
The Citadel Theatre, Canada, 2019

Celie (Tara Jackson),
The Citadel Theatre, Canada, 2019

against by the company and the production and my job. That's true with any work, but when there's music, you have to put it through the wringer and interrogate it a little bit more. Whether or not we succeeded I'll never know, because I'm sure there was some terribly nice white lady in an audience who was just, "What a wonderful time. Don't they sing brilliantly?" and then went home. Also, that's not to say that when you're in front of a Black audience, that's a safe space and everyone's going to get it. But it became particularly important on that tour, knowing that the show was going to feel different in different places, to ensure ourselves and do the work. And I think the work's better for it. It's win-win.

KIMBERLEY: That's it.

TINUKE: *The Color Purple* is for everybody, but it's dedicated to Black people. The book felt so specifically and unapologetically about Black women and for Black women. It felt like, if anyone else gets anything out of this then that's great, but it's not for you. Come along for the ride if you must, but we're not going to change any of the language. We're not going to stop and do an expansion comment for you about what's happening.

It's not a bad thing that people relate to Celie's character. They ought to. But the dedication ought to still feel like it's specifically for Black women—that it's a love letter to Black women, and if other people get to read

it that's great. That's how I wanted Black women in the audience to feel when they watched it.

KIMBERLEY: What's so amazing about Black women is that our experience is so grand in this world that everyone can find a connection to it. It's huge. I know for me especially, it's the sisters. My sister and I are incredibly close, and every time I read the book or see the movie and those two sisters are pulled apart…I could cry right now. Done. I am done, done, devastated. I was like, "How dare you write something so beautiful?"

TINUKE: Yeah, me too. I have a sister, and she's my best friend, and we're so tethered to each other. Connected isn't quite a good enough word. You're tethered to them somehow. It doesn't matter where they are in the world. They're always there. And you can't give up. You have to keep going. That came up so often in our room of, why doesn't she just give up? I would just give up. And you go, "Well, she can't." Because she physically is connected to somebody else.

KIMBERLEY: That's it. She can't. Unless she knew that her sister was gone from this earth, that life force between the two of them was always there. Then when she gets the letters—*hoo!*

Hope emancipates you, right? Hope can break all kinds of chains and all these women give it to one

Shug (Karen Burthwright) at Harpo's Juke Joint, The Citadel Theatre, Canada, 2019

another. It's a virtuous circle, and you see them lighting candles for one another.

But that's also one of the things that I like about the musical: having those three church ladies. That Greek chorus is bananas. I love it so much. Having more of a female presence and representing more points of view within a community—I love them.

TINUKE: And holding the real context of the world they're in. The kind of scrutiny you're under all the time. You know the church is this overarching thing, but because you only get it at the beginning, the church ladies become a way of regulating the rules under which Celie lives—in a good way and a bad way.

I also love the church ladies because it's where it's most theatrical. There's always this question of whether putting a work on stage gives us something new that we wouldn't get just from reading the novel. And the church ladies, for me, were the way I could answer that question. I could start to think about the specific theatricality that you can gain with a group like that. How you can then organize the world of the novel on stage in a way that feels visual and accessible and truthful. So I *love* them. And if you've got three great singers—

KIMBERLEY: Oh, my gosh, I still have it as a ringtone! [*sings*] "That's uh-uh-uh-uh-uh."

TINUKE: I was just going to say that! If you have great vocalists, the whole show cracks open.

KIMBERLEY: It cracks open. It's like sunshine on the stage.

TINUKE: And it tells everybody the kind of evening you're in for.

KIMBERLEY: I love the amount of truth they're able to speak. Because we don't hear Black women speaking enough on stage. They can see the truth when they're looking at Celie, but then there's also the truth of, "There but for the grace of God go I, and I'm continuing on with my day."

But then there's compassion. There's, "What's going to happen to this child? Wow, are you all watching what's happening?" Having these ladies on the stage is a way to talk about what it is to be in community and how complex it is. I love those church ladies.

TINUKE: Me too. So much.

KIMBERLEY: When a Greek chorus works, a Greek chorus works. That's who they were for me. The musicality and the classic device that they are in the theatrical space is fantastic. You don't have to work hard to make them ping or to help them do what they need to do. They're just perfectly placed, and they're able to move through the space more quietly than men. Everyone's like, "Oh, they're just doing their chores." But little do you know, they're watching everything. They are our eyes. You're like, "Oh, I didn't see that, but I'm watching Doris watching it."

TINUKE: The church is one of the spaces where women can hold a lot of power in a society that doesn't allow you to hold much power elsewhere.

KIMBERLEY: That's so true. I love, too, how it shows the church is dangerous sometimes. They showed the hypocrisy of it, wielding the big stick of judgment. And as you were saying, by singing directly to us, they implicate us, which is always one of the greatest things ever, when you can implicate the audience: "You're not a voyeur. You're in this. You're going to participate. You have to make some decisions with us in this play."

TINUKE: It's like, "You saw what I saw, right? Don't act like you didn't see that, too."

KIMBERLEY: "I saw you seeing that. I saw you seeing me seeing that."

TINUKE: "Now what are you going to do?" I agree. In terms of directing this show, I think it matters that we are both women, because moving through the world as a woman changes the way you experience it. You are living in a world that's not set up for you.

KIMBERLEY: The performances that the female actors gave, the depths they went down to and came back up from every show was profound. And I hope they trusted this Black director who was female and said, "She's going to hold space for me. She will help me come back out of this every day. She will help me do this work." To have the gift of being able to do that is profound. I got to be the strongest director that I've ever been because I was a Black female directing *The Color Purple*. I was the strongest director I've ever been because of that.

IX

JOY

*But I don't think us feel old
at all. And us so happy.
Matter of fact, I think this the
youngest us ever felt.*

—from Alice Walker's
The Color Purple

TO LAUGH IS TO SURVIVE

PHYLICIA PEARL MPASI (Young Celie, 2023 film): The music in the new film gives the audience a starting point of where we all begin as humans, which is in joy and innocence. Music allows the audience to fully go on Celie's journey, so you're not just hopping into trauma right away. You're actually seeing the full version of her, when she did have a lot of joy. She did have a lot of fun. She had so much happiness in her life in spite of the trauma she was facing. That is really important.

I'm very happy that this film is coming out again, and it's going to be something that my children will one day find. And then they'll find the 1985 version, and it will help them to build a legacy of Blackness that is maybe starting to get a little erased. Maybe not *erased*, but in trying to create more powerful Black stories, sometimes I

that is a survival technique. To laugh is to survive. For instance, when we were working on the show early on with Marsha Norman and Gary Griffin, Brenda and I were always fond of the church ladies' "Uh-Oh" scene, which is not in the movie. It's when the church ladies suddenly become the Greek chorus in the Juke Joint and they're thinking, "This is going to be entertaining because these two women are going to get into it. There's a domestic squabble happening in front of us. We're going to laugh." When Squeak hits Sofia and there's a laugh, I remember several white people in the room said, "That's not funny. That's not funny." Brenda and I said, "Well, it is."

We didn't articulate it this way back then, but had we known what we know now, we would've said, "Yeah, it's not *funny*-funny, but there are so many terrible things we've had to endure, we've had to keep our ability to laugh." We know that given the stakes here and where this is going, it's not going to some terrible place. It's a

"We can see how bad things are and still do the Electric Slide at the cookout."
—Taraji P. Henson

worry that stories like *Color Purple* are going to be talked about less because we don't want to sit in the trauma of it. What this adaptation of the movie is going to do is give us both. Give us joy and give us trauma and see how we're able to get back to our inner beings and almost our inner child.

This film is going to remind people about the incredible and amazing things that we are able to do in spite of the way the world wants to treat us. When I think about the messaging I received as a kid, and even today, the messaging around, "I'm not enough. I'm not worthy. I will never be where I want to be because I'm not white-skinned, blonde, blue eyes," it's a miracle that I wake up every day and I'm excited to take on the day. I think this film is going to remind people of all that we can do.

STEPHEN BRAY (music and lyrics, 2005 Broadway musical, 2015 Broadway revival, 2023 film): We're learning more and more about transgenerational trauma. In the presence of that trauma, we've evolved a sense of humor

skirmish. It's going to be over. We're going to laugh right now. It's a choice we make.

TARAJI P. HENSON (Shug, 2023 film): This is the thing about Black people: We're incredible with turning our trauma into joy. We can see how bad things are and still do the Electric Slide at the cookout. On social media we see injustices happening every time we scroll with that thumb. But then right behind that is somebody Black with an incredible joke. Even the ugliest moments, we tend to put a funny spin on it because we have to. Otherwise, we'll wither up and die. You can't steal our souls. You can keep us locked in an economic pocket, but we gon' slip through the cracks.

PHYLICIA PEARL MPASI: Once I got the role, I worked with an acting coach, Ashley Ware Jenkins, who actually played Celie on the *Color Purple* national tour. This show has been in her lexicon and in her being for years. We went through scenes, and her biggest note for me was always, "You need to bring yourself to this, because that's why they booked you. Anyone can say these lines. Anyone can be this character. But there's something special about you," she kept telling me, "that you need to bring in." Where I always start is comedy and joy, so I looked for those moments. That helped inform the more dramatic moments I had to play, because as children, we start from that joyful place until we get other information. I thought, "If I can really find out where that joy comes from, then I can look at the other aspects of her life that take that away." And the joy was Nettie. So anytime Halle [Bailey, Young Nettie] and I were together, I thought, "This has to be joyful. It has to be beautiful. It has to be rooted in an innocence about Celie."

SCOTT SANDERS (producer, 2005 Broadway musical, 2015 Broadway revival, 2023 film): Life, for most people, is challenging. Life for the characters in *The Color Purple* is in many instances exceptionally challenging. One thing that we have all learned from humanity, and in particular from Black culture, is that humor and music are two tools that are used to mitigate pain. There are characters in *The Color Purple* who are incredibly funny. Obviously, Sofia comes to mind first, but Celie also has a really good sense of humor. It's particularly great to see the women use humor to get them through their days. In terms of music, this story sits between 1909 and 1949, which birthed

incredibly rich genres of Black music, from gospel to jazz to blues. Having the opportunity to bring humor and music into the storytelling really makes the story more buoyant, more entertaining, and more authentic.

SEEING YOURSELF FOR WHO YOU REALLY ARE

AISHA HARRIS (co-host/reporter, National Public Radio's "Pop Culture Happy Hour"): In the book and the 1985 movie, people keep telling Celie she's ugly. And that was something that a lot of critics of the movie latched onto. But you watch that movie, and I, at least, don't think Celie is ugly at all. Part of that is the way that she is framed: Even though other characters are saying this to her, the camera doesn't believe that. It doesn't convey that. It shows that this is what those other characters are projecting onto her.

To some extent, that moment where Celie smiles at Shug is cute, but it's also very beautiful. Whoopi Goldberg is so radiant. I don't know if she's ever been as radiant onscreen. Even though the character can be very meek, we watch her grow stronger and stronger. And when she says, "I'm here," that is her finally realizing that even if she is "ugly" to other people, she deserves to be loved and deserves to exist. That's both an inner and outer beauty that the movie was really able to tap into. I credit Whoopi Goldberg's performance, but also the filmmaking and the way the characters were originally written.

PHYLICIA PEARL MPASI: This story has a way of finding people who not only are talented enough to tell it, but also there's something within them and their being that has to tell the story. That combination is magical and sets this story apart from others. Not anyone can tell the story of *The Color Purple*. I'm not trying to boast myself up, but it requires a special person to tell the story. I'm very grateful I was chosen.

We as people sometimes can feel lost on this journey of life, and watching Celie find herself, and then find herself again in her sister, is like she's coming back to herself. That's inspiring for people. To think that you can experience the worst of the human condition and you can still find love and joy in the end, that's just a very inspiring message that people hold on to.

Celie (Whoopi Goldberg) and Shug (Margaret Avery), 1985 film

Sofia (Danielle Brooks), 2023 film

Clockwise from top left: Corey Hawkins, Blitz Bazawule, Colman Domingo, Taraji P. Henson, Ciara, Fantasia Barrino, and Danielle Brooks on the set of the 2023 film

NIIJA KUYKENDALL (former production executive, Warner Bros.): There's something so relatable and universal to Celie's story of having so much to overcome and then finally deciding to overcome it for herself. There's something that rings very true about being told that you're ugly, even if you're not explicitly told you're ugly. Being told that you're not worth it. Unfortunately, our world tells girls those things. Everyone can relate to that experience, and in America, Black girls can for sure. Even if you're beloved, from a middle class, very great family and a well-taken-care-of young woman, as I was, the world you existed in—the world I existed in, that we all existed in—just every day was saying you're just not worth it. I think that this book uniquely taps into that in terms of how to overcome it. That's why this story is so important and also so universal.

DANIELLE BROOKS (Sofia, 2015 Broadway revival, 2023 film): How beauty was going to be represented on the screen was important to me. Having always been plus-size, as a teenager and as a woman, it was important to me that we were represented in a more complex way, where we weren't automatically assumed to be ashamed about our bigger bodies. Playing Sofia, I feel she's the opposite. When I spoke with Blitz about the character, that was a huge thing for me, making sure that Sofia always looked beautiful, felt beautiful, and knew she was beautiful because I do feel like it's on the page. She's had five kids with Harpo before it goes awry with them, and then she easily gets another guy, Buster. Sofia has a sexiness about her. She has a sex appeal that draws men in. I wanted to make sure that that was not lost.

Perspectives about who can play which roles are definitely starting to shift in this industry and in society. People are just annoyed with Hollywood telling us that we're not worthy enough to play certain characters. The openings we're seeing are led by society more than by the film industry. People are starting to embrace their differences now, and the industry is just catching up to that and understanding the value of individuality. We express that fully in our production by having an array of different shades and body types represented. And sexual orientation, which we're leaning into more than the previous movie did.

I try to embrace who I am wholeheartedly every day. It's not always easy for me, but I want to continue to hold that space because I know how important it is to so many women to see people who are comfortable in their skin. So every day I strive to be that.

OPRAH WINFREY (Sofia, 1985 film; producer, 2005 Broadway musical, 2015 Broadway revival, 2023 film): [Steven] Spielberg told Reuben [Cannon, casting director] to call me and let me know I'd been cast as Sofia. Reuben found out that I was at a fat farm, and he said to me, "Spielberg said if you lose a pound, you could lose this part." Then when I next saw Spielberg, he said, "What were you doing?"

To hear that felt like relief. It felt like I'm not going to have to prove myself because I'm not enough: I'm not thin enough, I'm not pretty enough, I'm not enough. To have the director say that to me was the greatest validation I could have been given as a woman, and certainly as a want-to-be actress. Imagine doing that role, feeling the whole time, "I'm not skinny enough. I need to lose ten more pounds, or twenty more." For me, it would've been fifty more pounds.

I can imagine what that would've done to my whole psyche, my sense of security, my sense of confidence. My ability to step into the role of Sofia would've been hindered by feeling like I wasn't enough to play her. As I reflect on it, it brings tears to my eyes, because it is perhaps the most powerfully validating thing I've ever been told.

LAWRENCE DAVIS (hair department head, 2023 film): Even as a male Black kid, I remember playing with my friends in the community one day and this guy calling me over to his car where he was trying to impress these girls.

"Everything about *The Color Purple* feels like love to me."
—*Oprah Winfrey*

He was an older Black man, and he says, "Hey, come over." I say, "Hey, hey, what's up?" He goes, "You know what? You are the ugliest Black kid I've ever seen in my life." He says that to me, and I just run away from the car.

A lot of kids are told things like that from other kids and some adults when they're children, and it sticks with them and goes with them throughout their lives. I know that firsthand, because it happened to me as a young Black child. But when you embrace who you are, and the history of your people, and the history of your race, and know your inner beauty, you get stronger as a person. You know that it's not about what people say about you, it's about who you are and what you exude. I know that, historically, a lot of African American women in slavery went through abuse and were belittled and told that they weren't good enough. But when they learn who they are, and they get a voice, and they get a backbone, and they learn how to stand up for themselves, and they realize that they are beautiful, whether it's the skin color or the hair, it makes a difference in their life. It definitely does. But that moment was something I will never forget. I got over it, but I remember.

COLLECTIVE JOY (REJOICING)

OPRAH WINFREY: Filming *The Color Purple* was one of the true moments of joy in my life. I've kept a journal since I was fifteen years old, and during *The Color Purple* I wrote in the journal: "This morning I sat in the tree, and I watched everyone else work. I had no scenes today. But I can't wait to be here. Just being here, seeing everybody, seeing Alice, just being around Quincy makes me feel joy. This is what it feels like to love, I believe. Everything about *The Color Purple* feels like love to me."

"*The Color Purple* is my go-to comfort novel. Even though it touches on difficult subject matter like child abuse and forced marriage, this story believes that human kindness, courage, and love can defeat any challenge. Its big, beautiful happy ending is heartfelt and hard-won. Every single time I read this book, I walk away as a slightly better person than I was when I picked it up."

—TAYARI JONES
Author and academic

From "Celeste Ng, Ann Patchett, Min Jin Lee and Others on the Books That Bring Them Comfort" by Elisabeth Egan and Tina Jordan, *The New York Times*, 2020

JOHN LATENSER (supervising location manager, 2023 film): When we completed the [final] scene at the tree, our soundman put music on and the whole cast and crew broke out into the Electric Slide. It was such a great way to kick off the film.

TARAJI P. HENSON: The trauma is there in this story, but what we do with our trauma as Black people is that we always fight for the joy. We always find the joy. Yes, Celie's broken in all of this, but she has a damn imagination, just like every human, and we get to see it. And Black people, we understand that. We understand because we're always hearing, "Can't do that. Don't be loud. Sit down."

So immediately in this film, you'll see what we do miraculously as Black people. We tap into that joy each and every chance we can—you're going to see it through the music, through the choreography, instantly.

Blitz is of the African diaspora. This movie deals with that. This movie deals with two sisters who have been separated. Not only that, how far removed are we from coming over on the ships? Our roots are still tied. We're still connected. We're always going to be connected.

God, this movie is so deep. It's so deep. I'm just so glad and honored to be reimagining another aspect of this incredible piece of literature so that we can continue to keep this conversation going and this story very much alive and give these millennials and the Generation XYZ something to talk about and be proud of.

Celie (Fantasia Barrino) rejoices, 2023 film

JON BATISTE (Grady, 2023 film): It's important for us to really love each other, and to really know what each other's going through, and know that it's more alike and more united than it is separate. Stories like this help us to see that Celie's struggle for identity and her search for self-worth and self-esteem is every one of our struggles. We have a mental health epidemic in this country. We have an epidemic of people not knowing their own value, and I think it's triumphant when someone discovers that they have a purpose and they have a depth. I'm just glad to be a part of anything that can help to spread that message and awareness.

COLMAN DOMINGO (Mister, 2023 film): I had the best time working with Fantasia because it was her first film. I think we realized how much we needed each other for this, for her to do the work that she needed to do and for me to do the work that I needed to do. But there had to be so much love between us, and trust, and friendship, and laughter. We just laughed a lot together. We're playful, we're flirty. So, I always enjoyed laughing with her. For us to do such deep work together, we laughed a lot. I love any scene when the main cast is in one room together, like the Juke Joint scenes. Fantastic. The scene where Taraji is dancing, it's such a celebration of movement. All the dancers, the background—it was extraordinary, those scenes.

HALLE BAILEY (Young Nettie, 2023 film): There are so many examples of Black joy and Black beauty in this film. I think the beauty is from everyone all around. Shug's character, even when I was younger, seeing Margaret Avery in the red dress and her red lipstick, it just ignites something within you. I remember looking at her and then looking at my skin and being like, "I'm like that." She's beautiful, and to all of these people in this film she's beautiful. She was a powerful beauty image for me in the film.

PHYLICIA PEARL MPASI: In the story, Celie eventually believes in herself and sees her own beauty. That's after my part ends, but I kept walking with, "If I don't do the job, it doesn't matter how far Fantasia goes. If I am not sitting in this trauma, it's not going to be worth the payoff in the end." So I was able to take one for the team. I mean, it was Fantasia. I feel like just getting to watch her was joy enough for me. Someone I idolized as a kid. They always say, "Don't meet your heroes." Meet your

Cast and crew spontaneously dance on the set of the 2023 film

heroes. Because it was incredible to have her care for me and look out for me, and any kind of question I had, any hard day, she was like, "Please call me." And I would.

OPRAH WINFREY: The most joyful moment for me in the entire new film is the ending around the tree—the symbolism of the strength of the tree and connection to family. No matter how separated you've been, forgiveness and opening your heart to other people changes everything.

Also, in general, from being involved with *Color Purple* all these years, these decades, I have the full-on recognition that prayers do get answered. I have been able to share everything that I have felt about the book, the play, the Broadway version, the original movie, the story, Alice Walker. I have witnessed again and again how it makes people feel when they watch it, experience it, and are changed by it. They've reopened connections within their own families, were willing to speak about their own abuse, were willing to feel for themselves that maybe for the first time they were enough, were able to forgive somebody who had done great harm to them.

When you release art into the world, you have no idea how many people will be touched by it and in what ways they will be touched. The very offering of the release means that many will be. The joy for me has been to do what Toni Morrison speaks so strongly of in her *Song of Solomon* passage when she says you've got to bend it, break it, shape it, make it, and pass it on.

For me, it's the passing it on that brings me great, great joy. Great joy that another generation will get to experience it and have all those feelings.

CELIE'S PANTS

In the novel, Celie's hard-earned autonomy bears fruit when she launches Folkspants, Unlimited. A boundless enterprise indeed, Celie puts her imagination and skills into redefining what trousers can be—and who can wear them. Costume designer Kara Harmon, who worked on *Purple*'s stage adaptations for Portland Center Stage (Portland, Oregon, 2018), and Signature Theatre (Arlington, Virginia, 2022) reflects on how she interpreted these iconic symbols of liberation and self-actualization.

Miss Celie's Fancy Pants store interior, 2023 film

"The reason we create is to tell stories and evoke conversation, feelings, emotion, dialogue. And as a creative team, even before rehearsals begin, we have a lot of dramaturgical conversations around the themes of the play. The pants hold so much weight in this production. They are the turning point in a lot of ways. There is conflict between some of the women, and in this particular moment, the pants are what pull them all together. But they also demonstrate the women's power and their ability to literally and physically move.

"Up until this moment in time, pants were socially forbidden for women. We get glimpses of them in World War I as women start to go into the workforce, and then a little bit in the '30s when we see Hollywood celebrities dabble in the world of pants. In the '40s, we come into World War II, where women again take on traditionally male roles in the workplace. And slowly, by the 1950s, it's like, "Oh, we get to have clamdiggers!" And then we finally get pants. So thinking about that kind of liberation—all of those thoughts go into the design. There's that element of history.

"There's also the element of our production and what that visual is. And, of course, the language and the text of the script. In our particular production, visually, there's a simplicity and rawness to it. In designing the pants, it was important to me that they felt in the world of it holistically, but also that they would be something we hadn't seen before.

"When Celie is describing the pants, she says she's got a million patterns in her head, and she talks about all the different fabrics she could use. We were trying to get this look where pants feel like they're for everyone. No matter your shape or size, Celie can provide the thing that makes you feel strong and beautiful. In designing the shape, I was looking at the period patterns, but also, what is something that you put on and just feel like you have to strike a pose?

"I would have moments where I was experiencing in the fitting room what Celie would have been experiencing in her fitting room. We start the process with muslin mockup fabric, and then patterns are made for each person. With muslin, we can adjust the tailoring, figure out the shape, the drape, and the detail elements. That's an informative fitting. The next time we fit, we do it in the fabric. And every time we tried pants on people in these fittings, it really did change the person. The way that they stand and move and wiggle and flaunt the pants. It was always very fun, and that's exactly the spirit of this moment, that it's playful and joyful and sort of encourages you to move.

"Very early on in the process, Timothy [Douglas, the director] said that he didn't think anything should be purple except Celie's pants and the single flower that blooms on stage. So they are purple, but they are a whisper of purple."

Celie (Naomi Van Der Linden, center) and cast sing "Miss Celie's Pants," NDSM Wharf, the Netherlands, 2018

Celie (Nova Y. Payton, center) and cast in the pants designed by Kara Harmon, Signature Theatre, Arlington, Virginia, 2022

MISS CELIE'S PANTS

[Celie] (spoken)
Dear Nettie, I went back home to Georgia. The house wasn't too bad, but the store was a dusty mess. I fixed it up, though, and now I'm makin' pants for anybody that wants 'em. I change the cloth, I change the waist, I change the print, I change the pocket. Only thing I can't do is quit makin' em!

[Celie]
*All I need's a needle and a
    spool of thread
Got about a million
    patterns in my head
All the ladies' legs are
    gonna love to dance
When they're in Miss
    Celie's pants.*

[Shug and Squeak]
*Gabardine,
    velveteen, satin
    or lace
Buttons and
    bows all over
    the place*

[Celie]
*Styles that make you feel
    like a queen*

[Shug, Squeak and Sisters]
*That at woman's a wiz
    with a sewin' machine*

[All]
*Who dat say
Who dat say
Who dat?
Who dat say
Who dat say
Who dat?
Who dat say
What you say
In Miss Celie's pants!*

*Who dat say
Who dat say
Who dat?*

[Sofia]
*Lookit here
Get out my way
Sofia's back
And I'm here
    to stay*

[All]
In Miss Celie's pants!

[Shug]
Girl, you swept out
the mem'ries,
Filled this place with joy

[Sofia]
In this big ol' store

[Doris]
Got your sewin' machine

[Darlene]
Mirrors shiny clean

[Jarene]
And a fittin' room
Smell like
sweet
perfume

[Sofia]
That man might have

[Sofia, Doris,*
*Darlene and Jarene]
Done you wrong

[Celie]
But look
I said look
Are you lookin'?

[Sofia]
We all lookin' honey

[Celie]
Look who's wearing the
pants now!

[Everyone]
Who dat?
Who dat say
Who dat say
Who dat?
Who dat say
Who dat say
Who dat?
Who dat say
What you say
In Miss Celie's pants!

[All scat]

[All]
Who dat say
Who dat say
Who dat say

[Celie]
5, 6, 7, 8

[All scat]

Cast of the Broadway musical
revival, Bernard B. Jacobs Theatre,
New York, 2015

X

A NEW PURPLE RISES

*Wonder who
that coming yonder?*

—from Alice Walker's
The Color Purple

Sofia (Danielle Brooks) and
Celie (Fantasia Barrino), 2023 film

VISION QUEST

SHEILA WALCOTT (senior vice president of creative development, Warner Bros.): We landed on Marcus [Gardley, the screenwriter], and then I left Warner Bros. for a couple of years, and then Niija left the company. Then Courtenay Valenti [then president of production and development] asked me to come back. She said, "Sheila, if you come back, you can be the senior executive on *The Color Purple*." I thought, "OMG, that's fantastic, because obviously I have to work on the movie."

I came back, and by this point they had greenlighted the movie. It was also COVID, and we were set to start shooting in three months and were in preproduction. That's what I walked into.

everyone is making the same film. And the bigger the ensemble, the more important it is that we are all making the same film. Costume has to be talking to production design; production design has to be talking to photography; photography has to be talking to choreography. When we all watch it together, we know very quickly if everyone is on the same page or not.

When I started putting it together, besides the storyboarding, I also had a very basic acronym that I used to synthesize all the groups, and it was SPA, with *S* standing for scale, *P* for proximity to audiences today, and *A* for authenticity. This film has to have scale. It has to be the biggest version of *The Color Purple* that's ever been made, otherwise there's no reason to make it. It has to have proximity to audiences today. We cannot create a film that makes the audience think, "Oh, that's dated." If

"This film has to be the biggest version of *The Color Purple* that's ever been made."
—*Blitz Bazawule*

BLITZ BAZAWULE (director, 2023 film): My style of filmmaking is to get a lot done in the prep period. I start with storyboarding every scene myself. I don't hire an on-set artist because then it's their movie, not mine. I've been a visual artist for many years, so that's quite a cheat that I can rely on. With this project, I went even further. Not only did I sketch every scene, but I also stitched them together and hired voice artists to read. Everyone who was hired had to sit through a two-hour viewing of this pre-movie movie. These pencil sketches tell you very quickly if your film works or doesn't. I found problems in that phase that I didn't carry into production. For instance, Celie and Shug were supposed to sing "What About Love?" with microphones, and it was very obvious in our sketches that it was going to be boring, watching two people stand and sing on microphones. I couldn't draw it dynamically, so I knew that I couldn't film it dynamically. I had to call Fatima [Robinson, the choreographer] and ask her to figure out an elegant way of motion.

That pre-vision had everything: It had music, it had dance, it had sound effects. The goal is that I know

that's the case, there are other versions they can experience. And while doing so, we could not forget that it has to still feel authentic. We still have to feel, "I'm living in Celie's life from 1910 to 1950."

Everybody can't be doing everything at the same time, so in a given scene, I will know that maybe production design's going to give us scale, choreography will give us proximity to audiences today, and then maybe costume will anchor us in authenticity. We were always passing the baton around.

TARAJI P. HENSON (Shug, 2023 film): Blitz is very delicate. It's almost like he comes in and gives you the mood. It's very nurturing. When you feel like you're cared for in that way, you become uninhibited. I feel the safety net there. I'm going to leap feet first because I know he's got me. That's how magic happens. He's the captain of the ship. If you don't have a clear vision for steering us, then what do you expect from me? How is my instrument going to feel free to create? That's what he creates. He creates the safest, most loving environment.

— PIANO CART

RICKY DILLARD (MYSTERIOUS WAYS)
CHOIR ROBE/
GLASSES.

THINK CARNIVAL FLOATS
OR SOUND SYSTEMS.
FASTEN PIANO AT BACK
OF CART FOR CHOIR
MASTER. WILL ADD
DIEGETIC ELEMENT
TO OPENING SEQUENCE

MISTER: COLMAN

STYLE MUST EVOLVE
NEEDS PERIOD HAT
THAT FEELS COOL TODAY
EARTH TONE WORK
CLOTHES. STYLE CHANGES
WHEN SHUG ARRIVES
BACK TO DISTRESSED
LOOK AFTER CELIE
LEAVES.

Director Blitz Bazawule's sketches
for the 2023 film drew on his experience
as a visual artist

Blitz

SHUG : TARAJI
MOST STYLISH CAST
MEMBER. USE RED
OFTEN AS COLOR OF
POWER WHICH SHE
WILL PASS TO CELIE.
FUR COATS AND FANCY
HATS SHOULD BE NORM.
MAKE UP, NAILS ETC
MUST REFLECT THE
TIMES.

CELIE : FANTASIA
FUNERAL LOOK FOR ALFONSO FUNERAL
ALL BLACK. HAT WITH
IVET. MAYBE ADD FUR COAT
TO REFLECT HER NEW
STATUS > BAG, AND GLOVES
A MUST. LIGHT
MAKE UP
GREY STREAK IN
HAIR?

NETTIE : HALLE
MODEST STYLE.
CLOTHES SHOULD BE
WORN BUT NOT DIRTY
HAT SHOULD BE MEMORABLE
IDEALLY STRAW.
MUTED COLORS IDEAL.
NO MAKE UP

COREY HAWKINS (Harpo, 2023 film): For me, working on this required all of myself. *In the Heights* required all of myself artistically, but this also required myself spiritually and as a Black man, the history, my ancestors. Being part of a project like this is a once-in-a-lifetime thing. We've never seen it. Yeah, they did the original film, but now we have characters who take on a different nuance and the music that'll live forever on film.

This was the first time that I felt truly, from the top down, that this film was, as we say, "for us, by us." We had so much support. We had Mama O [Oprah Winfrey] up there. We had Quincy [Jones]. We had allies like Scott [Sanders], like Mara [Jacobs], who have believed in this story for years.

From the beginning, I realized how special this was going to be. Everybody at the top realized it too. Usually, when the Warner Bros. executives come to visit, we call them the Suits. The execs aren't Suits anymore. There were women, Black women executives, who spent time on set, and they recognized and felt how beautiful it was. Every day we were on set, there would be tears shed or people in the back clapping. I'd look over at Gayle [King] and Oprah singing along with a song. It was a hard shoot, but it did not get old. Sometimes, working on films, after a while the magic goes away and you're like, "OK, it's a job. Got to keep going." But the magic never went away.

JON BATISTE (Grady, 2023 film): Blitz is a musician as well as a film director, and there was so much musicality to his approach. The way that he would direct reminded me of how a bandleader would get the best out of their musicians. He would give notes that were very musical, almost like telling the drummer, "Loosen up on the snare." He would say, "Loosen up in the scene" in a way that was very special. With the music that was played in "Miss Celie's Blues," it would turn into these jam sessions. He would allow us to have the moment play out and be a natural segue into the next take. There was a real beauty and flow to the way he had the set feel like it was a natural, inevitable flow from scene to scene.

BLITZ BAZAWULE: I really believe in thoughtful planning. It alleviates a level of anxiety, which then allows you to see the magic in real time. If you are too pressed because you are unprepared, then you can't see the blessings that float up because you're so in the tunnel of unpreparedness.

I showed up on set two hours before call. Played a little guitar, sat down, walked the sets, felt at home—because once it gets flooded, as much as you would like to, you can't see. It's just people in your frame. So I show up when no one's there, when the grips are still loading the lights in, and I'm able to see the entire

Gayle King and Oprah Winfrey
on the set of the 2023 film

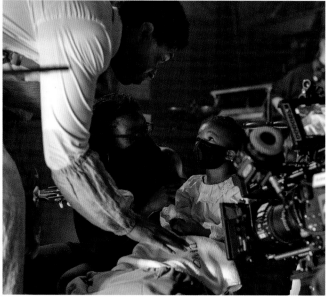

Deon Cole encourages a young cast
member on the 2023 film set

Blitz Bazawule plays guitar on the 2023 film set

day play out. Some days I just know, "It's going to be a rough one, but I'm prepared for it. I'm prepared for it."

DEON COLE (Alfonso, 2023 film): Blitz is one of the most talented, amazing directors I've ever met. His guidance was unreal. There was one situation where we were in the store, and this is when Celie was talking to the baby, and I had to scream at her and tell her to get back to work. Every time I did that, the baby would lose it. We had fifteen or sixteen takes because the baby would cry, to the point where we had to start dancing and trying to make the baby smile and laugh and look like I'm really not a bad guy. They brought Blitz a guitar, so he was playing the guitar while I was dancing, and all the cameramen were sitting there just waiting around for the baby to smile. And that went on for an hour and a half.

DANIELLE BROOKS (Sofia, 2015 Broadway revival, 2023 film): The fact that we shot scenes out of order wasn't so challenging for me because I had played this character for a year. I know this story in and out, dissected, in between, turned on its head, flipped upside down. I know this story. It didn't throw me at all because I knew exactly how much paint I wanted for each section of the canvas. I knew exactly the tools I was going to use, the texture of paintbrush I wanted. I knew exactly how rich I wanted the color to be. I was able to do that with the film because of having this long journey with Sofia. I had always approached Sofia starting with the book. It takes you on a deeper journey. It's so much more specific. I would read it over and over, little points that would open up something else in me or make me think of something else.

What changed the most for me since I played Sofia on Broadway was that I got married and had a child. My daughter changed a lot for me. Having a family and understanding love in a different way really contributed to what I was able to bring into this production.

BLITZ BAZAWULE: There's a continuum in African American culture and history that has held it all together, and that continuum is something this film helps unpack. Very few properties allow us to explore African American existence in a thirty- to forty-year span of history and culture, where it's not purely through the prism of either enslavement or subjugation but through a domestic life and the evolution of that domestic life. It was a great opportunity for us to find and meet African Americans at an equilibrium in this story, existing as people, with all the ups and downs that happen as they will with any culture.

of her parents; her sister is taken from her. She's raped by this man who she has to live under, and his kids are abusive to her. She doesn't have the power, at least at the beginning and midway, to say, "Stop treating me like this."

How do we tell her story? How do we depict her circumstance? It came to me so naturally, because the content and the art form are in concert with each other in a beautiful way. I leaned on the visual. My first pass through, I didn't do any dialogue. What does this film look like if it has no dialogue in it? All of these images start popping up.

The dialogue wasn't hard to do, because there are so many iconic lines. I really made a list of, "If I don't include this, I'm never going to be able to walk the streets again." I made that list, and then I did the iconic scenes. It was also important for me, being brutally honest, to bring my own self to it. I thought, "What about this book do I often think about? If this was my story, what's that ver-

"I was in everybody's trailer at some point, multiple times throughout, especially on heavy days."

—Blitz Bazawule

FRANCINE JAMISON-TANCHUCK (costume supervisor, 1985 film; costume designer, 2023 film): When my agent called to ask if I was available to meet with the people from *The Color Purple* musical film, I was finishing up *Emancipation* and thought, "Maybe I should take a rest after that particular epic." But I just really couldn't resist, and even though it meant doing films back-to-back, I ended up saying yes.

MAKING THE MAGIC

MARCUS GARDLEY (screenwriter, 2023 film): With this particular show, which is why the magical realism is so important, I really sat back and thought, "This central protagonist has few words. Her voice, in a lot of ways, has been robbed from her. She was molested; she lost both

sion?" That came through a choppy dialogue; staccato is the best way to describe it. It's very sharp dialogue these characters have. That's my family, that's growing up in a massive family.

I had a beautiful opportunity as a child to experience this. My great-grandmother died the day I was born, and our family, even though they're super-Christian, believe in superstition. They said, "That's her. She didn't want to leave the earth. That little boy is her." I got the honor of sitting around them, where no other male could, until I turned thirteen. I got to sit amongst them when they were cooking. All of this language, all of these beautiful Black women, the way they spoke, the way they sang, the way they loved on each other, the way they experienced heartbreak—all of that is in my body, because I got to be this little kid in the corner, listening to them. It's all there. I wanted to give that to this screenplay. Also, my father and the men of my family played dominoes, so there's a scene of that in there, which nobody wanted. I said, "I have to," and they let me have it.

One of the biggest gifts writers receive is the opportunity to add their own thread to any story they write or adapt. You become a piece, a patch of a larger quilt—something that ultimately brings people comfort and stays with them forever.

ALICE WALKER (author of *The Color Purple*, 1982): I love the magical realism. Gabriel García Márquez is one of my favorite writers because of that. We tend to feel like—of course we do—nature is extraordinary. But nature *is* extraordinary. The whole thing is extraordinary. It moves in ways that are incredible, in the way you see things, the way they appear to the soul, not just to the eye. The way you can be looking at something and somebody else can be looking at the same thing and you're seeing two different things. I love it. To play with that, and to just get all into that and to stretch it, is what artists do.

BLITZ BAZAWULE: The Africa section was highly researched. We had to ground every bit of it in reality. I know Ghana, and I know that the dominant tribe is the Ashanti, so that's who I leveraged for this. There was an entire well of culture we could pull from: language, cadence, musical history, and style. So why make it up?

We treated Georgia the same way. It's coastal Georgia. When you see the landscape, you know that you are in a real place, and this place has history and culture. The groundedness of this film is what then gives us license to expand and create hyperbole. You can't do that if your ground is shaky. I'm sure some of my collaborators will attest to this: We let nothing slide. In one scene, where there's a large orchestra playing, we were running behind, so we decided we couldn't custom tailor [their costumes]. We bought suits in bulk for the thirty-plus orchestra players, but the problem was that the lapels were not the right period. Any other team might say, "So what? They're going to be in the background anyway."

But we banded together, Francine [Jamison-Tanchuck, the costume designer] leading the charge, working overtime and on weekends to make sure that every single lapel was altered correctly. Now you look at the cut, you can't even see them; they're in the background. But it matters. In every sense and at every turn, we created a world of support. It was obvious how Colman [Domingo] cared for Fantasia [Barrino], how Corey cared for H.E.R. So much love and help was offered

Young Nettie (Halle Bailey) carries Celie's daughter, Olivia, in Africa, 2023 film

to some of our newer entrants, like Jon Batiste, who'd never quite done this before, or Halle Bailey, who's fairly new in her career. It was such camaraderie, from the first rehearsals until the day we wrapped.

I was in everybody's trailer at some point, multiple times throughout, especially on heavy days. We talked. I always made myself available, and I often showed up uninvited because it was important that support was felt and it wasn't just that they were hired to do a job. We had minors there, and if they weren't minors, they were young: our Young Celie, our Young Nettie. There are many traumatic scenes in this film that they had to endure. My job, more than anything, was to be there to talk through the implications, the emotional weight that they were bearing. The actors bear it all, and I've never once taken for granted the personal sacrifice it takes to embody a character. Colman Domingo is the nicest guy you will ever meet, but he has to find a place in himself that is brutal, and we have to believe him, otherwise we do not have a movie. Beth [Marvel], who plays Ms. Millie, is one of the nicest people you'll ever meet, but she had to be stone-cold and mean.

LOCATIONS

Purple's creative team scoured Georgia for buildings and backdrops to
use in the new musical film. Thanks to preservation and, sometimes, neglect, they
found the texture and authenticity they needed in locales ranging from Jekyll
Island to Senoia, Macon to Savannah, and Atlanta to Grantville.

Rendering of the closing scene, 2023 film

Celie (Fantasia Barrino) reunites with Nettie (Ciara), 2023 film

THE ANGEL OAK

JOHN LATENSER (senior location manager, 2023 film): Locations are basically actors. Yes, they're in the background, but they're telling just as much as anything or anyone else. My favorite part of making films is when I'm driving around with the production designer and the creative juices are flowing and we're thinking about where these characters would live. Why would they be here?

PAUL AUSTERBERRY (production designer, 2023 film): We drove for five weeks.

JOHN: We drove in my car. I had to get it serviced.

PAUL: I don't know how many thousands of miles we put in.

JOHN: Our goal was to find these amazing locations that tie the story together and make it look like we're all in one place. That was also tricky for the art department because we filmed all over Georgia and on stages in Atlanta. In fact, our greens department actually brought the fine, sandy soil that they have on the coast to all of our locations and spread it out, which made the film look amazing but drove the crew crazy because they got so dirty.

PAUL: Our job, in a way, is to have the backgrounds just become part of the background. The story is the story. That's what you want to tell. Our backgrounds help elevate the story and make everyone believe they're right there.

JOHN: One of the main characters in the film is actually this Angel Oak tree. This film's about Celie's roots. It's about where she came from, where she's gone with her life, and who she's connected to. This tree represented so many different things, including family history, the family tree. But it also put us in the right geographical place where this film should have been filmed. That's coastal Georgia, which has these grand oaks with Spanish moss hanging down. To make it even more cinematically appealing, we went out and found the best possible tree we could find. We found a place that had pretty much been untouched for over a hundred years, and it's where the folks in this film would've lived.

WATERFALL

OPRAH WINFREY (Sofia, 1985 film; producer, 2005 Broadway musical, 2015 Broadway revival, 2023 film): I am, believe me, a die-hard loyalist to the original film, so this reimagining took me a minute. At first I said, "Celie wasn't near the water. She lives in North Carolina. She didn't see no ocean. We weren't playing on the beach. How you gonna do that?"

Once I went to Georgia, I was like, "Oh, OK." These locations bring a broadened sense of longing to the story. The thing that knocks my socks off is Young Celie [Phylicia Pearl Mpasi] singing "She Be Mine," walking through the chain gang and then coming to the washerwomen. Just visually stunning.

JOHN: Blitz said to me, "What about the scene where the women are washing clothing in the river? Do you have something special?" And I said, "Yes, there's this old mill in Senoia that has a waterfall. I've seen it over and over again, but it's never been filmed." Getting a film crew in there was super-hard, but when Blitz saw it, he said, "That's what I'm talking about."

We walked up to the waterfall, and then it occurred to us, "How deep is it, really?" We grabbed a stick and pushed down, and it went all the way till the stick disappeared. We got a longer one. [Then] we hired a marine unit to put on scuba gear and measure the depth. It'd be 2 feet deep here and 7 feet deep there. We said, "There's no way we're going to be able to film this unless we build a platform."

PAUL: At great expense and a lot of labor and people in wetsuits, we built an underwater stage. It was almost 100 feet long and 14 feet deep. We put scaffolding in about 3 inches below the water. We painted two layers of plywood to look a bit like sand and smooth rock. We had to scribe it all carefully to the shore, because they come from the shore onto it, do their dance, and then they walk back off. It looked beautiful live, watching them.

FATIMA ROBINSON (choreographer, 2023 film): There are always challenges in the moment. You'll do things one way in a dance studio, and then you get to the location and you're almost rechoreographing in the space. Once we got to the waterfall, we had to restage it for camera, so we had to move the girls around to fit the different

On location at the waterfall in Senoia, Georgia, 2023 film

Purple Rising

Crew members build the waterfall platform for the 2023 film

The set of Harpo's Juke Joint, 2023 film

Rendering of Harpo's Juke Joint, 2023 film

camera angles. We had to move rocks around. The stylists had made shoes for them that looked like feet, but that didn't work, so the girls had to do it barefoot. It was slippery with the water and the moss that grows on rocks. Restaging it so that everybody felt safe and we'd get it right with camera was one of those things that took some time. You have to keep working and working on it until it comes together, but it was so powerful to see Phylicia singing as the washerwomen got up and danced.

JUKE JOINT

JOHN: This starts out as Old Mister's house, then it becomes Sofia and Harpo's, then it becomes the Juke Joint. We decided the most efficient way to do this was to film it in reverse order and build the whole Juke Joint, then strip it down. We had scouted real swamps in the Savannah area that looked amazing. But there were other challenges, like they have alligators. We found a swamp that didn't have alligators.

PAUL: Building out in the middle of the water is not easy. We chose this location because it was a fishing pond that had been artificially dammed. The beauty of this place was that we had control: We could pump water in or out.

It may not have been the easiest place to shoot, but we were able to drain it down to a muddy bottom and then put swamp mats down—heavy fiberglass mats that interlock. You can make a path over swampy ground, then drive little machines out there to drive the piles into the water to build everything.

We went back to this place three times because we had three different time frames in our film. We needed to have it drained to build that big structure, so we worked backward.

The Juke Joint is one of my favorite sets. It was quite difficult to plan out. It's not a highbrow set. It's not particularly difficult design-wise, but it was just tricky to execute. Harpo spent three years working on the Juke Joint. He would have scavenged a bunch of wood and windows, so that's what we did. We actually scavenged windows, and we actually salvaged a bunch of wood to put on there. And old tin for the roof, just to give it all free patina. It's just so character-filled when you see it.

COREY HAWKINS (Harpo, 2023 film): When I saw what they'd built, it blew my mind: the level of detail and quality that made it look like it had been there for years. I was in awe. But then I also thought, "Uh-oh. I got to show up and show out because this is for me. This is Harpo's Juke Joint. I can't let them down. I don't want them to catch me sleeping."

Halle Bailey and Blitz Bazawule
on set, 2023 film

MEMORABLE MOMENTS

ALICE WALKER: When I was visiting the set, the scene that made me just weep before I even understood what I was weeping about was where Mister, who would've been my young grandfather before I knew him, talks about how he had wanted to sing, to be a musician. I thought my heart would break. My grandfather's heart had been broken: maybe not that he wanted to be a musician, but after Reconstruction, he actually thought he was going to have a place that he owned that was truly his.

The direction of that scene brought me to tears. I realized Blitz's power as a thoughtful, compassionate director. I didn't know his work before that. I'd seen one or two things that I liked the magical realism of,

that scene, everyone on set knew: Phylicia's going to need some help.

The two days we filmed that, especially the first day, there was so much joy and love, and I felt so taken care of, especially by Halle and Colman. We had such a bond in the cast holding area. We were all freezing, but we were still able to have fun. The first day was leading up to the separation, kind of the "Let us stay, please." The second day was the actual separation. It was pushing 3 a.m., 4 a.m. Halle had left, and it was me and Colman. Something happened where we had a two-hour break. I was defeated, I was soaking wet because they had to wet us between every take. I was exhausted.

I started singing some Hilary Duff song. I don't know what I was going through. I felt: "I need to not be in this space because I don't know if I can do any more takes."

> # "[When] Mister, who would've been my young grandfather before I knew him, talks about how he had wanted to sing, to be a musician. I though my heart would break."
> ## —Alice Walker

and some of the ways that he creates wonder from the natural I truly, truly resonate with. His film *The Burial of Kojo* had some scenes on the water that made me think, "This is someone seeing wonder his own way." I like that. I really affirm that in people: See wonder your own way.

PHYLICIA PEARL MPASI (Young Celie, 2023 film): I was stressed out about the scene where Nettie and Celie were going to be separated by Mister. Anytime someone would mention it, I would think, "What am I going to do?" One of the reasons I was so resistant to this piece for so long was from watching that scene in the Spielberg film. I had a younger sister; I never wanted to know what that's like. And it was in an iconic scene: Danny Glover beating the hands. I remember watching that as a kid and thinking, "Oh my gosh, I can't believe these two girls have gone through this." By the time we got ready to shoot

And Colman pulled me aside and said, "We are here to create art, and we're here to create magic. This is not a film. This is your real life. I'm going to take your sister away." He kept repeating it: "I'm going to take your sister away; I'm going to take your sister away." And he said, "Just leave every single thing that you have here on the ground, and we never have to talk about it again."

That gave me everything I needed to get through. Especially from someone like Colman. It wasn't even about him getting his take, it was about me being able to be in that space and be in that moment and get through it. I will always remember that.

After we filmed that, I didn't talk for two days. I could not separate myself from the character. I remember thinking, "Am I in this situation because I'm not pretty? Because I'm not beautiful? Because I've done something to manifest this?" I wanted this dream job; I wanted this role. But this night was so hard. "Is this what it's like to be an actor? I don't know if I want to do this. I have to rethink my life. I don't know if I'm strong enough to keep diving into old emotion and old trauma and showcasing it for people."

When you film something, everybody else is focused on the camera and the lights and the costumes. I felt like no one cared about me. They had me do it over and over and over again. Afterward, I was going to call my managers and say, "I think I have to quit. I can't do this," when I got a text message. "Hi, it's Oprah. Do you mind if I call you?" And I responded, "Ha ha ha, who is this?" She was like, "Oprah." I said, "OK, yes, you can call me. No problem." She called, and she had been there the whole time watching. When I felt so alone and like no one saw me, she was watching. She said, "I was going to come over, but you were so locked in and triumphant and dynamic. I did not want to pull you from where you were as a character." She said, "I'm so proud of you. You did phenomenal work, and I hope you hold on to this moment and know that you did something really beautiful and profound that a lot of people cannot do."

I had been at my lowest point, and a woman who I've admired my entire life was watching me. I had no idea.

OPRAH WINFREY (Sofia, 1985 film; producer, 2005 Broadway musical, 2015 Broadway revival, 2023 film): I could see how much she gave—she gave us her soul in that scene.

Mister (Danny Glover) separates Celie from Nettie, 1985 film

"It was a very hard scene for us to play, but we got through it."
—Halle Bailey

HALLE BAILEY (Young Nettie, 2023 film): Right before I get thrown out of the house, Colman, Mister's character, is coming on to me. He comes into my bedroom. It's nighttime and thunderstorming. In the original, [Nettie] gets thrown out in sunlight. This version feels dark; the mood feels dark. Colman helped me so much throughout that whole scene, because we were really fighting each other. It was physical. I was tussling, fighting against him, pulling him. He was throwing me. It was very emotional, and I had to go somewhere deep for that, but then, when we started the rain scenes, after he had thrown me onto the dirt, I'm kind of falling, and there's a moment where I'm on my knees. Right before they called "Action," they'd say, "OK. Get in your positions." I'm in the mud, waiting for the rain to start. I was on my knees, and I closed my eyes, and they said, "OK, we're starting the rain in 3…2…1." The rain started, and it was washing over me, and it was freezing, and it was so cold at night, but it almost felt like an awakening for me and my soul.

We had to do that over and over and over again, but I remember, even though it was freezing, I was really excited for that one moment when the rain would start, and I closed my eyes and got into it. When I opened my eyes, I felt like I was Nettie. It was a very hard scene for us to play, but we got through it. That was one of the best moments for me because I felt like I grew so much after it. I don't know if I healed something within myself. I felt empowered.

DANIELLE BROOKS: One of the real bonuses was getting to work with Colman Domingo. I've always been a huge fan of his, and I feel like we're similar actors in that we never go for safe choices. We're always trying to find the most interesting way of telling the story. For so long, I thought, "I cannot wait to get on a project with him and see what we come together and find."

Mister (Colman Domingo) throws out Young Nettie (Halle Bailey), 2023 film

DANIELLE BROOKS:
ON STAGE VS. SCREEN

Sofia (Danielle Brooks), Bernard B. Jacobs Theatre, New York, 2015.

"When I was playing Sofia on Broadway [in 2015], I felt a freedom of artistic expression. In that production, we were coming from a very minimalist place where we could use our imagination to create the story. That was so much fun. I had gotten my start working in black boxes. When you're a first-year student at Juilliard, you're taught how to bring a story to life with a box and maybe a bag, just one or two things. Working with [director] John Doyle on the stage, I was creating a baby out of a sheet. You're bringing the audience into your world by creating those things; it all has to come from you, the actor.

"There were times that it was challenging to be without actual props or space or people. I think about the scene where Sofia is getting beaten by this mob of white men. When I was on stage, I did that scene with no one else there; I had to use my imagination and come up with a way of expressing to the audience the internal pain Sofia was going through when externally, nobody was seeing me get hit. When we did it in the film, it was easier to tap into that scene, being that I did have all of the elements and all of the players right there.

"For the film, I actually had a mob. But that presented its own challenges, too, physically and mentally. To have to continuously go through a scene like that, to go through being beaten by white men in the 1930s—I thought about my own family's history. It was really quite traumatizing to the body, to the point where my back went out and I had to do physical therapy afterward. Doing that over and over and over definitely had its challenges, but I preferred having all of the elements available to me, feeling the ground under my feet and the dirt and being on an actual plantation and having the water surrounding me. It's a whole different ball game when you can use all your senses to tell the story."

Sofia (Danielle Brooks) confronts the mayor (Charles Green), 2023 film

Mister (Colman Domingo, center) plays dominoes at Harpo's Juke Joint, 2023 film

The first time Sofia gets to meet Mister was one of my favorite scenes, because she comes in with such innocence and excitement to meet her soon-to-be father-in-law. The energy he gives her is like watching two bulls go at it. It was so much fun to play with Colman. Every take was different. The subtleties of him cutting his eyes at me and what that would make me do. Or while he and the other men were at the table playing dominoes and he said something smart to me, I would take a tile from the table, then flick it back at him at the end of the scene like, "I always will have one up on you." There were all these little beats we were able to find in the moment.

COLMAN DOMINGO (Mister, 2023 film): There may be very few white characters on camera, but their impact is implicit. It's permeating all the choices. You know the systems that you live under, and you're trying to become human and navigate and have power and agency in your own life, but you know that. That's the container that you're in. This book—and this film and musical—shows this so very clearly. I love that no one says anything directly about the white man or what he's done. They're just operating and moving through space, trying to get by and figure it all out for themselves. That says a lot about Black people in America. It's been our constant since we've been here. We're navigating this land that's not ours and then trying to find our plots of land and make our families and make our lives in every single way. That's what this film does.

The first thing I truly understood about Blitz was after we finished rehearsal of the ending, a scene where music and dance play throughout. The first thing I said to him with tears in my eyes was, "You love us. You love us." Because that scene was such a celebration of who we are, from the inside. It's not from an outside purview. It is from the inside. "Oh, you love us, you love your grandmother, you love the African descendants, you love all of us."

BLITZ BAZAWULE: You've got to start with love, and I'm talking about the deep kind. And you also have to start with the responsibility. I'm very, very aware of the responsibility that's on us to tell the story right and to tell it in all its majesty and greatness because of how few opportunities like this exist for the actors. The big thing was to try to make sure that if we never, ever made a film again, which is implausible, but if we never made a film again, this has to be a beacon of how to do it right. And all it is for me is submitting. I hired people that could submit. You didn't have to be Black [to work on this film] but you had to have love for Black people and love for Black culture. And not the superficial kind, either, because it will show. If Dan [Laustsen, the cinematographer] has no love for Black people on this planet, you will know from when you look at one frame. It's that simple. And that doesn't make that person a bad person or a good person, it just means, "I don't have love and appreciation for this thing or these people or this experience."

That's how I picked everybody. Sure, there are talented people who can act their asses off and film and choreograph and do all this, but I needed people who had love for this particular version of Blackness that we were trying to exalt. When you have that many people who are there for the right reasons, you cannot fail, because the love *for* is what allows all this brilliance to exist. It was really special to put together an army, pretty much, of brilliant people who I have love for, and it had to start with me. I had to have a deep love and appreciation for me, mines, and my larger diaspora. If I had that, then I knew that I would be able to pull people who were seeking the same thing.

And there was no *I*. It's a cliché, but there was no *I* in this set. It was always *we*. Nobody ever endured anything alone. No one ever was made to feel isolated or alone. I saw it in how the actors interacted with one another. There was a true love, joy, and appreciation from the most experienced to the least experienced.

COREY HAWKINS: If you grow up in Ghana as a Black person and you grow up in the United States as a Black person, there's a difference in the way that you may see the world. Honestly, I thought about that. I thought, "We have this Ghanaian-born director directing a story about Black people in the South. Is he going to get it right? Can he touch that? Can he access that? Well, what if a Black person from the South directed it? What would it be like if a Black American went and directed a Ghanaian film or a film in Nigeria?" We have to start having those conversations. Blackness is bigger than Black American or Ghanaian or Nigerian or Kenyan or a Black British person who grew up in London.

SHEILA WALCOTT: This was a tough shoot. We had four COVID outbreaks. In the scene where Celie finally confronts Mister at the dinner table, every single day someone got COVID, and then we'd have to break and go down for two or three days, if not more. There's only one shot when all of the actors were actually there. All of our actors gave beautiful renderings, but Danielle in particular went through this range of emotion from laughing to crying and grateful, and the whole time, she was talking to a stand-in.

For the most part, that scene had to be shot in increments, and then Blitz put all of those pieces together to make it feel cohesive. But when you watch that scene with an audience, it's one of the most well-received scenes in the movie.

Left to right: Sofia (Danielle Brooks), Celie (Fantasia Barrino), and Harpo (Corey Hawkins), 2023 film

JON BATISTE: I really enjoyed being with Louis Gossett Jr., sitting at the table doing the Easter dinner scene, and this scene was captured over multiple days. Planned for two days, and all of these setbacks happened. One of the most incredible things to see for me was how, over the course of two days, Louis would change his approach and mold his response to the moment based on what everybody else was doing, and really live it out authentically every time. He's such a true, true veteran. In every sense, he's elite, and I remember it transferring so much knowledge to me as to how to live in front of the camera. That was such an incredible experience. A lot of the cast was on set and a part of that scene, and you could see everybody watching him and learning and soaking it up. Something about that moment was profound for us all. I remember Taraji looked at me at the end of one

of his own experience being from Ghana and then living in America. You feel that in his visual language, how colorful and robust his staging is. Then the scale: It is Africa and it's the Americas, and it's that convergence. It's all that he knows. I rarely feel this way while working on a film, but I felt like, "This looks beautiful." I could tell with the lighting and his incredible director of photography. I felt like I was in a gorgeous painting that was all set up for me. All I had to do was work to help that become more animated.

A lot of times you can't tell what it's going to look like on camera. But on this set, you could tell because it had such deep, layered lighting sources, plus the staging, where they placed the cameras. You feel the movement of the camera. You felt like, "I'm in a film that moves, and it flies, and it turns around, and it turns in on itself, and it expresses itself from the inside out."

"Blitz made it bigger than life in a fantastic way. He's a renaissance guy in that true sense of the word."
—Stephen Bray

of his takes and she kept saying, "Y'all going to learn today. This is a master class right here. Y'all going to learn today."

TARAJI P. HENSON: Oh my God, Jon is so incredible in this. I had so much fun working with him, because he's the guy who's going to make whatever he does shine. Grady's not a huge role, but he is totally memorable. I'm telling you, he steals the scene.

GETTING THE LOOK

COLMAN DOMINGO: Blitz is an incredible visual artist. I feel like there is some beautiful amalgamation happening there; he knows in his mind that he's painting these images. That's why it feels fresh. It feels like a crossroads

DAN LAUSTSEN (director of photography, 2023 film): I'm trying to tell the director's vision in a very visual way. And that, for me, is using the camera, writing with the camera, and painting with the light. That is a director of photography's work.

For me, this job was like a dream come true because I really wanted to do a musical; I had been very interested in doing that for a long time. There were a lot of things that were really thrilling for me to do that I hadn't done before. That period, around 1900, is super-interesting, and I wanted to be a part of telling this important story about Black history. I'm from Denmark, so it's not a part of my history, but of course, I know the history about Black people, and there was [slavery] in Denmark in the early 1800s. That's something we have talked about in Denmark. It's something we're not proud of. For me, it was like, "Wow, it's important and it's very, very interesting." I'm proud of being a part of that storytelling.

BLITZ BAZAWULE: In terms of the photography, Dan and I talked very early about how we were not going to photograph this film the way a lot of period films are photographed, which is to affect a sepia tone. Instead of using photographs that have survived a hundred years as our reference point, we were like, "No, let's go into the photo. What was it like when these people were living? Sepia is just what's survived."

Proximity to the characters—the sweat, the smoke, the richness of their world—is something that you rarely see in period films because, again, most people are using photographs as the reference point, as opposed to saying, "Well, let's imagine ourselves there. What would it feel like in Harpo's Juke Joint?" It's all part of the conversation of figuring out how to make sure that this is not an external gaze of these people, which often creates extremities: They have to be so beautiful that it's unreal. Sometimes you watch a period film and it feels like everybody shopped at the Sears and everything was perfect, and I go, "That's improbable."

We cannot be afraid to show Black people as themselves, as beautiful as they are. Here, we're talking about a period when there was no AC, and it was hot. It's the rural South, so people sweat, and it's important that you show that, because the authenticity is what then gives you the license to create fantastical elements: because the audience knows that you've been diligent about the time. That's ultimately what magical realism is—it's as real as it gets, but there are elements of fantasy. Sometimes it's subtleties. It's the costume that's leaning toward something that's real but not quite. It's the dance movement where you say, "Wait, I recognize that, but do I?" The audience is constantly in this oscillation of, "What's real?" to the point where the elements all start to speak to one another and you stop feeling them as real and unreal. You start looking at all of them as an experience.

STEPHEN BRAY (music and lyrics, 2005 Broadway musical, 2015 Broadway revival, 2023 film): Blitz brought a painter's eye to the whole thing, and one example is the scene when Celie is bathing Shug. The bathtub is on a record, on the old phonograph player, and the light is very shadowed and dreamy. It's almost like an Edward Hopper painting, the way the light is hitting that record and the old Victrola. Yet at the same time, Blitz is exploding that because he's got the jazz. It's like she's hearing this jazzy intro to the song from the show, which we call "Dear God – Shug," when Celie says she's got "a million tingles rolling."

Celie (Fantasia Barrino) sings "Dear God – Shug", 2023 film

A rendering of Shug's Juke Joint outfit and the real thing, 2023 film

He definitely did what you want in a film: He made it bigger than life. Musicals are, in a way, bigger than life—obviously in an audio way, but they're not necessarily bigger than life in a visual way. But Blitz made it bigger than life in a fantastic way. He's a renaissance guy in that true sense of the word. He's a musician, he's a painter, he's a writer, he's a film director. He's really got it all going on.

FATIMA ROBINSON (choreographer, 2023 film): For period pieces, especially that long ago, there isn't much dance you can look up and reference. You really have to use your imagination. There's one scene where Shug Avery comes into town, and I used stepping in one of the breakdowns. Stepping had to come from somewhere. Every time I do research, I always find some move we thought we created in hip-hop that turns out was completely from our ancestors.

Whether I'm watching African dance or looking as far back as I can, I understand that the movement we have now is ingrained in us and we're just reinventing it with each generation. The question I had to answer was, "How do I take that generational movement and make it entertaining and exciting, but also feel like it's true to the era?" The fact that Blitz knows African dance and music, and that he's an artist himself, really helped. He did so much of my job by handing me good music to work with—which was very different from the play. That in itself was heaven sent.

As for the dancers, Blitz and I wanted to pick people with interesting faces that felt like the era. I told the ladies to come dressed in the era for the audition. I told them to take off the lashes and the wigs and the weaves and the this and the that. They didn't have that back then. As much as you can dress the part, it helps us see you in that era. It also helped that we were in the South. It was easier. The pool of dancers is bigger in Los Angeles, but when you get to Hollywood, you become polished, whereas it's a different kind of energy in the South. I was born in Little Rock, Arkansas, but have lived in L.A. since I was five. Every summer I'd go back. It's a different energy.

FRANCINE JAMISON-TANCHUCK: When we're talking about the principal costumes, as well as background, as well as dancers, we're looking at, I would say, over 10,000 costumes. Adult Celie alone had thirty-two changes of clothing.

Period pieces can be more challenging, depending on the period. The earlier the period, the more challenging it is. If you're going through a period that is pre-photography, you have to rely on museum pieces and paintings and etchings and diaries. Also, bodies change. Trying to fit 2022 people into 1920s outfits can be challenging. A lot of women were not big then. Even sizes were different, because a size 8 in 1920 or 1930 is equivalent to a size 4 now. Eight was considered big. You didn't have fast foods, jobs were more laborious, and people walked everywhere, so you had that going on.

When we were dealing with the general background talent, there were major differences. With the dancers, many of them were petite, but they were also muscular in certain places. So a lot of garments, even in the background, had to be built by us because we could not take apart the rentals that came out of the costume house.

Then we had Shug Avery, who was bringing all types of flash to the town. Her Juke Joint costume went through some major fitting. We were trying on different things and looking at different fabrics for Shug. There was a garment that I wanted to try on, but it needed a lot of refashioning because it wasn't quite there for the character. I added layers of beaded fringe to the outfit and made sure that it was the drop of the '20s, but I also needed to give Shug, Taraji, a waist, so it didn't look so sacky on her.

The sheath of the 1920s doesn't work for everyone.

CAROL RASHEED (makeup department head, 2023 film): The thing that resonated with me with Blitz is that he wanted me to make us look like ourselves. He wanted our skin to look rich on camera and have a rawness to it as well. I loved that in terms of taking part in this project: being able to make us look like we look, but in a beautiful way. So often you see people onscreen, particularly Black people, and they're overly made up, overdone. It's too much everything: too much eyeshadow, too much lipstick, too much foundation, too much lash, too much everything.

The standard of beauty is very narrow in America for Black people. Not from our perspective, but from others outside of our realm. It's so interesting that a word like *flawless* is used in terms of beautifying people. The reality is that we're flawed individuals. We are all flawed. So guess what? A gap in your teeth or a scar is still a form of beauty; it's all about how it's carried.

"I wanted to make sure that when Taraji arrived at the Juke Joint, she was looking fabulous and felt great."
—Francine Jamison-Tanchuck

I wanted Shug to really stand out, so I took a certain license here in making it fitted, but the tier at the bottom, the drop, still told us we were in the '20s. In giving it more of a waist, I wanted to make sure that when Taraji arrived at the Juke Joint, she was looking fabulous and felt great. You can look at her and tell she was having so much fun.

For the headdresses, I added pearl beading around to make it a bit more fashionable for her, but still keeping in that era. I had brought up different research of headdresses back in the early and mid '20s for how that could work. This whole costume ended up being substantial. If you picked it up, it had weight to it. Taraji said, "Oh, I've worn things heavier than that." She was really into it. She loved the outfit. For her entrance on the barge, I created what I called the cocoon coat, which was very much the era of the '20s. When she came in, she discarded the coat to reveal this fabulous dress.

When I think about Mister, for example, he was a very flawed individual. When Mister was younger, even in the midst of him doing things that were completely wrong, there was still a sexiness about him. Some of the discolorations and the marks that the actual actor had were left there in order to show his beauty coming through. I covered some of it up, but then I left some of the rawness to his face. I didn't take all the darkness from underneath his eyes.

Fantasia entered the movie as an adult Celie, so I ended up aging her about twenty years. Not to the extent of the forty years [as in the Broadway version], because we had somebody else playing the younger Celie. For Fantasia, we started with a look that was very downplayed. This is when Mister was still treating her like crap, before she really fully recognized her womanhood and who she was. The makeup was hardly anything at that point. It was her natural beauty. I told Fantasia to

"Blitz lets our skin show through, letting us be seen in our fullness. It is very powerful to see us depicted in all shades and sizes."

—Carol Rasheed

please let her brows grow in. I even distressed her a little bit under her eyes. I took the color out of her lips because they looked too vibrant and pink and nice. I wanted them to look dark, a little down and dim. We had her take off her fake nails, and I made her skin look a little sallow. As she progressed, she got a bit more color into her skin.

The second look for her is when Shug comes to town and Celie starts singing to her. Celie starts feeling better about herself, and we followed that with the makeup. I put more color back into her face.

And then, of course, we got to the aging stage, where I ended up graying her brows. I added age spots. I also used a product called Bluebird Aging around her eyes to introduce wrinkles. I saw Blitz on set at one point and he said, "Yeah, can you give a little bit more wrinkle?" But when we wrinkled the top of her eye, it was too much. He's like, "We don't want her to look that old. Can you bring it back a little bit?" We had to find the happy medium that would resonate on film, because when film blows up onto a big screen, everything kind of spreads out.

The place where we used the most makeup on her was during her imaginary ballroom scene with Taraji. At the moment when she and Taraji touched lips, we wanted her to have the same color of lip Taraji had. I mixed up something so that when they kissed, it looked like the same lip color. That's the one time we used lashes on her. I did a burgundy smoky eye, but it was minimal. It looked like something Celie would've done for herself, whereas Taraji's character was very polished. I didn't use anything matte on Celie because I really wanted it to look like something she would've tried to do herself—or something that Taraji's character would've done to her. So Celie was never really glammed in the movie, but she was picked up in terms of a red lip and a little lash that didn't look like a lash. Then I gave her skin some rosiness, some life to the skin in terms of foundation colors. It still looked like her skin, but it had more sheen and shine to it to make her look happy and healthy.

Throughout, Blitz lets our skin show through, letting us be seen in our fullness. He and Dan [Laustsen] together—because, of course, Dan had to light it and shoot it—but Blitz had the vision to see and to express that this is what he wanted to see. Black people in their rawness, in their beauty, in their natural talent. Nothing's covered up. It is very powerful to see us depicted in all shades and sizes. It will resonate with audiences, whatever color they are, that our beauty, our realness, our humanness comes in all these different forms.

PHYLICIA PEARL MPASI: Blitz wanted to show what it's like to have melanated skin. He wouldn't let us hide behind makeup. It forced me to really get comfortable with what I looked like. I really had to do it. I had to look at that mirror every day and say, "Millions of people are going to see this face. You need to get comfortable." It was very minimal makeup; some days it was none. As someone who's darker, I really appreciate that, because the messaging I've gotten is, "You need to lighten these dark spots. You need to get rid of that acne. You need to have perfect skin." He was really intentional in wanting to show our full Blackness, and it starts with our skin tone.

LAWRENCE DAVIS (hair department head, 2023 film): My job was to tell the story through hair. I had to make sure the looks were authentic and period appropriate. To help show that, the looks in the beginning of the film were kinkier and not as glamorous. Well-groomed, but kinkier hair was prevalent. Although [the entrepreneur] Madam C.J. Walker had come about by then and had introduced the relaxer and hair pressing, a lot of these women still didn't have access to it.

As a hairstylist, I love to have a little bit of the kinky hairline. To me, it's a good lead-in to the history behind the hair. When it's bone straight, it's beautiful. When you can see that there's a little kink there and know that it took a little work to get what's going on outside of that, I appreciate it much more. I also like it when it comes to wig wearing. If there's a wig that's not custom, adding it right behind the hairline makes it look more realistic on camera.

When it comes to film and hair, we have to consider the weather, the lighting, and the activity of the actor, whether it's a physical scene or a bedroom scene or shower scene. Some of the hair we used was synthetic, which was a lifesaver because we didn't have to worry about it reverting. I actually welcomed reverting in this film, only because it gave a more authentic look. Everybody was not silky, pressed out. It's not realistic to the time period or the characters. So I wasn't as afraid of the Georgia humidity as I would've been on a current-day film where a woman needs to be silky and glamorous. I wasn't as freaked out by a 99-degree, 70 percent humidity day. In all, we used about sixty-five wigs, including background characters. When it came to the Juke Joint and townspeople, we tried to use as much of their natural hair as possible. It was a lot to keep up with.

Building Celie from a young girl to a well-groomed, mature woman was a journey for me, and I loved that. In the beginning, we kept her pretty much a woman who wasn't confident in the way that she looked, but she was consistent. She had a particular braid she wore and a particular scarf she wore in the house. Most of the time, she wore her hair covered. Once she got older and started speaking for herself, coming into her womanhood and learning things about beauty and what made her feel pretty, she wanted to explore more of the big city look that Shug had. My favorite look for her was what we called Celie's glam look, this beautiful flapper style hairdo she imagined for herself when she went to this fantasy place with Shug.

My greatest challenge, at least in the beginning, was Nettie's hair. Halle Bailey has dreads pretty much down past her shoulder, mid-back. It's a lot of hair, and we had to compact that flat enough to the head to put a wig over it. I thought, "How are we going to do this?"

It took me and my key [hairstylist] maybe a half a day to realize the logistics of it. I split her wig up the back, to right above the occipital bone. It was almost putting a puzzle together. So that wig was cut in half, the dreads were compacted, we'd press and pin and tuck them, and then we'd put a wig cap over the back and make sure everything was nice and firm and not slipping. Then we'd put the wig over top of it. Once we got that wig pinned down, we inserted another clip-in weft to cover the middle. It was almost like an envelope. It was amazing

Celie (Fantasia Barrino) during a fantasy sequence with Shug, 2023 film

Nettie (Ciara), 2023 film

Squeak (H.E.R.), 2023 film

once we figured it out. After a while, once we got the rhythm going, we could do it in fifteen minutes, and it was a no-brainer. In the beginning, though, it definitely was mind-boggling.

DAN LAUSTSEN: We didn't want to shoot it like it was a shampoo commercial. We wanted it to look real. They have to be beautiful and strong and Hollywood, but on the other hand, they have to be very strong Black women—and guys, of course, but it's a lot of women in the movie. It was important we have a lot of organic structure in the faces and in the sets. That's the reason sometimes you have to paint the walls darker, so you don't have to fight the darker skin tones with the walls. That's something Paul [Austerberry, the production designer] and I talked a lot about, together with Blitz. The same with the costume designer. We want to have strong colors that could bounce into the skin tones. I think we have a lot of romantic, beautiful skin tones and see the actors very well.

We used a little bit of old-fashioned lighting, with big lights far away outside a window so the light would move naturally into the room. We have a lot of shadows. I'm not afraid of getting dark, but you can get lost there if you don't see anything, and we didn't want to do that. We wanted to do a character-driven lighting setup. Sometimes we went for the warm side and sometimes very dark and very dramatic and a little bit blue.

MUSIC FOR A NEW GENERATION

QUINCY JONES (executive producer and composer, 1985 film; producer, 2005 Broadway musical, 2015 Broadway revival, 2023 film): There has always been an effort to diminish the African American experience and its cultural and societal contributions. For many years, jazz and the blues were considered to be unworthy of value and serious consideration as an art form by the institutional powers of the day because it was born on plantations and reared in juke joints. But the music was so powerful and honest that it could not be diminished, and ultimately became the Esperanto of the world.

I am of the belief that you have to know where you come from to get to where you are going. *The Color Purple* is a reflection of our African American experience, and each presentation allows another generation to know our story. Particularly at a time when some are trying to water down or, in some cases, erase that history completely.

ALICE WALKER: My favorite song is "Shug Avery Comin' to Town." I think it's because she represents a return of natural life to a dead culture and the people spontaneously understand that. They feel it viscerally that she is coming to town, and all the old BS and all the old stuff that's just dead from too much churchifying and too

Grady (Jon Batiste), 2023 film

much trying to be "good" and trying to live so right and all of that. They understand that, in a way, they've been stifled and that they have in themselves life, and she represents that life. I love that they understand this and that they're joyful about it.

STEPHEN BRAY: Blitz wanted people to have something to sink their teeth into other than just the legacy. Other directors might have said, "Let's be really faithful to the musical and let's let it be itself." But Blitz said, "Well, let's take a song like 'Shug Avery' and let's liven it up so that it can work at a faster tempo with a lot of jazz. Because when Shug arrives, I want the jazz to arrive." Blitz was full of concepts like that.

FANTASIA BARRINO (Celie, 2005 Broadway musical, 2023 film): The very smart thing that Blitz did was take the music and make it very modern. Not so modern that he took away the grit, the soul, the substance. But we're in a different generation, and we have to figure out how to speak to our younger generation. So he's taken the music and made it totally different: sounds, the beat of the drums. That's what attracted me to the [1985] movie in the first place when I was a kid. I'm a music baby, and today's music babies are going to connect in a crazy way to the music that they have produced for this film.

But also, each person he picked to play a role now is going to stand out in a major way. All of these young people that I was able to work with—H.E.R., Ciara, Jon Batiste, everybody that was a part of this film—a lot of young people watch them, follow them, and are listening to them. That's very, very smart. What we're bringing is nothing like what was done before, because you don't want to go bother a lot of that. That's respect. It's like a legend that came before me. Patti [LaBelle], Aretha [Franklin], they've done their thing. You don't want to touch it. You can't touch it, right? You don't want to bother it. What we are doing is leaving the meat on the plates, but dressing it up. We switched up the yams; we put a little salt and pepper on the collard greens. It's like we spiced it up a little bit and made pots and bigger plates of food so that we could bring in a much bigger crowd.

BLITZ BAZAWULE: In terms of the Broadway show, the specialness of it was the use of music and how that music vocalized the things that Celie could not say in real time. By the time we were coming around, we kind of had the cheat code. Somebody had already shown us how you can advance a character that didn't have agency. But we also had the music as an internal monologue that this character can have.

The music I inherited from Broadway is great on Broadway, but that doesn't mean it works cinematically. I needed it to have SPA: scale, proximity, and authenticity. The Broadway music doesn't have to do any of that. It just has to exist as one thing that lives on Broadway.

Left to right: Shug (Taraji P. Henson), Grady (Jon Batiste), Celie (Fantasia Barrino), and Squeak (H.E.R.) arrive in Memphis, 2023 film

Choirmaster (Ricky Dillard), 2023 film

Juke Joint band member (Keb' Mo'), 2023 film

Because our film is tracking time, we had to be specific in how we evolved the music. I split up the music into three parts: gospel, blues, and jazz. That was the continuum. I know that out of enslavement came the Negro spirituals that became the basis for gospel, which evolved into the blues when it became secular, and that evolved into jazz when we added scale to our lives, when we were allowed to exist outside of all of our confines.

I found practitioners in each of these categories. For gospel, I found Ricky Dillard, who is a master gospel composer, creator, choir leader, and director. For blues, I found Keb' Mo', who is undoubtedly one of the national treasures of blues. And for jazz, I found Christian McBride, who is another master of his craft. I gave them each a mandate to not only apply this SPA acronym to the musical numbers that fell within their categories, but also find a way that it could all synthesize as one, so we weren't necessarily listening to a gospel track or a blues track or a jazz track. We were listening to *The Color Purple* as an amalgam of all of these styles that are part of the same thread.

We took each Broadway track and said, "Let's break it down. Let's reconstruct it to feel like a motion picture." To do that, it needed to feel like the biggest thing ever. It couldn't feel like a small rural town, because how they experience it isn't small. From our vantage point, we see a juke joint and we say, "Well, it's a small little thing." No, no. To them, that's Madison Square Garden, and Shug

Avery is Beyoncé sold out ten nights in a row. For gospel, it is the biggest megachurch.

It was less about an external gaze as much as it was an internal gaze and how people see themselves. I come from hip-hop culture, I come from hip-hop music, so I know what these experiences are like. The first time I saw KRS-One, it was like seeing Michael Jackson. Externally, people will say, "Well, you can't even compare the two." But that's how the person experiences it. So what we tried to do was create an inward gaze of how these people existed and not how we saw them exist.

RICKY DILLARD (gospel music composer, 2023 film): I was in the process of producing my album *Breakthrough: The Exodus* when I got a call from my label, Motown. They said Blitz was interested in talking to me about participating in the remake of *The Color Purple*. I thought, "Whoa, me? Let me pinch myself. Guys, you've got to be kidding."

I got on the call with Blitz, and he told me, "I'm looking for a little of Ricky Dillard." I was shocked that he even knew my style of gospel, which comes through a connection to music I heard as a boy. I came from the Baptist church, and the sounds I was raised with were very Thomas Dorsey, Mahalia Jackson, [Sister] Rosetta Tharpe. Then there was a church next door, which was Pentecostal. It was magic. It was the New First Church of God in Christ, and the music ministry was led by the

Clark Sisters' mother, Dr. Mattie Moss Clark. I didn't hear that sound at my Baptist church, but I heard it next door. I was more drawn to the charismatic Pentecostal sound. So that's what Blitz wanted "Mysterious Ways" to be: the Ricky Dillard version of Mattie Moss Clark. Blitz wanted all of the hand clapping and joy.

This was my first time ever doing an arrangement for a movie. I got with one of my keyboard players and let him hear what I wanted to do. He started to play a more current version, but still keeping in line with the original "Mysterious Ways" song. What we did to that song is something we do all the time, and it's hard to explain because it's really from the soul. Because I do it so regularly and I have twelve albums out, I felt like I was just

when you come through on the other side, you're so happy to be out of it. You're so happy to breathe and to be liberated and to be lifted. That's what gospel music does. It lifts you. It puts a smile on your face. It dries the tears from your eyes. It gives you hope for tomorrow. You think today was something? Wait till tomorrow.

JON BATISTE: Ultimately, what I love most about this movie is that overall, it's a narrative of hope and overcoming anything that may come your way. It shows the capacity of the human spirit and the resilience that we all have to endure and still maintain our humanity. That's one of the things about being on set and the music that was made off-camera, in between these heavy scenes.

"I felt like I was just getting ready for Sunday morning service. I don't play nothing: I don't play no keys, I don't blow no horns, I don't play no drums—but I hear it in my heart and my soul."

—Ricky Dillard

getting ready for Sunday morning service. I don't play nothing: I don't play no keys, I don't blow no horns, I don't play no drums—but I hear it in my heart and my soul.

I wanted to make "Mysterious Ways" as authentic Black Gospel Charismatic Pentecostal as you could get. I wanted it to be the Black church experience such that when you hear this and you see the actors performing to it, it's going to take you straight to church. Like the *Blues Brothers* moment when the choir was there and people were flipping in the air, because that's what gospel music does. It is the joy. It is the happiness.

When you talk about Black struggle: After all the things that they endure weekly, come Sunday they finally get a space where they can rear off to their God and let him minister to them. And after he ministers, there comes this joy. So this joyous moment, when you hear it in the beginning of the movie, I want people to rise up and clap their hands, ready to dance, ready to go off. I want people to feel that when they hear it. That's the authenticity of the Black church experience. After going through a struggle,

It was almost an affirmation of the humanity that we all have, those moments in between scenes when Gabby [H.E.R.] and I would be making music, and then Fantasia would start singing, and we would create these moments of celebration. That's a beautiful thing to have at the heart of a narrative that deals with such heavy things: this affirmation of humanity, that no matter what you go through, you can find the light. I'm certain that we couldn't have had such a balanced experience on the set without having those moments of levity in between.

KEEPERS OF THE FLAME

STEPHEN BRAY: Every day that we were on set together, Scott [Sanders] and I were having a good time and pinching ourselves, saying, "Is this really happening? Is this really happening?" We'd been trying for so long to get them to make a film. But at this point in time, in the trenches, I felt

Sofia (Danielle Brooks, right) confronts Celie (Fantasia Barrino, left), 2023 film

like we were wearing whatever the hat is called of trying to be the keepers of the legacy and needed to honor the intention—or at least our perception of what the intention was, filtered through our own experience. To maintain what we believed to be Alice's intentions.

DANIELLE BROOKS: The Sofias who came before me left such a great blueprint for me, so I was really excited about getting to walk that path, but then do it my way. I'm very appreciative to Miss Oprah for being so generous and open with me about her past experience with this. Even before knowing her personally, she had such an influence on my life. Specifically, when she shared her own testimony over the years of getting the part in *The Color Purple* and how it came to her only after surrendering her will. I heard that story, and it resonated so much with me that I ended up getting "surrender" tattooed on my arm. I've always kept that in my mind, to surrender to the moment.

I didn't necessarily feel intimidated when Miss Oprah was there, but there was one time she came on set when we were shooting the "You told Harpo to beat me" scene, which has always been the most famous line in the movie. She created one of the most famous lines in the canon of American films, and here she was about to watch me say it on film. I definitely had to get in a Zen zone before that moment, so that I could surrender to what this moment

"The Sofias who came before me left such a great blueprint."
—Danielle Brooks

needed from me and not lose the moment trying to impress her. I know the purpose that I have in this story and in being a storyteller. It's so much bigger than one person's opinion of me, two people's, three people's opinions. I really try to remind myself of that, and that the same way in which watching Felicia Fields, LaChanze, and Ms. O have changed my life, I have an opportunity to do the same for someone else. I don't want for someone else to lose out on finding their purpose because I was in my head.

OPRAH WINFREY: The first time I saw Danielle Brooks on set, she was walking across a field. I'd come there to watch, and they were going to be filming the final scene around this enormous, gorgeous tree. Danielle was arriving on set for the first day. I burst into tears, because watching her walk across the field to the tree was a very Sofia-triggering moment for me. Then I went back to watch her do the "You told Harpo to beat me" scene, and I felt like, "OK, my work here is done."

I've seen multiple versions on Broadway and different people playing Sofia wonderfully, but I'd never felt like, "Oh, I've laid it down; it now has become somebody else's." But it now officially gets passed on to Danielle. She took it and made it her own in a way that is only her own. That's a hard thing to do for something so iconic, and so repeated, and so memed, but she did the work she needed to do to go inside and find that particular version for herself. On the day that she finished, we both hugged each other and ugly cried, because we knew that the baton had been passed.

Danielle Brooks and Oprah Winfrey on the set of the 2023 film

SHEILA WALCOTT: Scott [Sanders] will say it affectionately now, but I was kind of a broken record throughout production. I knew the cultural touch points before I ever watched the movie, and while I'm not saying you have to remake the first movie beat for beat, I do think there are these touch points that are important to honor.

In the filmmaking group, we all had different versions of what that looked like. Blitz is an African man; he has an African last name. I am an African American with an English last name. So even within that, there's a different history. We don't have a shared history. Our perspectives are different. Oprah is from a different generation, even though we are both African American, so she has a different touch point, and she was in the [original] movie. Two of the producers, Mara [Jacobs] and Carla [Gardini], are white women who have their own touch points. We all represent a segment of the audience for this movie.

phone where the line should go in the new dialogue. I'm thinking, "It has to be in the movie. I cannot go home and visit my family if the line is not there. You don't understand. I can't go home." I was panicking, calling, texting, sending screenshots of the page. But the line's in the movie. We dodged the bullet.

DAN LAUSTSEN: The first time I saw the whole movie, I fell in love. I was surprised about how much it took me in, because I'm not this kind of guy normally. I've made so many movies in my life that I'm a little bit, "I know the

> # "We have earned our way into another version of this film. It will be this generation's *Color Purple*. Hopefully another generation will come, and if they find any problems, they will be brave enough to take another swing and make it theirs."
>
> ## —*Blitz Bazawule*

Because this was not a coy group, we all were going to give our perspective. In the end, it was about creating that Venn diagram to find a balance between perspectives and making sure that we're honoring the core demographic of the movie. Because ultimately, as a Black woman, it's not just a movie for me. This is a part of my culture. It is a part of how the experience of being a Black woman has been represented for forty years.

One touch point was the line, "Harpo, who this woman?" I noticed it wasn't in the script. I said, "Can we put it back in, please?" They said, "Sure, no problem." The day they were shooting that scene, something changed, and they sent me the new pages. The line was gone again. They were in Atlanta; I was three hours behind in L.A., so I called the producers: "Is there a reason it's not in there?" They said, "OK, well we'll talk to Blitz. I think we can put it in."

Blitz was OK with it being in, and they asked me, "Where was it again?" So literally I am texting on my

screenplay; I know how we did it" and all that stuff. But I thought, "Wow, this is fantastic." It was great, and emotionally, it hit me hard. I'm not used to that.

JON BATISTE: What makes *The Color Purple* story unique in all these iterations is the cast and what they bring to it, their experience with the narrative, and how the narrative has formed and re-formed over time. That naturally happens because the cast is bringing something to it, based on all the other iterations they've seen and digested and experienced and even been a part of.

BLITZ BAZAWULE: Without a question, we have earned our way into another version of this film. It will be this generation's *Color Purple*. Hopefully another generation will come, and if they find any problems, they will be brave enough to take another swing and make it theirs the way that we've been able to make it ours. ∎

Celie (Fantasia Barrino) in her pants store, 2023 film

MEET THE INTERVIEWEES

The multitudes of people who've touched or been touched by the legacy of
The Color Purple crosses oceans, professions, ages, and artistic mediums. Those listed
below generously offered their experiences and insights for this book.

TADEU AGUIAR Brazilian actor and playwright Tadeu Aguiar produced and directed the 2019 Brazilian stage production (*A Cor Púrpura*), which opened in Rio de Janeiro and then toured the country.

PAUL D. AUSTERBERRY Paul Austerberry was the production designer for the 2023 film.

MARGARET AVERY Actress and producer Margaret Avery played Shug Avery in the original 1985 film, garnering an Academy Award nomination for her performance.

HALLE BAILEY Actress and singer-songwriter Halle Bailey played Young Nettie in the 2023 film.

JON BATISTE Actor, musician, singer-songwriter, composer, bandleader, and television personality Jon Batiste played Grady in the 2023 film.

BLITZ BAZAWULE Samuel Bazawule, known professionally as Blitz Bazawule and Blitz the Ambassador, is a Ghanaian musician, visual artist, author, and filmmaker. He directed the 2023 film.

STEPHEN BRAY Stephen Bray is a songwriter, drummer, and producer. Along with Brenda Russell and Allee Willis, he wrote the music and lyrics for the original 2005 Broadway musical, which received a Tony Award nomination for Best Original Score.

DANIELLE BROOKS Actress Danielle Brooks made her Broadway debut as Sofia in the 2015 Broadway revival of *The Color Purple*, earning a Tony Award nomination and winning a Grammy for Best Musical Theater album. Brooks revived her role in the 2023 musical film. The original Broadway production of *The Color Purple* was the first Broadway show Brooks ever saw.

REUBEN CANNON A television producer and the first Black casting director in Hollywood, Reuben Cannon cast the iconic roles for the 1985 film.

DEON COLE Actor, comedian, and writer Deon Cole played Alfonso in the 2023 film.

TINUKE CRAIG British theater director Tinuke Craig's 2019 stage production opened at Leicester's Curve Theatre and the Birmingham Hippodrome before touring nationally.

LAWRENCE DAVIS Lawrence Davis led the hair department for the 2023 film.

RICKY DILLARD An award-winning recording artist, gospel musician, and choirmaster, Ricky Dillard arranged music and appeared in the 2023 film.

BRANDON VICTOR DIXON Actor and producer Brandon Victor Dixon gave a Tony Award–nominated performance as Harpo in the 2005 Broadway musical.

COLMAN DOMINGO Actor, producer, writer, and director Colman Domingo played Mister in the 2023 film.

TIMOTHY DOUGLAS Theater director, actor, and educator Timothy Douglas helmed the 2018 Portland Center Stage, 2022 Arlington, Virginia, Signature Theatre, and 2023 Denver Center for the Performing Arts stage productions.

CYNTHIA ERIVO Actress, singer, songwriter, and producer Cynthia Erivo played Celie both in London at the Menier Chocolate Factory and then again in her Broadway debut for the 2015 revival, which won her Tony, Emmy, and Grammy awards.

FANTASIA BARRINO In 2007, actress and singer Fantasia Barrino succeeded LaChanze in the role of Celie in the original Broadway musical. She then played Celie in the 2023 film.

MARCUS GARDLEY Poet, playwright, professor, and screenwriter Marcus Gardley wrote the screenplay for the 2023 film.

DANNY GLOVER Actor, director, and producer Danny Glover played Mister in the 1985 film.

GARY GRIFFIN Gary Griffin made his Broadway debut as the director of the original 2005 Broadway musical, which received a Tony Award nomination for Best Musical.

PETER GUBER Entrepreneur, producer, and sports team owner Peter Guber headed several film studios and production companies and bought the original film rights to *The Color Purple* with partner Jon Peters.

KARA HARMON Kara Harmon was the costume designer for the 2018 Portland Center Stage and 2022 Arlington, Virgina, Signature Theatre stage productions.

AISHA HARRIS Writer, editor, critic, and reporter Aisha Harris co-hosts NPR's "Pop Culture Happy Hour" and the "Screening Ourselves" podcast series, whose final program recounts the debates ignited by the 1985 film.

COREY HAWKINS Actor and producer Corey Hawkins played Harpo in the 2023 film.

TARAJI P. HENSON Actor, producer, director, author, and mental health advocate Taraji P. Henson played Shug Avery in the 2023 film.

DANIELLE HOPKINS As a high school student, actress Danielle Hopkins played Shug Avery in the 2012 Northwest School of the Arts stage production.

JENNIFER HUDSON Actress, singer, and talk show host Jennifer Hudson played Shug Avery in the 2015 Broadway revival.

DANA IVEY Actress Dana Ivey played Miss Millie in the 1985 film.

FRANCINE JAMISON-TANCHUCK Francine Jamison-Tanchuck was the costume supervisor for the 1985 film and lead costume designer for the 2023 film.

BERNARD JAY Producer Bernard Jay helmed an all–South African cast in the 2018 stage production, which opened at Johannesburg's Nelson Mandela Stage at the Joburg Theatre and garnered 13 Naledi Award nominations.

TODD JOHNSON Author and singer Todd Johnson was a producer of the 2005 Broadway musical.

QUINCY JONES Quincy Jones is a songwriter, composer, arranger, and producer. He was a lead producer on, and wrote the score for, the 1985 film, then produced the 2005 Broadway musical, the 2015 Broadway revival, and the 2023 film.

GAYLE KING Author and journalist Gayle King made a cameo appearance during Sofia and Harpo's wedding scene in the 1985 film.

NIIJA KUYKENDALL Former production executive at Warner Bros. Pictures, Niija Kuykendall was the executive vice president of Warner Bros. Pictures when producer Scott Sanders pitched her the idea of adapting the Broadway musical production for the screen.

LACHANZE Actress and producer Rhonda LaChanze Sapp, known professionally as LaChanze, originated the role of Celie in the 2005 Broadway musical, which earned her a Tony Award for Best Actress.

JOHN LATENSER Location manager and producer John Latenser was the supervising location manager for the 2023 film.

DAN LAUSTSEN Cinematographer Dan Laustsen directed the photography for the 2023 film.

MEKHAI LEE As a high school student, actor, director, and writer Mekhai Lee played Mister in the 2012 Northwest School of the Arts production in Charlotte, North Carolina.

DESTINY LILLY Destiny Lilly was a casting director for the 2023 film, alongside colleagues Bernard Telsey and Tiffany Little Canfield.

TIFFANY LITTLE CANFIELD Tiffany Little Canfield was a casting director for the 2023 film, alongside colleagues Bernard Telsey and Destiny Lilly.

ELIZABETH MARVEL Actress, writer, and director Elizabeth Marvel played Miss Millie in the 2023 film.

COREY MITCHELL Theater director and teacher Corey Mitchell won a Tony Award for Excellence in Theatre Education; in 2016, the documentary *Purple Dreams* was made about his 2012 production of the show at the Northwest School of the Arts in Charlotte, North Carolina.

PHYLICIA PEARL MPASI Actor and writer Phylicia Pearl Mpasi made her film debut as Young Celie in the 2023 film.

MARSHA NORMAN Playwright Marsha Norman won a Pulitzer Prize for Drama for her play *'Night Mother* on the same day as Alice Walker won the Pulitzer for Fiction for *The Color Purple* in 1983. Norman went on to write the book for the 2005 Broadway musical.

WILLARD E. PUGH Actor and producer Willard E. Pugh played Harpo in the 1985 film.

KIMBERLEY RAMPERSAD Canadian actress and theater director Kimberley Rampersad helmed the 2019 stage production at the Neptune Theatre and Royal Manitoba Theatre Center, which earned Sterling and Merritt Awards for Outstanding Direction and Production.

CHARLES RANDOLPH-WRIGHT American film, television, and theater director, television producer, screenwriter, and playwright Charles Randolph-Wright introduced Brazilian director Tadeu Aguiar to the Broadway show, which Aguiar then brought to Brazil.

CAROL RASHEED Carol Rasheed headed the makeup department for the 2023 film.

FATIMA ROBINSON Dancer, music video director, and choreographer Fatima Robinson was the choreographer for the 2023 film.

BRENDA RUSSELL Singer, composer, and producer Brenda Russell wrote the music and lyrics for the 2005 Broadway musical, along with colleagues Stephen Bray and Allee Willis.

SCOTT SANDERS Scott Sanders was a lead producer of the original 2005 Broadway musical, the 2015 Broadway revival, and producer of the 2023 film.

HANK SANTOS As a high school student, actor Hank Santos played in the ensemble for the 2012 Northwest School of the Arts stage production in Charlotte, North Carolina.

E. R. SHIPP In 1986, American journalist and professor E. R. Shipp wrote a *New York Times* article covering the controversy surrounding the 1985 film, titled "Blacks in Heated Debate Over 'The Color Purple.'"

LETÍCIA SOARES Brazilian actress and musician Letícia Soares played Celie in the 2019 Brazilian production (*A Cor Púrpura*).

STEVE SPIEGEL Steve Spiegel is the founder and owner of Theatrical Rights Worldwide, which represents the live stage rights for the musical.

STEVEN SPIELBERG Film director, writer, and producer Steven Spielberg directed the original 1985 film and returned as a producer for the 2023 film.

BERNARD TELSEY Bernard Telsey is a casting director and founder of The Telsey Office, which cast the 2005 Broadway premiere, the 2015 Broadway revival, and the 2023 film.

SALAMISHAH TILLET Salamishah Tillet is a scholar, activist, and the author of *In Search of The Color Purple: The Story of an American Masterpiece*, published in 2021, which uses cultural criticism, literary history, and memoir to explore the cultural resonance of Alice Walker's novel.

GABRIELLE UNION Actress and activist Gabrielle Union is an outspoken advocate for women's issues and LGBTQ+ equality and against gender-based violence. Herself a survivor of sexual assault, Union credits *The Color Purple* with helping her to heal.

KOEN VAN DIJK Dutch theater director Koen van Dijk translated and directed the 2018 Dutch production (*De Kleur Paars*), which premiered in Amsterdam at the NDSM Wharf and was attended by the Netherlands' Queen Máxima.

SHEILA WALCOTT Sheila Walcott is the senior vice president of creative development at Warner Bros., which produced the 2023 film, along with Scott Sanders Productions, Amblin Entertainment, and Harpo Films.

ALICE WALKER Alice Tallulah-Kate Walker is a writer and activist. In 1982, she published *The Color Purple*, her third novel, which won the Pulitzer Prize for Fiction.

EVELYN C. WHITE Journalist Evelyn C. White authored the biography *Alice Walker: A Life*, published in 2004, which draws on papers, letters, journals, and extensive interviews with Walker, her family, friends, colleagues, and other cultural figures.

OPRAH WINFREY Actress, author, talk show host, producer, and philanthropist Oprah Winfrey made her film debut playing Sofia in the original 1985 film, which earned her an Academy Award nomination. She went on to become a producer for the 2005 Broadway musical, 2015 Broadway revival, and 2023 film.

YUMIKO YANAGISAWA Japanese literary translator Yumiko Yanagisawa translated the Japanese edition (紫のふるえ), published by Shueisha in 1986.

CREDITS & ACKNOWLEDGMENTS

Conceived by SCOTT SANDERS: Scott is an Emmy-, Grammy-, and Tony-winning producer. Having developed *The Color Purple* musical from its inception, he produced both its 2005 premiere and 2015 revival on Broadway, as well as the 2023 feature film adaptation. His producing credits also include the movie musical *In the Heights*, Disney's *The Odd Life of Timothy Green*, and Broadway productions including *Tootsie*, *After Midnight*, *Elaine Stritch: At Liberty*, and *The Pee-wee Herman Show*. Scott resides in Los Angeles and Provincetown with his husband, Brad, whom he married in 2008 in a ceremony officiated by Alice Walker.

Written by LISE FUNDERBURG: Lise is an award-winning author and journalist. Her books include the best-selling memoir *Pig Candy: Taking My Father South, Taking My Father Home*; the acclaimed oral history *Black, White, Other: Biracial Americans Talk About Race and Identity*; and *Apple, Tree: Writers on Their Parents*. The recipient of numerous fellowships and grants, she teaches creative writing at the University of Pennsylvania. Find out more at LiseFunderburg.com.

Cover art by JAMEA RICHMOND-EDWARDS: Jamea is a Detroit-born interdisciplinary artist known for her maximalist monumental-scale assemblages and immersive installations. Her work is invested in exploring the materiality of collage, and she often incorporates self-portraiture that exists within the realm of imagination and mythos.

This book was produced by Melcher Media, Inc.

MELCHER MEDIA

124 West 13th Street, New York, NY 10011, melcher.com

Founder and CEO: CHARLES MELCHER
Vice President and COO: BONNIE ELDON
Editorial Director: LAUREN NATHAN
Production Director: SUSAN LYNCH
Executive Editor: CHRISTOPHER STEIGHNER
Senior Editor: MEGAN WORMAN
Assistant Editor: CARLIE HOUSER
Editorial Intern: KEVIN LI

Art direction and design by MORCOS KEY
Additional interior design by CHIKA AZUMA
Project management by JILL ADAMS

ACKNOWLEDGMENTS: Scott Sanders would like to thank Albert Lee, Brad Lamm, Jill Benscoter, Drew Hodges, Carla Gardini, Mara Jacobs, and Amy Jacobs for their generous support. Melcher Media would also like to thank the following individuals for their contributions to this project: Madison Brown, Amelie Cherlin, Shannon Fanuko, Laura Helms, Elisabeth March, and Anna Wahrman.

ENDNOTES: 1 Evelyn White, *Alice Walker: A Life* (2004) 2 Evelyn White, *Alice Walker: A Life* (2004) 3 Chris Danielle, *Living By Grace* (Website) 4 Alice Walker, *Saying Goodbye to My Friend Howard Zinn* (2010) 5 Alice Walker, *Saying Goodbye to My Friend Howard Zinn* (2010) 6 Evelyn White, *Alice Walker: A Life* (2004) 7 "Alice Walker Shines Light on Zora Neale Hurston," *American Masters* (TV), (2014) 8 "Gloria Steinem on Alice Walker, Her Friend," *American Masters* (TV), (2014) 9 Alice Walker, *Gathering Blossoms Under Fire* (2014) 10 Alice Walker, *Gathering Blossoms Under Fire* (2014) 11 Alice Walker, *Gathering Blossoms Under Fire* (2014) 12 "Steven Spielberg and Whoopi Goldberg Reflect on Her Casting in *The Color Purple*," *The View* (TV), (2016) 13 "Banned Book: *The Color Purple*," Politics and Prose (Website) 14 Donald Bogle, *The Phil Donahue Show* (TV), 1986 15 Alice Walker, *The Same River Twice* (1996) 16 Salamishah Tillet, *In Search of The Color Purple* (2021) 17 Edward Wyatt, "Oprah Winfrey to Back 'Purple,'" *New York Times* (2005) 18 LaChanze, Tony Awards (2006) 19 Pratibha Parmar, *Alice Walker: Beauty in Truth* (Film), (2013) 20 Alice Walker, *The Beat with Ari Melber on MSNBC* (TV), (2018) 21 "Behind the Scenes with Samira Wiley, Narrator of The Color Purple," Audible.com (2021).

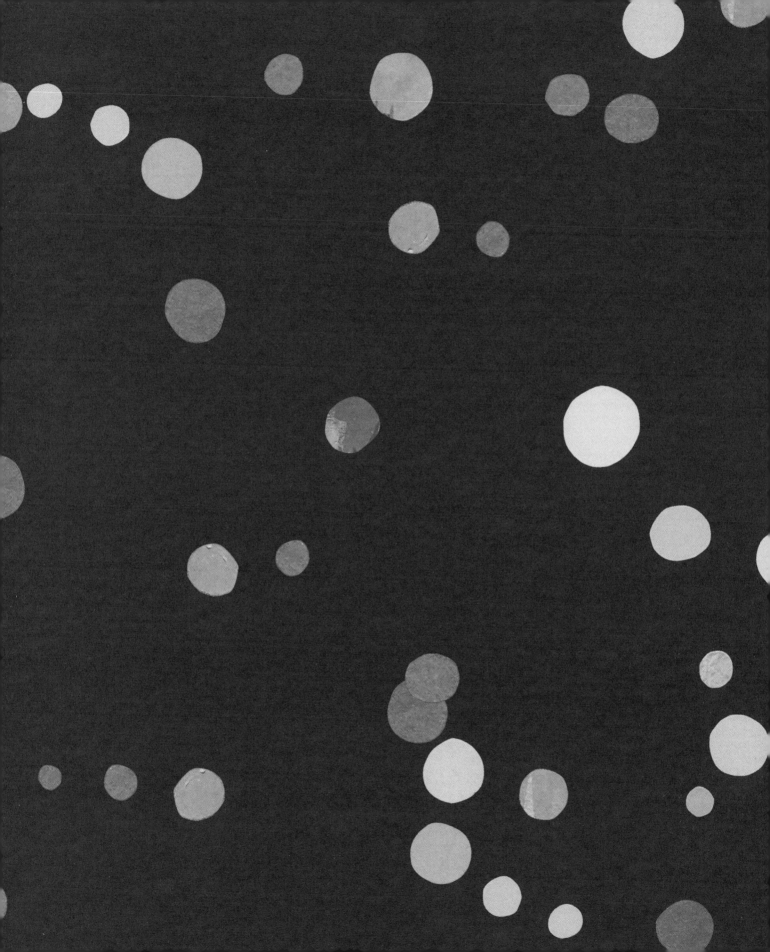